Anthony Trollope his Art and Scope

Also by P. D. Edwards

Anthony Trollope (Profiles in Literature series)
Some Mid-Victorian Thrillers
(As editor, with R. B. Joyce) Trollope's *Australia*

Anthony Trollope
his Art and Scope

P. D. Edwards

St. Martin's Press

New York

© University of Queensland Press
St. Lucia, Queensland, 1977

All rights reserved. For information, write:
St. Martin's Press, Inc., 175 Fifth Aveune, New York,
N.Y. 10010
Library of Congress Catalog Card Number 77-27915
ISBN 0-312-04271-X
First published in the United States of America in 1978

Printed in Hong Kong

Library of Congress
Cataloging in Publication Data

Edwards, Peter David.
    Anthony Trollope, his art and scope.

    1. Trollope Anthony, 1815—1882—Criticism and
    interpretation. I. Title.

PR5687.E3   823'.8   77-27915
ISBN 0-312-04271-X

Contents

Acknowledgments

The writing of this book has been facilitated by financial help, mainly in the form of study leave, from the Universities of Queensland and Sydney and by the award to me, in 1958–60, of a Walter and Eliza Hall Travelling Scholarship. I wish to express my gratitude to the two universities and to the trustees of the Walter and Eliza Hall Estate.

I wish also to acknowledge my deep sense of obligation to the late Geoffrey Tillotson: though there is much in this book that he would not have agreed with, it would not have been written at all without his encouragement over a number of years.

The book is dedicated to the memory of my mother, Marjorie Wood Edwards (1898–1966).

Texts Cited

There is no uniform edition of Trollope's novels. The nearest approach to one is provided by the World's Classics series, in which thirty-six of his forty-seven novels have been issued. Some of these have been allowed to go out of print, but they are still as a rule the most accessible texts of the novels in question. I have therefore chosen to refer to the World's Classics text of any novel that has been issued in this series, even if it is not still in print. For other novels the text I use is that of the first edition.

The novels are listed here in order of publication in book form, but dates of composition—taken in all but a few instances from the Trollope papers in the Bodleian—are also included. WC = World's Classics edition.

The Macdermots of Ballycloran, 3 vols., 1847. Written 1843–45.

The Kellys and the O'Kellys, 3 vols., 1848. Written 1847. WC (1929), 1951.

La Vendée, 3 vols., 1850. Written 1849.

The Warden, 1 vol., 1855. Written 1852–53. WC (1918), 1950.

Barchester Towers, 3 vols., 1857. Written 1855–56. WC (1925), 1960.

The Three Clerks, 3 vols., 1858. Written 1857. WC (1907), 1952.

Doctor Thorne, 3 vols., 1858. Written 1857–58. WC (1926), 1963.

The Bertrams, 3 vols., 1859. Written 1858.

Castle Richmond, 3 vols., 1860. Written 1859–60.

Framley Parsonage, 3 vols., 1861. Written 1859–60. WC (1926), 1949.

Orley Farm, 2 vols., 1862. Written 1860–61. WC (1935), 1956.

Rachel Ray, 2 vols., 1863. Written 1863. WC (1924), 1951.

The Small House at Allington, 2 vols., 1864. Written 1862–63. WC (1939), 1963.

Can You Forgive Her?, 2 vols., 1864. Written 1863–64. WC (1938), 1953.

Miss Mackenzie, 2 vols., 1865. Written 1864. WC (1924), 1950.

The Belton Estate, 3 vols., 1866. Written 1865. WC (1923), 1943.

Nina Balatka, 2 vols., 1867. Written 1865. WC (1946), 1951.

The Last Chronicle of Barset, 2 vols., 1867. Written 1866. WC (1932), 1958.

The Claverings, 2 vols., 1867. Written 1864. WC (1924), 1951.

Linda Tressel, 2 vols., 1868. Written 1867. WC (1946), 1951.

Phineas Finn, 2 vols., 1869. Written 1866–67. WC (1937), 1951.

He Knew He Was Right, 2 vols., 1869. Written 1867–68. WC, 1948.

The Vicar of Bullhampton, 1 vol., 1870. Written 1868. WC (1924), 1949.

The Struggles of Brown, Jones and Robinson, 1 vol., 1870. Written 1857, 1861.

Sir Harry Hotspur of Humblethwaite, 1 vol., 1871. Written 1868–69. WC (1928), 1950.

Ralph the Heir, 3 vols., 1871. Written 1869. WC (1939), 1951.

The Golden Lion of Granpère, 1 vol., 1872. Written 1867. WC, 1946.

The Eustace Diamonds, 3 vols., 1873. Written 1869–70. WC (1930), 1959.

Phineas Redux, 2 vols., 1874. Written 1870–71. WC (1937), 1952.

Lady Anna, 2 vols., 1874. Written 1871. WC, 1936.

Harry Heathcote of Gangoil, 1 vol., 1874. Written 1873.

The Way We Live Now, 2 vols., 1875. Written 1873. WC (1941), 1951.

The Prime Minister, 4 vols., 1876. Written 1874. WC (1938), 1955.

The American Senator, 3 vols., 1877. Written 1875. WC (1931), 1951.

Is He Popenjoy?, 3 vols., 1878. Written 1874–75. WC (1944), 1951.

An Eye for an Eye, 2 vols., 1879. Written 1870.

John Caldigate, 3 vols., 1879. Written 1877. WC, 1946.

Cousin Henry, 2 vols., 1879. Written 1878. WC, 1929.

The Duke's Children, 3 vols., 1880. Written 1876. WC (1938), 1957.

Dr. Wortle's School. 2 vols., 1881. Written 1879. WC (1928), 1951.

Ayala's Angel, 3 vols., 1881. Written 1878. WC (1929), 1951.

Kept in the Dark, 2 vols., 1882. Written 1880.

Marion Fay, 3 vols., 1882. Written 1878–79.

The Fixed Period, 2 vols., 1882. Written 1880–81.

Mr. Scarborough's Family, 3 vols., 1883. Written 1881. WC, 1946.

The Landleaguers, 3 vols., 1883. Written 1882.

An Autobiography, 2 vols., 1883. Written 1876. WC (1923), reset edition 1953.

An Old Man's Love, 2 vols., 1884. Written 1882. WC (1936), 1951.

The Letters of Anthony Trollope [referred to in the text as *Letters*], ed. Bradford Allen Booth, 1 vol., 1951.

Prefatory Note

I have assumed that the reader will be familiar with the plots of Trollope's better known novels, such as the chronicles of Barset, the "political" (or "Palliser") series, *The Eustace Diamonds*, and *The Way We Live Now*. For the others, I have endeavoured to work in enough details of the plots to make my commentary intelligible to the reader who has not read them or whose recollections of them are indistinct.

1 The Two Streams

Those happy tales of mystery are as much my envy as the popular narratives of the deeds of bread and cheese people, for they both create a tide-way in the attentive mind; the imagination pricking our credulous flesh to creep, the familiar urging our obese imagination to constitutional exercise. And oh, the refreshment there is in dealing with characters either contemptibly beneath us or supernaturally above! My way is like a Rhone island in the summer drought, stony, unattractive and difficult between the two forceful streams of the unreal and the over-real, which delight mankind—honour to the conjurors!

MEREDITH, *Beauchamp's Career*

One of the most remarkable features of Anthony Trollope's work is its homogeneity of style. Though indefatigable in experimenting with new subjects, he remained content with basically the same narrative techniques for nearly forty years. Apart from one of his last novels, *The Fixed Period*, and some of his short stories, all his tales were told in the third person, and in only one other—his first novel, *The Macdermots of Ballycloran*—was the narrator given an identity distinct from that of the author. In a broad range of situations all of his characters think, and many of them speak, in a language indistinguishable from his own. Whether the setting is revolutionary France (*La Vendée*), Middle Europe (*Nina Balatka*), the Australian bush (*Harry Heathcote of Gangoil*), or even the terra incognita of Britannula (*The Fixed Period*), the mores of Trollopian England are never far beneath the surface. With the single exception of *An Eye for an Eye*—in which the main story is told as a flashback—all of his narratives follow chronological order.

The mark of Trollope's narrative style, at its most characteristic, is levelness of tone. He is the least excitable of novelists, the least liable, as R.H. Hutton observed,[1] to lose himself in the emotions of his imaginary creatures; he takes moments of crisis in his stride, without any luxurious lingering over them. As narrator, he is always at hand to allay the reader's anxieties. Sometimes he intrudes directly to dispel false conjectures about the future course of events or to guide us in our judgment of his characters; and he is not even above

encouraging or admonishing the characters themselves. But, in a less obvious way, he is ubiquitous, forever editing and articulating the unspoken thoughts of his characters, translating them into his own superbly relaxed and lucid prose. Henry James's complaint that Trollope "took a suicidal satisfaction in reminding the reader that the story he was telling was only, after all, a make-believe" and that he, the novelist, "could direct the course of events according to his pleasure"[2] cannot fairly be applied to more than a few of the novels, and these among the lightest-hearted and most stylized. But it is certainly true of Trollope's art in general that it depends on a high degree of stylization—however "realistic" it may be in its effect— and that the pervasive presence of the narrator, whether intruding directly or not, is perhaps the most striking sign of this stylization.

To recognize this is to grant that Trollope's levelness of tone is maintained at some cost to verisimilitude, to lifelikeness. For while his method of translating his characters' thoughts into his own staple language will serve when only the general impression of a state of mind is required, it tends to leave him without an adequate notation for the actual processes of silent thought and the confused flux of emotions. At his best he is able, like all great artists, to make a strength of his limitations, even of this one; but often he unmistakably fails to achieve the effect he is seeking.

Such failures are best studied in their particular contexts, and I do not intend to go into instances now. It is worth remarking, however, that the narrator himself from time to time admits his own inadequacies. In *The Three Clerks*, for example, he at one stage characterizes his account of the adolescent heroine's feelings as "bombastic" and makes an apology that is by no means misplaced: "It is my fault if I cannot put into fitting language the thoughts which God put into her young heart" (p.361). And in *Doctor Thorne*, when he becomes aware that his "tedious way of telling it" may have given the impression that Mary Thorne had allowed Frank Gresham to hold her hand for longer than she ought, he is driven to bemoan his lack of a "quick spasmodic style of narrative" (p.103). Occasionally, as in the case of Alaric Tudor's confession to his wife in *The Three Clerks* (p.438), he simply balks at a difficult scene, owning that he "does not dare to describe the telling". This is perhaps intended to remind us of Thackeray throwing a veil over, or shutting the door on, an affecting scene; but Thackeray—from whom (as also from Fielding) much of Trollope's obtrusive, self-conscious narrative manner clearly derives—is a master at the art of modulating between his own language and a language appropriate to the character whose state of mind he is trying to catch.[3] For him, the problem of striking a balance between commentary and action,

and between description and "scenic" representation, seems hardly to have existed; for Trollope, it was always something of a bugbear. He could, it is true, joke about it, using it to illustrate the inevitable cumbersomeness and artificiality of the novelist's tools of trade. The problem, however, was serious enough when he found himself having to apologize time and again for keeping his characters waiting in the wings while he held the stage. In *Castle Richmond*—admittedly the most extreme example—we are not "brought down to the period at which our story was to begin" until chapter 5, and the story proper does not get under way until the beginning of chapter 8: "And now at last we will get to Castle Richmond, at which place, seeing that it gives the title to our novel, we ought to have arrived long since." In *The Bertrams* Trollope resolves that "for once" he will "venture to have a heroine without describing her" (I:72), and in *Castle Richmond* he keeps his description of Clara Desmond "very short" on the grounds that "ten, nay, twenty pages of the finest descriptive writing that ever fell from the pen of a novelist" will not bring a character home to the reader (I:18). A little later, speaking of Clara's "virtues" and "faults", he asks: "Will it not be better to leave them all to time and the coming pages?" (I:20) The answer is obviously yes, but his uncertainties persisted. His initial descriptions of his characters, and particularly his heroines, often continued to give too much away, making their careers entirely predictable; and some of his most memorable characters—Rev. Henry Fitzackerley Chamberlaine and Colonel Marrable in *The Vicar of Bullhampton*, for example—are little more than brilliant vignettes. In *The Duke's Children*, one of his very late novels, he did try "putting the horse before the cart" (though only for a "branch" of his story), by plunging "in medias res" instead of describing his characters and their circumstances first (chapters 9–10); but he did so in a spirit half of adventure and half of self-depreciatory hopelessness. He had made similar daring experiments much earlier, in *The Claverings* and *The Last Chronicle of Barset*; otherwise, he put the horse safely before the cart at the beginning of every one of his forty-seven novels.[4]

In dwelling on the stiffness and conventionality of Trollope's narrative, I do not wish to deny that it generally serves him well. What I wish to emphasize here is the impression of flatness that it creates. His unexcitable levelness of tone, his lumbering, strictly sequential unfolding of plot, his sameness of style in novel after novel have blinded most readers to the variety of his subject-matter and especially to his fondness for the sensational, the morally macabre, the exotic. Practically from the outset of his career a major delusion of Trollope criticism has been that he is essentially a chronicler of small

beer, of what Meredith (in the passage quoted at the beginning of this chapter) calls "bread and cheese people".

That this is a delusion can be demonstrated, prima facie, by a rough statistical summary. Sensational ingredients—such as hidden family relationships, lost wills, bigamy, murder and other crimes, threats of legal or illegal disinheritance, protracted court cases, seductions, insanity, and suicide—figure prominently in more than half his forty-seven novels. There are murders or attempted murders in eight: *The Macdermots of Ballycloran, The Kellys and the O'Kellys, Can You Forgive Her?, The Vicar of Bullhampton, Phineas Redux, Lady Anna, An Eye for an Eye,* and *The Landleaguers.* Other crimes, such as bigamy (actual or suspected), blackmail, forgery, embezzlement, and theft, occur in nine others, as well as in some of those already named: *The Three Clerks, Castle Richmond, Orley Farm, The Last Chronicle of Barset, The Eustace Diamonds, The Way We Live Now, The Prime Minister, John Caldigate,* and *Dr. Wortle's School.* And "sensational" happenings play a crucial part in seven others: *Doctor Thorne, The Bertrams, Phineas Finn, He Knew He Was Right, Cousin Henry, Marion Fay,* and *Mr. Scarborough's Family.*

Even allowing that evidence like this is not conclusive, the durability of the notion that Trollope largely avoids crime, violence, and illicit passion is puzzling. It first found expression in 1859, when the *Times,* remarking that Trollope's style is "the very opposite of melodramatic", complained that he "carries his aversion from everything melodramatic to an extreme, and though he errs on the right side, still he errs".[5] Ten years later, when Trollope's career had reached its zenith, a writer in the *Fortnightly Review* asked: "Is there nothing deep, dark, and deadly in human nature and human sin to be painted vividly so that our souls may be purged by terror, and pity, and stronger thoughts than amusement at unmarried jilts, married flirts, and young mothers?"[6] Another contemporary critic felt that Trollope's novels "have this grand recommendation, that they show how popular a writer may become while dispensing with anything like vulgar sensation. There are but a couple of murders, so far as we remember, in the whole range of his novels".[7] The *Times,* after his death, found "more of the sensational" in his *Autobiography* than in "any of his novels".[8]

Many subsequent critics have echoed these opinions. The most illustrious is Henry James, who pronounced that Trollope's "inestimable merit was a complete appreciation of the usual" and that he "walked with his eyes comfortably fixed on the familiar, the actual".[9] A. Edward Newton pictured Trollope as the ideal companion for drowsy fireside reading because there is "very little blood

and no thunder" in his work and because he "did not care to deal much with the disagreeable or the shocking, as those whom we call realists usually do".[10] And Bradford Booth, in his full-length study of Trollope, saw the three "criteria" that he "habitually applied to fiction" as a "sound moral and ethical tone, the avoidance of the sensational in plot, and realistic characterization". To illustrate the second of these he quoted Trollope's remark, apropos of Hawthorne, that "great and glowing incidents", though they may interest, will not "come home to the minds of readers", and pointed out that Trollope objected to the "falsely sensational" in Mrs Stowe's novels. His conclusion was that "Trollope, the realist, opposed the selection of plot materials favored by Dickens and the 'sensation novelists'."[11]

Surprisingly, however, Booth completely overlooked Trollope's long paragraph on "realism and sensationalism" in chapter 12 of his *Autobiography*. There the use of so-called sensational materials is vigorously, and sensibly, defended. Without them, Trollope believes, "tragedy" in prose fiction is impossible; and the novelist who can "deal adequately with tragic elements is a greater artist and reaches a higher aim than the writer whose efforts never carry him above the mild walks of everyday life". This is unequivocal, and it was stated not only in writing but more than once to a "live" audience.[12] For supporting evidence Trollope turns to *Ivanhoe*, *Old Mortality*, *Jane Eyre*, *Henry Esmond*, and his own *Orley Farm*: who could say that the authors of these novels "have sinned in being over-sensational"? Gratuitous horrors, "would-be tragic elements" heaped one upon another, will of course be "dull" and "useless". But as long as there are "men and women with flesh and blood, creatures with whom we can sympathise" and "truth of description, truth of character, human truth as to men and women", a novel can hardly be too sensational. It is a mere fallacy that while the "realistic" novel depends on character interest, the "sensational" is content with plot interest. The good novel depends on both and fails in its artistic purpose if it does not achieve both; it should be both realistic and sensational, and "both in the highest degree".

It is true, as the examples given by Booth suggest, that Trollope's views on these matters are not fully consistent; but his own practice unmistakably reflects his desire to "deal adequately with tragic elements", to reach higher than the "mild walks of everyday life". And though the effect is generally not sensational, the plot materials often are. He may speak of plot with contempt ("the most insignificant part of the tale") and lament that he never could plan a tale beforehand in such a way as to be sure the end would fit the beginning (*Autobiography*, pp. 109, 296). But many of his novels, and nearly all of the best, have very fine plots, not only in the sense James

gives to the term *story*—"the subject, the idea, the donnée of the novel"[13]—but also in the looser sense of good yarns, stories that would sound interesting and unusual even in bare outline. Such novels make nonsense of Trollope's well-known dictum that a "novel should give a picture of common life enlivened by humour and sweetened by pathos" (*Autobiography*, p.109); for their art is certainly more than pictorial and the life they reflect is often far from common.

There are, then, two streams running through Trollope's work. One is the stream of common life, of Meredith's "bread and cheese people"; the other the more "sensational" stream of "great and glowing incidents". In some novels it is evident, despite the author's belief that a good novel should be both realistic and sensational, that the first stream alone is being followed and the second deliberately excluded. Some of these Meredith would no doubt have considered "over-real", as many contemporary reviewers did. Trollope's best work, however, does stand, like Meredith's Rhone island, "between the two forceful streams of the unreal and the over-real"; often it seems barely to escape being inundated by one or the other, but without both it would not exist as an island, whole and self-sufficient, at all. Its fineness, like that of all great art, consists in the sense it conveys at once of the strangeness of common life and of the naturalness, the inherent ordinariness of seemingly out-of-the-way experience.

My object in this study is partly to assess the range and quality of Trollope's attempts at what he thought of as "fiction shorn of all romance",[14] and partly to show how persistent and varied were his efforts, throughout his career, to "deal adequately with tragic elements" above the "mild walks of everyday life". One conclusion, predictably, is that all his best work, regardless of its subject matter, displays essentially the same qualities of style and imagination. But I think it should be stressed that neither the predominance of a particular kind of subject matter nor the presence of all or most of what seem his characteristic qualities of style and imagination is in itself a guarantee of success. In insisting on this, I have in mind the traps into which it seems to me the best modern critics of Trollope have fallen. One such trap, which often claims Michael Sadleir for example,[15] is the idea that applause for Trollope's apparent fidelity to real life, or for the attitudes and values that he appears to uphold, necessarily entails applause for the novels as novels. Another is the idea, which pervades A.O.J. Cockshut's study,[16] that "serious" subjects necessarily make "serious" novels and that serious novels—in this sense—are worthier of attention than non-serious, that is to say comic, ones. The truth, I believe, is that Trollope at his most

"realistic" is often Trollope at his dullest, and that in attempting to be serious he often becomes pretentious. A balanced view of his work must distinguish between his best and his merely average performances, and the best can be and deserve to be judged by the most exacting standards, in which truth to life (at one level or another) and seriousness (in one sense or another) do not need to be demonstrated but are axiomatic.

In the discussion that follows I generally group the novels in terms of their subject-matter and consider them in chronological order within their group. Where there seem good reasons for doing so, however, I depart from this arrangement; the spreading of my discussion of such novels as *Orley Farm* and *Can You Forgive Her?* across two chapters is a case in point. Though my particular interests and emphases vary from chapter to chapter, my grouping of the novels is not to be taken as an attempt at a new classification along generic, thematic, or stylistic lines.[17] It simply represents the framework which will best enable me to emphasize the variety of Trollope's oeuvre without understating its essential homogeneity, and to discriminate as many as possible of the elements, whether common or distinctive, that make for the success of some novels and the relative failure of others.

Fifteen years ago Professor Booth marvelled at the "chaos", the endless "divergence", of opinion about the relative merits of different Trollope novels, and the three full-length studies that have appeared since Booth's[18] have not altered the situation. The last critic to try to "grade" the novels comprehensively was Michael Sadleir in 1927;[19] but his system of awarding them three, two, one, or no "stars", in imitation of Baedeker, predicates clearer-cut judgments than most readers will arrive at. My own grading, which for the most part is implicit rather than explicit in the ensuing discussion, is limited to singling out what seem to me the very best and the very worst of the novels. In respect of the much larger number in between, I generally indicate those which I see as falling little short of Trollope's best novels. *The Warden*, *Phineas Finn*, *The Vicar of Bullhampton*, *Ralph the Heir*, *Lady Anna*, *Is He Popenjoy?*, *John Caldigate*, and *Cousin Henry* are works that I place in this category. Above them, as will be seen, I place *Barchester Towers*, *Doctor Thorne*, *The Claverings*, *He Knew He Was Right*, *The Eustace Diamonds*, *The Way We Live Now*, and *Mr. Scarborough's Family*, all of which seem to me among the major Victorian novels. At the opposite end, I regard as Trollope's distinct failures the following: *The Kellys and the O'Kellys*, *La Vendée*, *Castle Richmond*, *The Struggles of Brown, Jones and Robinson*, *The Golden Lion of Granpère*, *Harry Heathcote of Gangoil*, *The Prime Minister*, *Kept in the Dark*, *Marion Fay*, *The Fixed Period*, and *The Landleaguers*.

NOTES

1. In his review of *Orley Farm*, *Spectator* 35 (11 October 1862): 1136–38. Though the review was unsigned, it is generally held to have been written by Hutton: see *Anthony Trollope: the Critical Heritage*, ed. Donald Smalley (London: Routledge and Kegan Paul, 1969), p.21. A number of the *Spectator* reviews of Trollope's novels which Smalley feels unable to attribute decisively to Hutton seem to me, on grounds of style and content, to be clearly Hutton's.
2. Henry James, "Anthony Trollope" (1883), reprinted in *The House of Fiction*, ed. Leon Edel (London: Hart-Davis, 1957), p.101.
3. This point is tellingly made by R.H. Hutton in his review, already cited, of *Orley Farm*; also by G. Tillotson in his *Thackeray the Novelist* (Cambridge: Cambridge University Press, 1954), chap.5.
4. Counting only those which were published in book form, and on their own, during his lifetime or soon after his death. The merits of different ways of beginning a novel are also canvassed at some length in the opening pages of *Is He Popenjoy?*, another late novel.
5. "Anthony Trollope", *Times*, 23 May 1859, p.12.
6. J. Herbert Stack, "Mr. Anthony Trollope's Novels", *Fortnightly Review* 5 (February 1869): 198.
7. [A. Innes Shand], "Mr. Anthony Trollope's Novels", *Edinburgh Review* 146 (12 October 1877): 460.
8. *The Times*, October 1883, p.10.
9. *The House of Fiction*, p.91.
10. "A Great Victorian", in *The Amenities of Book-Collecting* (London: John Lane, 1920), pp.257–58, 261.
11. Bradford A. Booth, *Anthony Trollope: Aspects of His Life and Art* (London: Edward Hulton, 1958), pp.142, 145.
12. As part of Trollope's lecture "On English Prose Fiction as a Rational Amusement" (1870), reprinted in *Four Lectures*, ed. Morris L. Parrish (London: Constable, 1938). Parrish notes (pp.91–93) that the lecture was given on at least four occasions.
13. "The Art of Fiction", reprinted in *The House of Fiction*, p.39.
14. See below, chap.3, and *Letters*, p.138.
15. In Michael Sadleir, *Trollope: a Commentary*, rev.ed. (London: Constable, 1945).
16. A.O.J. Cockshut, *Anthony Trollope: a Critical Study* (London: Collins, 1955).
17. There is a table showing three attempts to classify the novels—by Spencer Van B. Nichols, Michael Sadleir, and Hugh Walpole—in W.G. and J.T. Gerould, *A Guide to Trollope* (Princeton: Princeton University Press, 1948), pp. xviii–xix.
18. Robert M. Polhemus, *The Changing World of Anthony Trollope* (Berkeley and Los Angeles: University of California Press, 1968); Ruth ap Roberts, *Trollope: Artist and Moralist* (London: Chatto and Windus, 1971); David Skilton, *Anthony Trollope and His Contemporaries* (London: Longman, 1972).
19. Sadleir, *Trollope: a Commentary*.

2 The Boundaries of Barset

It is a commonplace of criticism that Trollope failed to find his mé-
tier until the idea for Barchester came to him one evening during a
stroll around Salisbury close. He was then in his late thirties.
Previously, over a period of ten years, all he had produced were two
Irish novels and a French historical romance. So *The Warden*, the
first of the chronicles of Barset, marked his discovery not only of a
new county but also of England itself. The point is worth noting
because, although Barset has always been his best-loved and best-
known creation, he was never content to withdraw into its boundaries completely. His next novel after *The Warden* and *Barchester
Towers* was *The Three Clerks*, a novel of London life in which the
world whose distant thunderings had occasioned such alarm in the
cloisters of Barchester is the main arena. The next of the Barsetshire
novels, *Doctor Thorne*, was followed, in *The Bertrams*, by another
study of the sick hurry and divided aims of modern life, with the
scene shifting restlessly all over England and half-way round the
world. And even after *Framley Parsonage*, his first major success,
Trollope continued to alternate between chronicles of Barset and
kindred counties and novels dealing with the troubled mainstream
of modern life.

The significance of this pattern of alternation is not as self-evident
as it may appear. Obviously such a prolific author as Trollope could
not restrict himself for long to one area, even one so congenial to
him as the clerical and lay society of rural England. And however
much his imagination may have hankered after rural fastnesses, his
real-life pursuits and interests were clearly those of a townsman. But
Barset had other limitations—for his imagination and his craft—
which are perhaps less obvious and which do not apply at all to other
rural counties. It was his own creature, his "dear county"
(*Autobiography*, p.132); and it came to occupy a place in his affections and his scheme of values which no real-life setting could have
filled.

Ostensibly, it is true, Barset almost is a real-life setting. In the

very first paragraph of *The Warden* it is stated that Barchester, though not a real city, could have been any one of several: "Wells or Salisbury, Exeter, Hereford, or Gloucester" Readers during and since Trollope's own lifetime have pressed the claims of one city over those of another, and have also, on good grounds, added Winchester to the list of contenders.[1] But whichever of these Barchester is most like, the important fact is that people have persisted in trying to identify it with places they know in real life. Many of the events that occur within it also invite comparison with well-known events in contemporary history. Early in *The Warden* we learn, for instance, that Archdeacon Grantly, the principal champion of inaction in the matter of reforming Hiram's Hospital, had taken a similar stand in the real-life case involving the St Cross Hospital at Winchester (pp.11–12). He also has strong views on the scandal connected with the dismissal of Dr Whiston from the mastership of Rochester Grammar School.[2] One case or the other is referred to no fewer than six times in the course of the novel. The object, one assumes, is partly to make it clear that the Hiram's Hospital case is not the Winchester or the Rochester case, and hence that the novel is not dealing in personalities; but at the same time the device serves to keep real-life analogues constantly in mind, so emphasizing the closeness of the novel's world to the real world.

A similar purpose is served by the reminders of contemporary history that are scattered throughout the Barsetshire series—and through the Palliser series which grew out of it. The period of most of the novels is precisely indicated, though on only one occasion— Frank Gresham's birthday in *Doctor Thorne*—is an actual date given to an event in the story.[3] There is, moreover, a clear attempt to keep the chronology of the series as a whole more or less in step with historical chronology.[4] *The Warden* is something of an exception in that the events it relates cannot be dated any later than 1847 or 1848, given the interval that is supposed to elapse between them and events in later novels; whereas the archdeacon's intervention in the Rochester case could hardly have occurred earlier than 1850. But in general the other Barsetshire novels are in accord, as regards both their internal chronology and their references to historical events, with the date given for Frank Gresham's twenty-first birthday, 1 July 1854 (pp.8, 44). A more detailed account of the historical references is given in appendix 1 below.

Even admitting that there are more inconsistencies of chronology than this account draws attention to, it is evident that the private lives related in the novels are placed in a very precise historical context, so much so that Barset almost demands to be squeezed into the history as well as the map of England. The gain in terms of

realism—and, in some of the novels, of piquant topicality—is obvious. But these benefits sometimes entail disadvantages. In particular they tend to conflict with Trollope's growing attachment to Barset, his increasing reluctance to allow any real sway within its borders to the forces of social change that were at work outside. His attachment to it makes it something more than a replica of a real county with precise geographical and historical boundaries, a world that Meredith might have considered "over-real". From the beginning it has the air of an imaginative sanctuary, with a faintly mythic otherworldliness, and this becomes more pronounced in each new chronicle. Barset in fact evolves, showing in the process how deep and devious as well as how shallow and artless the stream of domestic realism[5] in Trollope's novels can be. To explore this stream and chart the course of Barset's evolution I shall look at the novels one by one.

The Barchester that Trollope discovered on his evening stroll in Salisbury is a haven of traditional order under threat from new men and new ways. In its outward aspect it is the epitome of the "snug", the "picturesque" (pp.5–7). Some "scandals" it has already known, for instance the suspicion of nepotism in Mr Harding's appointment to a precentorship (p.2); but then it "scandalises" easily, as shown by its disapproval of Mr Harding's black neck-handkerchief (p.8). Of the major scandal about to break over it no more than "murmurs, very slight murmurs" have been heard (p.5). Ominously, however, the London road passes by the "ponderous gateway" that is so "unnecessary", but so "conducive to the good appearance" of Hiram's Hospital (p.7); ominously because it is from London that most of Barset's great upheavals come, including the one over Hiram's Hospital.

Confrontation between London and Barset runs right through the series. In *The Warden* it reaches one climax with John Bold's struggle against Tom Towers in the London office of the *Jupiter* (pp.188–92): Bold, though styled "the Barchester reformer", is in fact half a Londoner and half a Barcastrian (pp.13–14), but at this point he indignantly repudiates his alliance with the London radicals who had taken up his call for the reform of Hiram's Hospital. The most memorable climax comes, however, at the end of Mr Harding's "long day in London" dancing attendance on Sir Abraham Haphazard, the attorney-general (chapter 16). Here the utter strangeness of London in Mr Harding's eyes is conveyed by an account of his visit first to a cheap eating-house, then to a tawdry "cigar divan". It is a masterly piece of reportage, never far removed from stream of consciousness and eventually, by one of Trollope's

most imaginative strokes, dissolving into surrealism as Mr Harding dozes off and, in a dream, his familiar images of Barchester become submerged in the vivid and baffling images of his last few hours in London.

Mr Harding's unsophistication is of course extreme even by Barchester standards, but he embodies in their purest form those traditional values for which Barset stands. In later novels these values sometimes find more formidable champions—Dr Thorne, Lady Lufton, and Mr Crawley—but only Mr Harding is absolutely pure in his motives. It is to him that Trollope returns at the close of *Barchester Towers*, in what amounts to an apology for the foibles and pettinesses of his other clerical characters:

> The Author now leaves him in the hands of his readers; not as a hero, not as a man to be admired and talked of, not as a man who should be toasted at public dinners and spoken of with conventional absurdity as a perfect divine, but as a good man without guile, believing humbly in the religion which he has striven to teach, and guided by the precepts which he has striven to learn.

No other character in any of Trollope's novels receives or merits such unequivocal praise; and certainly no other could lead even the "wordly" Archdeacon Grantly to question for a moment the whole basis of his own life:

> "The fact is, he never was wrong. He couldn't go wrong. He lacked guile, and he feared God,—and a man who does both will never go far astray. I don't think he ever coveted aught in his life,—except a new case for his violoncello and somebody to listen to him when he played it." Then the archdeacon got up, and walked about the room in his enthusiasm; and, perhaps, as he walked some thoughts as to the sterner ambition of his own life passed through his mind. What things had he coveted? Had he lacked guile? He told himself that he had feared God,—but he was not sure that he was telling himself true even in that. [*The Last Chronicle of Barset*, II:421-22][6]

In this rare exalted moment the archdeacon can even credit Mr Harding with having shown "all the spirit of a hero" in giving up his wardenship of Hiram's Hospital. This, however, had not been his opinion at the time, and if we can judge by the passage at the end of *Barchester Towers* it had not been Trollope's either. "Had I written an epic about clergymen," Trollope remarks at the end of *The Last Chronicle*, "I would have taken St. Paul for my model", and in that novel Mr Crawley actually does measure himself against Saint Paul. But Harding is altogether too nervous and irresolute, and certainly too modest, to be cast in such a role. In the archdeacon's view, he cannot lay claim even to the less spectacular "heroism" that a man may show in triumphing for a time over his weakness. For the archdeacon still believes that Mr Harding's resignation, though

"right" for Mr Harding, would have been "wrong in any other man" (*Last Chronicle*, II:421).

A corollary of the archdeacon's view must be that, however right Mr Harding's motives, however consonant with his unworldly purity, his resignation was a betrayal of the "right" cause, indeed a betrayal of Barchester itself. If so, his position as the conscience of Barset, the embodiment of its truest values, is seriously compromised, perhaps even undermined. But judging from Trollope's comments in his *Autobiography* (pp.81–82), he didn't intend that the novel should appear to endorse the archdeacon's view. Rather, Mr Harding's resignation was to be taken not only as a surrender— and essentially an honourable surrender—to the reformers but also as a gentle moral rebuke to the complacent self-interest of his own party, led by the archdeacon. Trollope's stated aim was to draw attention to "two opposite evils" that he had observed in recent controversies about alleged misuse of charitable endowments. The "egregious malversation of charitable purposes" was of course one of these evils, but he wished also to stress the equally deplorable injustice which newspapers and others displayed in their "undeserved severity" towards the unwitting culprits. He accused himself, in retrospect, of an "absence of all art-judgment" in imagining that he could present both sides of the case, refusing to "take up one side and cling to that", and believed that, as a result, the novel had "failed altogether" in its "purport". The right weapons for dealing with such a controversial subject were not, as he had hoped, moderation and impartiality but satire and caricature.

If the novel does, as Trollope intended, remain neutral on the main points at issue between the reformers and the supporters of the status quo, then the moral satisfaction that accompanies Mr Harding's resignation is not shallow and delusory, as it must appear if he has mistaken his own motives, but the just reward for a right action. He is entitled to the sense of inner harmony and exalted moral vision that he displays in the scene where he forbids Sir Abraham Haphazard to take up the legal cudgels on his behalf:

> He was standing up, gallantly fronting Sir Abraham, and his right hand passed with bold and rapid sweeps before him, as though he were embracing some huge instrument, which allowed him to stand thus erect; and with the fingers of his left hand he stopped, with preternatural velocity, a multitude of strings, which ranged from the top of his collar to the bottom of the lappet of his coat. Sir Abraham listened and looked in wonder. As he had never before seen Mr. Harding, the meaning of these wild gesticulations was lost upon him; but he perceived that the gentleman who had a few minutes since been so subdued as to be unable to speak without hesitation, was now impassioned—nay, almost violent. [P.222]

It is typical of Trollope to inject an ironic note—Sir Abraham's prosaic incomprehension—even into such a solemn moment as this; but there can be no doubt that he means us to take the purest of the arts, in this instance, as expressing the purest of moral sensations.

Yet in the novel as a whole some doubt does persist about the purity of these sensations. What if Mr Harding's sense of the real issues has as little substance as his imaginary cello? What if the imaginary cello is not a higher vision, but simply his cowardly refuge from reality? Such questions have been asked, and—misguided as they are—one can see why. The *Athenaeum*, for example, found the novel's conclusion—Mr Harding's resignation—"lame and unsatisfactory", and accused Trollope of showing "too much indifference as to the rights of the case"; it complained of the "*laisser-faire, laisser-aller*" spirit of the book.[7] Trollope perhaps took this sort of criticism as evidence of his want of "art-judgment" in failing to take sides between the reformers and the clerical party. But the *Eclectic Review* left no such room for misinterpretation, remarking that the novel lacks a "*moral*" because the impression it leaves is simply one of "regret at the affairs of the hospital having been brought into question".[8] A similar complaint is implicit in Saintsbury's blunt assertion that Mr Harding is "nearly as much of a coward as of a conscientious martyr".[9] Flying, as they do, in the face of Trollope's apparent intentions and Mr Harding's own estimation of his motives, these misjudgments can only derive from an impression, produced by the novel as a whole, that the evil to which Mr Harding appears to submit in resigning the wardenship is a good deal blacker than the evil he would be condoning if he retained it.

It is all too easy to see how such an impression might be produced. For while the novel is eloquent about the evil of vicious newspaper campaigns, sensational "reformatory" novels, and indiscriminate enthusiasm for change, it is surprisingly reticent about the opposite evil—the misuse of charitable funds—which the reformers have uncovered. Indeed, there is little evidence that this is an evil at all. We are very early reminded that "old customs need not necessarily be evil, and that changes may possibly be dangerous" (p.15). We are also assured that whatever comes of the reformers' campaign it can only be an "unmixed evil" for Hiram's bedesmen themselves, who already have everything they need (p.40). And when the bedesmen decide to petition for a larger share of John Hiram's money, the narrator accuses them—with a perfectly straight face—of forming a "vile cabal" (p.258) and displaying "deep ingratitude" to their warden (p.255). Considering that Mr Harding himself has defended their right to get up their petition, such strong language can only be taken as betraying the warmth of the narrator's own distaste for the

methods of the reformers. Certainly, no comparable animus is shown towards the clerical party. At first the archdeacon is presented in an unfavourable light, presumably to place him more or less on a par with brash young John Bold: an unflattering picture is given of his family and of the chilly ostentatious luxury of his household (which may seem hard to square with his secret fondness for Rabelais); he berates the bedesmen in a manner which, the narrator concedes, is bound to arouse anger and disgust (p.62); and he rejects John Bold's penitent advances with brutal rudeness (chapter 12). Later, however, he softens marvellously, even to the extent of accepting the warden's decision to resign with barely a trace of rancour, and by the end we hardly need the novel's final plea for our forebearance: "We have seen only the weak side of the man, and have lacked the opportunity of bringing him forward on his strong ground." (p.250) No such softening occurs in or towards any of his opponents—except John Bold, who changes sides.

Trollope's failure to strike a balance between his two "evils" is epitomized in his attack on the *Times* (the *Jupiter*), Carlyle (Dr Anticant), and Dickens (Mr Popular Sentiment). In this he not only drops any pretence of impartiality, or, as he had promised at the beginning of the novel, of avoiding "personalities", but resorts to the very weapons of satire and caricature that he is attacking and that he claimed to have dispensed with altogether in his own novel. The editor of the *Jupiter*, for example, has to withstand this alliterative onslaught: "Quite true, thou greatest oracle of the middle of the nineteenth century, thou sententious proclaimer of the purity of the press—the public is defrauded when it is purposely misled. Poor public! how often is it misled! against what a world of fraud has it to contend!" (p.191) Carlyle is pictured, in the same spirit of angry exaggeration, as "reprobating everything and everybody" (p.182), and Dickens as specializing in "pattern peasants" and "immaculate manufacturing heroes" who "talk as much twaddle as one of Mrs. Ratcliffe's [*sic*] heroines" (p.193).[10] Such are the men who presume to teach Barchester its duty and to whose pressure Barchester, in the person of Mr Harding, is made to submit.

The cleverest and least exceptionable part of Trollope's attack on the real-life reformers is his parody of Dickens, which takes the form of a version of the Hiram's Hospital case as it might have been pictured in one of Dickens's novels. It shows an ugly, rapacious, port-besotted warden living in luxury on the money that should have been shared among the inmates of the hospital, while the inmates themselves, simply and saintly, are half-starved. Such a picture, the now repentant John Bold reflects, must be disqualified by its "absurdly strong colouring" from "doing either harm or good"; but the narrator disagrees:

The artist who paints for the million must use glaring colours, as no one knew better than Mr. Sentiment when he described the inhabitants of his almshouse; and the radical reform which has now swept over such establishments has owed more to the twenty numbers of Mr. Sentiment's novel, than to all the true complaints which have escaped from the public for the last half century. [Pp.195–96]

Here Trollope is in effect inviting us to contrast his way of writing a "novel with a purpose" with Dickens's, but he is also foreshadowing his admission of failure in the *Autobiography*, a failure that he attributed to his moderation in confining himself to "true complaints". Ironically, however, the chief weakness of *The Warden*, both as a novel with a purpose and as a work of art, is the very one that it was designed to expose and counteract. It is this weakness, as I have suggested, that blurs the significance of Mr Harding's fine moral gesture and in doing so compromises Barset itself in a way that Trollope clearly did not intend.

Michael Sadleir speaks of Trollope at this stage of his development and for several years afterwards as given to "tilting at windmills of contemporary abuse or misery" and "airing personal distaste for other folks' opinions".[11] The prime example is his long journalistic jeremiad *The New Zealander*, which was written between *The Warden* and *Barchester Towers*;[12] but *The Warden* also—as Sadleir implies[13]—needs to be considered in the same connexion. Although its great achievement was the establishment, however uncertainly, of the Barchester ethos, it is generally different from the later Barsetshire chronicles. None of the others could seriously be considered as a "novel with a purpose" designed to contribute to a public debate; and in no other does Barset appear so vulnerable to outside influences, to socio-historical processes beyond its control and emanating largely from beyond its borders. In the later novels Barset remains, as I have said, closely related to contemporary history, mirroring many of its changes; but at the same time it acquires a complexity and solidity of its own, and, with these, a resistance to, a power of excluding, aspects of contemporary life that it cannot comfortably assimilate.

The beginnings of this process can be seen in *Barchester Towers*. Next to *The Warden*, this is the most obviously topical of the Barsetshire novels, the one that belongs most clearly to a particular moment of history: the immediate aftermath of the Oxford Movement and of the first period of church reform. It also resembles *The Warden*—more than any of the later novels—in that it consists, basically, of a series of confrontations between old Barchester and the outside world, the latter being represented most conspicuously by the low-church Bishop Proudie, his wife, and his chaplain Mr

Slope, but also by the raffish, cosmopolitan family of Dr Stanhope, the high-and-dry prebendary. But although, as in *The Warden*, Barchester is only partially successful in its resistance to these alien influences, there is little of the bitterness that disfigures the earlier novel. *Barchester Towers* is, on the contrary, the gayest and most comically inventive of all Trollope's novels, the freest from that gloomy sense of "change and decay in all around" which is so marked in most of the other novels he wrote about this time.[14] Barchester is still, as it had been in *The Warden*, one of the arenas of a fierce and nationwide debate, and this gives the novel a topicality that is a large part of its appeal even for the modern reader. But any views it may have as to the rights and wrongs or the likely outcome of this debate are incidental and well disguised: it could never be mistaken for a "party" novel, a "novel with a purpose", as contemporary critics—almost to a man, and from George Meredith down[15]—noted with grateful relief. The old Barset is now much surer of itself and of its ability to wage an equal struggle with the forces of historical change; and Trollope's delight in the comic relish that both sides show for the struggle, the vitality and resourcefulness that they bring to it, carries far stronger conviction than his "true complaints" about the existence of such struggles.

It is in *Barchester Towers* and *Doctor Thorne*, the next novel in the series, that the struggle is fiercest and most exciting; in *Framley Parsonage* it becomes narrower in scope and less momentous, in *The Small House at Allington* it stiffens into deadlock, and by *The Last Chronicle* it is effectively over. One result of this progression is that the earlier novels, *The Warden*, *Barchester Towers*, and *Doctor Thorne*, appear more tightly constructed than the later ones: they have a definite animating idea; they are, relatively speaking, "well-made books" with the advantages that derive from a degree of compression and concentration. But more important they also have an imaginative freshness, a dynamic, a sense of direction, which are lacking in many of Trollope's other essays in domestic realism.

Barchester Towers, it is true, is not usually thought of as a well-made and dynamic book. Laborious Homeric similes, and thee-thouing authorial addresses to the reader and even to the characters, are more frequent than in most of the later, "mature" novels. Caricature and slapstick, styles of humour that don't usually suit Trollope, are more prominent than in most of his best work. And the love-plot is among his most protracted and dull. *Barchester Towers* is also supposed, wrongly I believe, to be unusually discursive even for Trollope, the episodes connected with Mr and Miss Thorne coming in for special condemnation on this score. All these elements, however, seem to me conditions of the novel's strength, which con-

sists above all in the finely sustained note of informality, mocking and self-mocking, that disguises both its sharpness of focus and its deep emotional commitment to the world it describes.

Seen in this light, it is much less artless than it pretends to be and is often taken to be. A case in point is the seemingly heavy-handed use of the "authorial I", to which James in particular took exception. In *Barchester Towers* Trollope intrudes into the novel not only in order to pass judgment on or admonish his characters, or to appeal to us to share his own feelings about them, but also at times to mock the whole ritual of narration. When he chips in to reassure us, well in advance of the event, that Eleanor Bold will certainly reject both Mr Slope and Bertie Stanhope (pp.129–31), he is merely exercising the narrator's privilege of breaking with strict chronological sequence, and he is doing so on respectable grounds—to put pointless speculations out of court. However, when he asks, by way of explaining Eleanor's failure to display the womanly tenderness that would have averted a misunderstanding between her and Mr Arabin, "But then where would have been my novel?"(p.285); and when he pronounces that the "end of the novel, like the end of a children's dinner-party, must be made up of sweetmeats and sugar-plums" (p.502), he may well seem, as James complains, to be delivering "slaps at credulity" and reminding us that the story is "only, after all, a make-believe" [16] But in fact he is not admitting that he has invented the story—which is what James accuses him of doing; all he is saying is that he has chosen a story, perhaps from life, that has the ingredients a conventional reader is likely to expect. The effect, then, is not necessarily harmful to the realistic illusion that the novel as a whole clearly aims at, though no doubt it may induce us to take some things—such as the manner in which the love-plot strings itself out—less seriously, with more of a feeling of déjà vu, than others. It may also, and this I think is of more consequence, accustom us to the idea that a good deal that happens in the novel is every bit as strange as fiction, but is not, for that reason, to be taken less seriously or as less true to life.

For *Barchester Towers* probably contains more to tax the credulity of the prosaic mind than any of Trollope's other "domestic" novels. Some of the characters are obviously caricatured, Mr Slope being only the most notorious example; farce and slapstick are used with memorable effect in many scenes, notably in those of Mrs Proudie's reception (chapters 10–11) and Mr Slope's "parting interview" with the Signora (chapter 46); and there is a flavour almost of fantasy in the story of the Signora's marriage (pp.67–70) and in the description of the Thornes (chapter 22). Yet at the same time, as I have suggested, the novel is very closely related

to contemporary history, and it offers not only what seem like highly realistic details of the customs, manners, and preoccupations of particular social groups at a particular point of time, but also, for example in the biographical sketch of Mr Arabin (chapter 20), a realism that can only be described as documentary. The art and imagination that assimilate all these elements into a unity—or a close approximation to one—hardly deserve to be called immature.

What is most impressive about the novel's formal and imaginative unity is the number of contrasting perspectives it accommodates. These have the effect, primarily of keeping us in constant doubt as to the reality, if any, that underlies the ostensible values of Barset. The crucial question in this regard is very much the same as in *The Warden*: whether in human and in objective ethical terms there is anything to choose between the old Barset and the new and foreign ways that threaten it. But much more than in *The Warden*, the elusiveness of old Barset's own special qualities is acknowledged. In *The Warden*, it will be recalled, the repetition of the word picturesque seemed to provide an essential clue, but the picturesqueness of Mr Harding's position was not sufficient to allay his doubts about its ethical correctness. In *Barchester Towers*, however, the epithet that catches our attention at the outset is *worldly*. It is applied to the archdeacon no fewer than three times in chapter 1, and on the last occasion (p.9) is accompanied by what amounts to an authorial manifesto: "Our archdeacon was worldly—who among us is not so?" This is but the first of many reminders that the clergyman, like any other professional man, is worthy of his hire and not usually backward, however exemplary his piety, in claiming it. The idea is one of the novel's great comic themes, and indeed becomes for Trollope an inexhaustible mine. And although Mr Harding and his liturgical music still haunt the cloisters, although in the chapter called "The Rubbish Cart" there is a further cry of petulant nostalgia for the good old days, quite in the manner of *The Warden* at its worst ("New men and new measures, long credit and few scruples, great success or wonderful ruin, such are now the tastes of Englishmen who know how to live"), worldliness has clearly become the dominant spirit even of old Barset. Picturesqueness, moreover, is now personified not only by Mr Harding but more vividly by the Thornes of Ullathorne, in whom it is shown running to delightful but bizarre excess.[17]

The Thornes (and, in a less likable way, the De Courcys) represent Barset in its "feudal" aspect, about which Trollope waxes so lyrical in *Doctor Thorne*. But the Thornes also reflect, in a distorting mirror, many aspects of Archdeacon Grantly and his worldly colleagues. For the archdeacon's seemingly prosaic worldliness in-

cludes at least a dash of poetry, as Trollope implies when he observes that it is not to be mistaken for mere "love of lucre": "He would be a richer man as archdeacon than he could be as bishop. But he certainly did desire to play first fiddle; he did desire to sit in full lawn sleeves among the peers of the realm; and he did desire, if the truth must out, to be called 'My Lord' by his reverend brethren" (p.9). Of his three main reasons for wishing to be a bishop, we note that two relate rather to the picturesque emblems of the office than to the actual power and worldly advantage it might confer. And it is noteworthy too that right through the novel he is cast in the role of defender of picturesque anomalies—of the "meretricious charms of melody" in cathedral services, though he will not tolerate "intoning" in his own church (pp.41, 46); of a wardenship with virtually no duties but a high salary and comfortable house attached to it; and of a deanship that carries great authority and status but virtually no duties ("'New duties! what duties?' said the archdeacon, with unintended sarcasm ... 'And where on earth can a man have peace and rest if not in a deanery?'" [p.462])[18] The archdeacon and his friends, we are told, are "all of the high-and-dry church" (p.45),[19] and in many of their attitudes they appear scarcely less high and dry than Miss Thorne and her brother—Miss Thorne who is a "pure Druidess" in her passion for the past, and Mr Thorne for whom Peel's "apostasy" on the question of free trade meant that "politics in England, as a pursuit for gentlemen, must be at an end", and whose heroes are "those fifty-three Trojans" who brought down the Whig-Peelite government in November 1852 (p.194).

Yet the dominant feeling that the picturesque side of Barchester's highness and dryness leaves with us is one of incongruity. For in its most characteristic manifestations the spirit of old Barchester is nothing if not practical and contemporary. This is brought home to us in the early scene (pp.1–7) where the archdeacon, at the bedside of his dying father, lays his plans for ensuring that he will succeed him as bishop. It is also dramatized in the anxious chatter of the clergymen gathered outside the room where Dean Trefoil lies dying (pp.294–97). Here solemn, but conventionally parsonical, solicitude for the sick man struggles with an in every sense livelier solicitude about who will be the next dean. The archdeacon is shocked by such discussion at this time, but even he turns pale and quite forgets Dr Trefoil when a "meagre little prebendary" mentions Mr Slope as a possible successor. A tersely businesslike argument about stipends and reports then follows. And although the impression of worldliness is softened by the clergymen's touching confusion about the facts which matter so much to them, and ironically punctuated by the choric repetition of the quaint titles which are their sole iden-

tifying marks, their prosaic absorption in questions of preferment and money must be judged unseemly.

In human terms, of course, these men are decidedly more agreeable than their low-church adversaries. They don't smell, or exude grease, like Mr Slope; they aren't rigorous about Sunday observance; they remember with pleasure a time when, without provoking censure, parsons played cards and hunted and enjoyed their wine like other gentlemen, and when, as Mr Harding recalls with some contrition, they were sometimes "very idle" (*Last Chronicle* I:224–25); they are not, in ordinary circumstances, aggressive or impolite in propagating their own tenets. Trollope, in the novel, makes no secret of his liking for them, nor, though he tries to be casual about it ("My readers will guess from what I have written that I myself do not like Mr. Slope; but I am constrained to admit that he is a man of parts" [p.56]), of his loathing for the worst of their enemies.

But on balance—in *Barchester Towers* if not always in other novels—Trollope recognizes that whatever his personal feelings, the high and dry cannot be represented as markedly more altruistic or morally aware, and certainly not as more truly religious, than the low. Even Mr Slope has taught himself, by "that subtle, selfish, ambiguous sophistry to which the minds of all men are so subject", to believe that "in doing much for the promotion of his own interests he was doing much also for the promotion of religion" (p.123). In any case, Mr Slope finally discredits himself even with his own party, so that we may take it that his grossest exhibitions of greed and duplicity place him outside the low-church pale. As to his lesser faults, the gist of the indictment seems to be that he is not a gentleman, as all of the high and dry unmistakably are. The archdeacon snarls that he has been "raked up ... from the gutters of Marylebone" (p.47); but this, we must remember, is after Slope has affronted the archdeacon by seeming to hold him personally accountable for the inadequacies of the plumbing and other amenities of the bishop's palace (pp.34–36). (Ironically, we later find that the archdeacon is not above interesting himself in such matters after all, for he looks into the domestic arrangements at Mr Arabin's parsonage with housewifely minuteness: pp.189–90.) Despite the fact that Slope had been at Cambridge—though only as a sizar (p.22)—the archdeacon's doubts about his social status may be justified. Not even the archdeacon, however, would deny that Bishop Proudie is a gentleman; and when in a moment of fury he unconsciously degrades the bishop to the same level as the bishop's chaplain, the laugh is clearly against the archdeacon himself:

"He is the most thoroughly bestial creature that ever I set my eyes upon," said the archdeacon.
"Who—the bishop?" asked the other, innocently.
"Bishop! no—I'm not talking about the bishop. How on earth such a
creature got ordained!—they'll ordain anybody now, I know; but he's
been in the church these ten years; and they used to be a little careful ten
years ago."
"Oh! you mean Mr Slope." [P.39]

The archdeacon's wildness here is only one of many indications
that high-and-dry Barchester is neither more reasonable nor always
more gentlemanly in its prejudices than are its enemies. Indeed
there are innumerable hints that both sides are tarred with much the
same brush. Petticoat government, for example, may seem the
special bane of the low-church party, but it is not unknown, either,
in the household of the archdeacon himself: he finds himself
badgered by his wife to put a stop to Mr Arabin's flirtation with the
Signora (pp.457–58) just as the bishop is badgered by Mrs Proudie
about Mr Slope's association with the same lady; and we observe,
too, that it is the archdeacon's wife, not the archdeacon himself, who
drops the few discreet words that silence the "intoning" curate of
Plumstead Episcopi (p.41). In a more general way, attitudes to
women, and the behaviour expected of them, represent an important bond between the two parties. If Barchester is united in any
respect, it is in its mingled cruelty and vulnerability to women. The
Signora highlights the vulnerability because she can exploit, and
brilliantly expose, a situation in which there is a universal assumption
that unattached woman is the weaker vessel, both intellectually and
morally. In the eyes of the men, the outrageous promiscuity of the
Signora's flirtations (with Arabin as well as Slope, Mr Thorne as well
as the bishop) is the sign of an essentially feminine weakness and
dependence, too flattering to themselves not to be readily forgiven
and enjoyed. But when the same male superstition convicts Eleanor
Bold, unheard, of being infatuated with Slope, she is cruelly
ostracized because she refuses to simulate feminine weakness. So
long as she takes her stand on rational moral grounds—arguing that
Slope need not be her enemy simply because he is of the low-church
party—she is misunderstood. And eventually, though it has been
maintained that she achieves some degree of heightened self-
knowledge,[20] she is driven, as I see it, to the same abject surrender,
the same admission of weakness, as nearly all of Trollope's heroines
who try to assert their own judgment on matters outside the
domestic sphere.

Admittedly, Eleanor's marriage to Arabin may appear, and may
be meant to appear, a marriage of true minds. Arabin is ostensibly
the most serious and least rancorous of the high-church party, and

he alone seems to see the Barchester struggle in something like its correct perspective. "Wars about trifles," he points out, "are always bitter, especially among neighbours." But he will not have it that "such contentions bring scandal on the church". The only alternative to them would be "that of acknowledging a common head of our church, whose word on all points of doctrine shall be authoritative". Having nearly followed Newman into the Roman church, he is aware that "such a termination of our difficulties is alluring enough" (pp.184–85). But in the existing situation his view clearly coincides with that already expressed by the narrator:

> Moderate schism, if there may be such a thing, at any rate calls attention to the subject, draws in supporters who would otherwise have been inattentive to the matter, and teaches men to think upon religion. How great an amount of good of this description has followed that movement in the Church of England which commenced with the publication of Froude's Remains! [P.170]

On the evidence of the novels, one may wonder whether Trollope's sense of this "good" was really as strong as he suggests here. But Eleanor, at any rate, hears Arabin's ideas "not without a certain pleasurable excitement, that this new comer among them spoke in a manner very different from that to which she was accustomed". It is a surprise to her to learn that there is a spiritual dimension to the disputes that she has seen raging about her and that at least one of the participants can admit that neither side has a monopoly of the truth (p.186). Yet it does not appear to shock either her or Trollope that Arabin should share and vociferate the general eager dislike of Slope, even before he has met the man!

Neither Eleanor nor Arabin, then, attains to anything like complete detachment from the fray. For this, and for the sense of how little there is to choose, objectively, between the contending parties, it is to the Stanhopes—particularly Bertie Stanhope and his sister the Signora—that we must turn. These are the jesters, whose function is to expose the common denominator of humanity that is overlaid by distinctions of rank, opinion, and deportment. Their great qualification for the role is not their ethical sense—for they are all "heartless" (p.63) and all, in varying degrees, unscrupulous—but their complete aloofness and disinterestedness, their impervious blandness. They are, in fact, the only absolute outsiders ever allowed into Barset, and after they leave it never recovers the same animation or has its lovable and unlovable absurdities exposed with the same sharpness and joy. Subsequently, I suggest, Trollope became too attached to the county—just as, for example, he became attached to the archdeacon during the course of *The Warden*—to feel comfortable with observers so unattached, so oblivious of its

traditional values. But it may also be that he took to heart the suggestion of his publisher's reader that the Signora in particular might shock the Young Person,[21] and the emphasis of friends and reviewers on the book's "manliness".[22] It is, at all events, unhappily true that none of his later novels—not even *The Eustace Diamonds*—can compare with *Barchester Towers* for gleeful irreverence, especially on the subjects of sex and religion. "Is it not a pity", he asks at one stage (p.314), "that people who are bright and clever should so often be exceedingly improper? and that those who are never improper should so often be dull and heavy?" But too often in his later novels, and especially those in his domestic stream, we sigh in vain for improper people who are also bright and clever.

The impact of the Stanhopes on Barchester, and on our view of Barchester, is seen at its strongest in three scenes: Mrs Proudie's reception (chapters 10–11), the confrontation of the Signora, Lady De Courcy, and Mrs Proudie at the Ullathorne sports (chapter 37), and the Signora's humiliation of Mr Slope (chapter 46).

At Mrs Proudie's reception (p.75 ff.), Bertie's unintentional chaffing of the bishop is not only funny in itself—because of the bishop's discomfiture and Bertie's obliviousness of it—but also very pointed as a commentary on the temporal preoccupations of the Barchester clergy generally. Bertie assumes unquestioningly that one addresses a bishop as man to man: "Bishop of Barchester, I presume? I am delighted to make your acquaintance." Instinctively polite, he easily finds common ground between them: "Do you like Barchester on the whole?" he asks, recalling that the bishop is as much a stranger in Barchester as he is. The next question, naturally, is how the bishop likes his new job and whether it is a promotion or just a transfer:

> " ... you are changed about sometimes, a'nt you?"
> "Translations are occasionally made," said Dr. Proudie; "but not so frequently as in former days."
> "They've cut them all down to pretty nearly the same figure, haven't they?" said Bertie.

"They", in this connexion, are presumably the bishop's own Whig friends and patrons, but the real sting is less in Bertie's casual way of referring to the church reforms that have meant so much to the bishop and, in a more distressing way, to Barchester, than in the implication that a bishopric nowadays is not a very lucrative or even a very dignified position: the word *figure* must strike the bishop as cruelly double meaning. Perhaps, however, there is not much for a bishop to do at Barchester? Bertie's query foreshadows the archdeacon's scornful mirth at the idea that deans have duties. The bishop replies, "with considerable dignity", that a bishop of the

Church of England never has an easy lot. Bertie confesses that he "once had thoughts of being a bishop" himself, or rather, he corrects himself, "a parson first, you know". What put him off, he remarks with crushing but still quite unconscious irony, was not the prospect of hard work—though he admits that his father has found it too much ("I fancy he didn't like saying the same thing over so often")—but his preference for the Church of Rome and more recently for the Jews. Here Bertie, and not Arabin, stands forth as the prime representative in the novel of contemporary religious unrest. And one cannot help wondering whether he is not a better guide than Arabin to Trollope's own attitude to this unrest. For Trollope at times seems to find as much to respect in Bertie, with his harebrained involuntary parodies of clerical attitudes, as he does in any of the clergy, and the tone of some of his references to the clergy in general, while inoffensive enough, is a good deal more flippant than he usually allows it to become. The "preaching clergyman", for instance, is characterized as "the bore of the age" (p.47), and it is suggested that, if deacons were prohibited from preaching as well as from pronouncing absolution, they would never be allowed by their congregations to advance to full priesthood but would be "bribed to adhere to their incompetence" (p.208).

Bertie's exchange with the bishop is followed by the near-slapstick incident in which Mrs Proudie's lace train is damaged by the castors of a rolling sofa, probably the very sofa from which Mrs Proudie herself is wont to preside in the bishop's study and which, it has been suggested before, is a fitting emblem of the new regime at the bishop's palace: "a horrid chintz affair, most unprelatical and almost irreligious: such a sofa as never yet stood in the study of any decent high church clergyman of the Church of England" (p.30). It is now the throne of the crippled Signora, conspicuous under the blazing gas lamps that are another of the Proudies' innovations at the palace (cf.p.35). As the substructure of Mrs Proudie's train begins to tear, and crack, and gape open under the assault of the sofa, every detail in the mélée that follows is beautifully calculated: Bertie's involuntary homage to Mrs Proudie as an enraged goddess; Mrs Proudie's misconstruction of Bertie's poetic promise to "fly to the looms of the fairies to repair the damage [to her lace]" as a "direct mockery" of her; the manner in which "Bertie" becomes "Ethelbert" as he attempts to respond to Mrs Proudie's "Unhand it" (opportunely recalled from some "scrap of dramatic poetry") with something equally poetic; the collocation of Bertie's blasphemous reference to the "cursed sofa" with the devotionally "imploring" face he turns to Mrs Proudie; the suggestive vagueness of the word *belongings* as applied to Mrs Proudie's nether garments; and the telling redundancy

of the Signora's "audible" laugh. In real life the niece of an earl, albeit a "Scotch" earl, would not say "Unhand me", or would say it more effectively; but incredulity gives way to sheer delight at the stylized eloquence of the scene.

The importance of Bertie's and Mrs Proudie's contretemps for the novel as a whole lies in its sexual overtones. Bertie and Mrs Proudie are clearly terrified of each other, Bertie because Mrs Proudie's stateliness unmans him, accentuates his usual effeminacy ("I'll fly to the looms of the fairies"), Mrs Proudie because she feels, no doubt unconsciously, in danger of a sexual assault. The irony of Mrs Proudie's fear is that here as always—as, for example, in her usurpation of her husband's prerogatives both in the home and in the diocese—she is playing the man's part and would be in little danger of losing her dignity but for this. The Signora, who specializes in humiliating men, and who succeeds in making not only Slope and the bishop but also, on the other side, Arabin and Mr Thorne look foolish, probably senses that her effeminate brother is unconsciously using tactics very like her own—a "poetic" affectation of weakness—to humiliate the mannish Mrs Proudie. Of Charlotte Stanhope, Bertie's other sister, the narrator observes that she "was a fine young woman; and had she been a man, would have been a very fine young man" (p.66), and the same, with minor variations, could be said of Mrs Proudie. Both of them, like the Signora herself, and to some extent like Mrs Grantly and even Miss Thorne (with her passion for muscular medieval sports), are natural man-tamers. Bertie, however, though Charlotte likes to feel she has him under her domination, nearly always wriggles out, obeying her according to the letter—for example, by proposing to Eleanor—but resisting her according to the spirit. He is, in fact, the sole exception to the male pomposity which, as I have noted, makes so much misery for Eleanor, and which, chiefly as a result of the wiles of the Signora— reaching their climax in chapter 46 with her dressing down of Mr Slope—we come to see as a crucial weakness that the old Barchester shares with its enemies.

Why did Trollope choose to make the Signora a cripple? One's first impulse is to say that he was simply playing safe: a sexually incapacitated siren would not compromise her male admirers to the same extent as one they could be suspected of hoping to seduce. But is it credible that she could have cast such a spell over so many men? The realistic answer must be no. But if we consider it as another of those elements in the novel which border on comic fantasy, the Signora's remarkable seductiveness can be seen to serve a distinct satirical purpose: that of showing up the sexual timidity of the Barcastrian, and perhaps the Victorian, male. In *The Ordeal of Richard*

Feverel, published two years after *Barchester Towers*, Adrian Harley mockingly observed that unless he happened to go to the ballet a Victorian young man might well remain ignorant of the fact that women possess legs; and it is presumably this comforting ignorance that beguiles the Signora's male coterie. What is certain, however, is that her sexual incapacity is one of the conditions of her emancipation from conventional standards, just as her brother's effeminacy is one of the conditions of his; and it is by contrast with this emancipation that the timidities of Barchester appear most absurd.

The Signora's satirical gaze of course takes in more than the sexual quirks of Barchester. She is also fully alive to the absurdities of its caste system, of which we are given a not altogether farcical parody in the imbroglio over the "classless" Lookalofts at Miss Thorne's fête. It is, for example, her amused awareness that Mr Slope is not the stuff of which Barchester deans are made that gives her such an advantage over him in the scene where she publicly ridicules him (pp.452–53). And she can use her own patently apocryphal claim to exalted rank—as the "last of the Neros"—with a perfect simulation of innocence: for example, when she sets out to embarrass the bishop by seeming to hint that he might personally prepare her daughter for confirmation. But her greatest moment is when she outstares the Countess De Courcy:

> She opened her large bright lustrous eyes wider and wider, till she seemed to be all eyes. She gazed up into the lady's face, not as though she did it with an effort, but as if she delighted in doing it. She used no glass to assist her effrontery, and needed none. The faintest possible smile of derision played round her mouth, and her nostrils were slightly dilated, as if in sure anticipation of her triumph. And it was sure. The Countess De Courcy, in spite of her thirty centuries and De Courcy Castle, and the fact that Lord De Courcy was grand master of the ponies to the Prince of Wales, had not a chance with her. At first the little circlet of gold wavered in the countess's hand, then the hand shook, then the circlet fell, the countess's head tossed itself into the air, and the countess's feet shambled out to the lawn. She did not however go so fast but what she heard the signora's voice, asking—
> "Who on earth is that woman, Mr. Slope?"
> "That is Lady De Courcy."
> "Oh, ah. I might have supposed so. Ha, ha, ha. Well, that's as good as a play." [Pp.356–57]

This is a scene that Trollope often attempts but never does so well again. But then, except perhaps in one of his last novels, *Mr. Scarborough's Family*, he never again allows himself to portray such an emancipated spirit as that of the Stanhopes with the same imaginative freedom.

Certainly, Barset is never afterwards exposed to quite so unblink-

ing a gaze. At the end of *Barchester Towers* the Stanhopes return to Italy, where, it is reported in *Doctor Thorne* (p.234), Dr Stanhope soon after dies (though in *Framley Parsonage*, p.279, he is reported to have come back and lived at Barchester before his death). Slope also departs, and with Arabin ensconced in the deanship the old Barchester is left to carry on its struggle with the Proudies on equal, if not advantageous, terms and in no further doubt as to its own survival. In the later Barsetshire chronicles, even when clerical characters play a major part, the struggle becomes essentially social and political, with religious, or at any rate sectarian, issues receding into the background.

The opening pages of *Doctor Thorne* constitute Trollope's fullest general description of Barset and of the particular historical and geographical influences that shaped it. They also foreshadow a significant shift in its centre of gravity and, in effect, an extension of its boundaries. Its location is now given as "the west of England", and it is described as "purely agricultural; agricultural in its produce, agricultural in its poor, and agricultural in its pleasures". It has a number of market towns, all more or less the same, but its greatness depends on the "clerical aristocracy" of Barchester and on the "landed powers", the "county squirearchy": in *Doctor Thorne* interest centres almost exclusively on the latter. The most important new revelation, however, is that there are in fact two Barsetshires. East Barset, which is the "more purely Conservative", is dominated by smaller land owners—minor nobility and untitled squires; West Barset is "overshadowed" (a word that proves to be aptly chosen) by two "great Whig magnates", the Duke of Omnium and the Earl De Courcy. The whole county is noted for its "frequent Tudor mansions", of which Greshamsbury, the main scene of action in *Doctor Thorne*, is accounted one of the purest examples, worthy to vie with Longleat and Hatfield (p.10); but significantly Courcy Castle dates from the reign of William III, and Gatherum, the seat of the Duke of Omnium, is of quite recent construction (pp.181, 231–32).

Barsetshire's division into eastern and western parts was only one consequence of the first Reform Bill, which was clearly an even more traumatic experience for the squirearchy than the church reforms of the 1830s and 1840s were for the Barchester clergy. True, members are still returned to parliament "generally—in spite of Reform Bills, past, present, and coming—in accordance with the dictates of some neighbouring land magnate" (p.1), and England is still a "feudal" or "chivalrous" rather than a "commercial" country. In Barset at least, if not in "some of its manufacturing leviathan brethren in the north" (p.1), the old symbols remain: " … and may

such symbols long remain among us; they are still lovely and fit to be loved. They tell us of the true and manly feelings of other times; and to him who can read aright, they explain more fully, more truly than any written history can do, how Englishmen have become what they are." Foremost among such symbols is the institution of a landed aristocracy, for in England, unlike any of the other great European countries, "there still exists the closest attachment to, the sincerest trust in, the old feudal and now so-called landed interests". If England is a commercial country, she is so as Venice was: "She may excel other nations in commerce, but yet it is not that in which she most prides herself, in which she most excels." (pp.11–12)[23]

Trollope is no doubt serious, but the novel as a whole hardly endorses this reassuring picture. Indeed its chief theme—introduced with brilliant precision and economy in the early chapters[24]—is the divisive effects of the Reform Bill and of the competitive, commercial, "democratic" spirit of which it was partly symptom and partly cause. Conservative Barset is shown to be locked in battle both with its own Whigs, who betrayed it by throwing their weight behind the Reform Bill (p.3), and with the new commercial plutocracy represented by, among others, the tailor's son Moffat, the ointment heiress Martha Dunstable, and the Scatcherds: Sir Roger Scatcherd, now a railway magnate, had been "an extreme demagogue, in those noisy times just prior to the Reform Bill" (p.20). Standing more staunchly for the "old symbols", for conservative Barset, are Dr Thorne and the Frank Greshams, father and son. These belong to Barset's oldest families (the doctor being related to the Thornes of Ullathorne) which claim to be much older than the De Courcys (p.18). All three, however, are victims of the new divisions in Barset society: Dr Thorne has had to make his own way in the world, largely because of his aristocratic relatives' disapproval of his brother's association with the Scatcherds at the time of Sir Roger's early demagoguery (pp.18–20); Frank Gresham senior is gradually losing Greshamsbury to Sir Roger because of the expense of election contests that probably would not have been contests but for the Reform Bill (and but for his having incurred the distrust of many conservatives by marrying a De Courcy); Frank Gresham junior, as a result of his father's financial setbacks, is under pressure to marry for money, sacrificing in the process both his own inclinations and his pride in his rank—since the money, Martha Dunstable's, is "commercial".

From this account—given that the Thornes, the Greshams, the De Courcys, and the Scatcherds dominate practically every episode— the novel will sound schematic; and indeed it is, by common consent, one of the most tightly constructed of Trollope's novels. In no

other early novel are his apparent aims at once so consistent and so undisguised. They are indicated by such unmistakable barings of the authorial breast as the "old symbols" passage, already discussed, and the lament for the old coaching town of Courcy left high and dry in the railway age:

> And how changed has been the bustle of that once noisy inn to the present death-like silence of its green courtyard! There, a lame ostler crawls about with his hands thrust into the capacious pockets of his jacket, feeding on memory. That weary pair of omnibus jades, and three sorry posters, are all that now grace those stables where horses used to be stalled in close contiguity by the dozen ...
>
> Come, my friend [the ostler], and discourse with me. Let us know what are thy ideas of the inestimable benefits which science has conferred on us in these, our latter days. How dost thou, among others, appreciate railways and the power of steam, telegraphs, telegrams, and our new expresses? But indifferently, you say ...
>
> ... There is nothing left for thee but to be carted away as rubbish—for thee and for many of us in these now prosperous days; oh, my melancholy, care-ridden friend! [Pp.182–84]

These sentiments are, of course, among the commonplaces of the early Victorian novel, and the mélange of Goldsmith ("Sweet Auburn") and Carlyle ("these, our latter days") is hardly felicitous; the passage also stirs unhappy recollections of Trollope's angrier outbursts in *The Warden* and of his one lapse into the same maudlin vein in chapter 13 of *Barchester Towers* entitled "The Rubbish Cart". But fortunately, for all the single-minded directness of its satirical purpose, the novel as a whole is not satisfied with such a simple view of the opposition between old symbols and new.

For one thing, the old symbols are already tarnished. Regret it as they may, the Greshams have allied themselves with the De Courcys, and there is at least a hint that the alliance was an inevitable one:

> "Gardez Gresham," had been chosen in the days of motto-choosing probably by some herald-at-arms as an appropriate legend for signifying the peculiar attributes of the family. Now, however, unfortunately, men were not of one mind as to the exact idea signified. Some declared, with much heraldic warmth, that it was an address to the savages, calling on them to take care of their patron; while others, with whom I myself am inclined to agree, averred with equal certainty that it was an advice to the people at large, especially to those inclined to rebel against the aristocracy of the county, that they should "beware the Gresham." [Pp.10–11]

This is Trollope's irony at its most delicate, for the question that has generated so much heraldic warmth is in fact the burning question of the whole novel: whether the people at large are to be regarded as the friends or as the foes of the aristocracy of the county. When

Frank Gresham senior married into the De Courcy family just before the Reform Bill, he was playing his part in closing the aristocracy's ranks; the alliance was probably as natural, as inescapable, and as painful to his family as, in many respects, is that which they make a generation later with Sir Roger Scatcherd's money, the property of his illegitimate niece Mary Thorne: both father and son, in opposite ways, have obeyed the injunction "Gardez Gresham". But in doing so they, or at any rate the family, have confessed their own weakness and dependence.

Neither father nor son, personable as they are, commands much respect. One of the main reasons, as with most of the men in *Barchester Towers*, is their ineptitude in their relationships with women. The father is bullied and has been nearly bankrupted by his wife and her female relations; yet the only matter on which he has been able to find the energy to resist them effectually is that of keeping his beloved hounds, and now that even they are gone he is reduced to mere grimacing behind his wife's back. The son, too, makes a fool of himself with, and is made a fool of by, no fewer than three women, including the one he eventually marries. Even after Mary Thorne has accepted him, and he is "to her like some god come from the heavens to make her blessed" and as "bright as an angel" (pp.359–60), his inherited passion for dogs remains as strong as his passion for her; he attends to his dogs "quite as vehemently as though he were not in love at all; quite as vehemently as though he had said nothing [to Mary] as to going into some profession which must necessarily separate him from horses and dogs" (p.435); and at a period of crisis in his relationship with Mary his hounds are still his first concern: "He had now completed his round of visits to the kennel, master huntsman, and stables of the county hunt, and was at liberty to attend to his own affairs." (p.463) Earlier, by way of apology for his fickleness and frivolity, the narrator has repeated a favourite quotation, from Sir Henry Taylor's *Philip van Artevelde*, to the effect that "women grow on the sunny side of the wall" and consequently mature sooner than men (p.83). But by the time he wins Mary he is supposed to have outgrown his hobbledehoyhood and to have become capable of gaining the love of an apparently intelligent and fastidious woman.

Frank is admittedly a shade less barbarous than some of Trollope's other jeunes premiers—than, for example, Peregrine Orme, in *Orley Farm*, whose favourite occupation is ratcatching, or Lord Chiltern, in *Phineas Finn*, who with the whole world before him and a clever and sociable wife decides to make hunting his life's work. In his more rational moments, Trollope can see that men of such limited interests are bound to be tedious companions even for

women of moderate intellect (the eponymous hero of *Ralph the Heir* is one example); but all too often the mental level of his lover-heroes is not far above that of the Boy's Own world of Charles Reade. Certainly in *Doctor Thorne* Trollope is only half-aware that his lover-hero, on his own showing, is unworthy of his heroine.

By insisting, however, that Frank Gresham is not the novel's true hero—an honour that he accords instead to Dr Thorne (pp.7, 17)—he emphasizes that love is not of primary concern to him. As in *Barchester Towers*, it assumes importance chiefly as one of the focal points of a broad social conflict, and sexual inadequacies are of interest less for their own sake than as symptoms or reflections of other inadequacies brought to light in this conflict. Thus in the men of the Gresham family they point to a weakness of character and intellect which, no matter how indulgently the novel may seem to regard it in the sexual context, is taken fully into account in other contexts. We need only contrast the Gresham men with, on the one hand, Dr Thorne and, on the other, Sir Roger Scatcherd to recognize that the feudal or chivalrous England which they personify has become effete. And if to Dr Thorne and Sir Roger we add Martha Dunstable, as representatives of a more competitive commercial spirit, the impression of effeteness becomes even stronger.

Dr Thorne has at least as much pride in his "blood" as any Gresham and is at least as alive to the "advantage held"—according to Dr Johnson—"by men who have grandfathers over those who have none" (p.26).[25] But in his own profession he is happy to incur the wrath of his colleagues by practices that they consider "democratic" and commercial: by advertising a scale of fees and by mixing his own prescriptions like a common apothecary. These practices, characteristically, are old-fashioned—the kind against which Dr Lydgate had set his face twenty years earlier in Middlemarch—but like all of Dr Thorne's conservative quirks they stem from a hatred of genteel pretence. They go along with his "combativeness" (p.31), and with the "vehemence of character" (very different from the feckless vehemence attributed to Frank Gresham), which he has passed on to his niece (p.42) and which finds expression at times in a kind of yeoman-like egalitarianism: as, for instance, when he is snubbing Lady Arabella Gresham (née De Courcy) or conversing man to man with Sir Roger. It is true that he blenches at the idea of mixing socially with the Scatcherds, and of having his niece mix with them—though eventually, in defiance of his predictions, she does establish a friendly, if uneasy, relationship with Lady Scatcherd. But, as we see later (in *Framley Parsonage*), he is not so proud of his "genealogical tree" (p.26) as to be above marrying Miss Dunstable, a woman with no greater pretensions to a grandfather than Sir Roger's.

Scatcherd and Miss Dunstable are generally considered two of Trollope's finest "characters", and in terms of their individuality and vitality they obviously stand out—both in *Doctor Thorne* and in his work as a whole—in a way that the Greshams do not. They are among the most sympathetic pictures he ever drew of people whose manners and breeding are definitely not those of gentlefolk. This is not to say, of course, that either is a fully attractive figure: Dr Thorne is clearly justified in feeling that the sottish Sir Roger is socially ineligible, and the "plain Dunstable of the matter", once we have become fully accustomed to it, ceases to be very amusing—though it continues to amuse Trollope himself. But insofar as they stand for an unashamed appreciation of the usefulness of money, they can be seen as an altogether salutary corrective both to the genteel incompetence of the Greshams and to the genteel hypocrisy of the De Courcys. In this sense they partly assume the Stanhopes' role of dangerous interlopers in Barsetshire; or rather, one must now say, in both the Barsetshires, East and West.

Miss Dunstable's talent for satirical debunking is seen in some of her exchanges with Mrs Proudie, for example the one in which she loudly explains that "something about money matters ... something to do with the ointment" had forced her to cut short a recent visit to Rome (p.191). When Mrs Proudie hastily changes the subject, with a question about sabbath observance in Rome, Miss Dunstable replies, "with rather a joyous air", that "Sunday and week-days are all the same there"; and her response to Mrs Proudie's fear that "danger was to be apprehended" from visits to such places is "Oh!—ah! the malaria—of course—yes; if you go at the wrong time; but nobody is such a fool as that now."[26] Here, even down to the "Oh!—ah" with which she introduces her ʟunch-line, Miss Dunstable is almost a reincarnation of the Signora; and her loud reference to money matters and ointment makes it clear that she appreciates the weaknesses of Courcy Castle and the general run of its guests perfectly. (The Proudies, of course, are Whigs: hence their presence at the Castle).

But Miss Dunstable is, after all, willing to accept the hospitality of the De Courcys; and subsequently, when she comes to know East Barset—in the persons of Dr Thorne and his niece, and Frank Gresham—she throws in her lot with it. The Signora, it is true, had also discovered a rather surprising tenderness for conservative Barchester—in the persons of Eleanor and Mr Arabin—but this friendship had petered out after a single exchange of letters (*Barchester Towers*, p.506): unlike Miss Dunstable, she was in no danger of being permanently seduced by Barset. In *Doctor Thorne*, however, Barset's seductiveness is such that even Sir Roger

Scatcherd, a self-made follower of the Manchester school (p.186), is not proof against it. The evidence of his seduction is the son whom he has had educated as a gentleman and who has turned out, in accordance with a familiar pattern, unfit either for business or for Barset, a composite of the worst aspects of both.

In *Doctor Thorne*, then, the chief interlopers, Miss Dunstable and the Scatcherds, do not pose quite the same threat to the conservative gentry of Barset as do their counterparts in *Barchester Towers*. Nor does the contemptible Moffat, the London tailor's son who jilts Frank Gresham's sister. Moffat is first rejected by the voters of Barchester, suffering in the process worse indignities—including a rotten egg—than any other of Trollope's parliamentary aspirants, and is then given a whipping by Frank in front of his own club. The latter episode is related in a mock-heroic style that turns the irony as much against the swaggering victor as against the quailing victim: unlike Adolphus Crosbie—who jilts Lily Dale in *The Small House at Allington*—Moffat is easily cowed, and Frank's triumph is clearly hollow, his bloodlust facile and childish ("Frank, his heart leaping the while, saw his prey ... "). The novel leaves us in no doubt that, for every Moffatt whose nerve or ambition fails him, another more resolute will dilute the blood of England's aristocracy—as, for example, the London attorney Mortimer Gazebee does when he marries one of the De Courcy daughters.

It is the tacit willingness of this blood to be diluted—the blood of the Greshams by that of the Scatcherds, as well as the blood of the De Courcys by that of the Gazebees—which is the chief object of Trollope's satire in *Doctor Thorne*. Not that he regards the dilution as a bad thing: Mary Thorne obviously has more than her money to contribute to the future wellbeing of the Greshams, and Mortimer Gazebee, though a cold fish, is infinitely more prepossessing than any of the De Courcy males. But Trollope is fully aware that the mystique of "blood", irrational as it is, is an essential prop of Barset's and England's social system, a prop that is shaken when Frank Greshams marry Mary Thornes or De Courcy ladies marry their family attorneys. His feeling on the subject is no doubt very similar to that of Mary herself, who, to the question "what makes a gentleman? what makes a gentlewoman?" can return only a contradictory answer: "Absolute, intrinsic, acknowledged, individual merit must give [gentility] to its possessor, let him be whom, and what, and whence he might. So far the spirit of democracy was strong within her. Beyond this it could be had but by inheritance, received as it were second-hand, or twenty-second-hand. And so far the spirit of aristocracy was strong within her" (p.85). Thus in resolving to insist on her equality with the Gresham girls and

Patience Oriel, Mary "came forth armed to do battle against the world's prejudices, those prejudices she herself still loved so well" (p.98). Much later, Frank protests that these prejudices, the whole "theory of high birth and pure blood", are an "empty, lying humbug" (p.472), and up to a point his words are proved true when, with the discovery that Mary is an heiress, opposition to his marrying her dissolves. But even Frank, "democratic" as he is himself, is slow to recognize the humbug for what it is—as Miss Dunstable reminds him in words that momentarily echo Mary's:

> "... some people are sometimes valued rather for what they've got than for any good qualities belonging to themselves intrinsically."
> "That can never be the case with Miss Dunstable; especially not at Courcy Castle," said Frank, bowing easily from the corner of the sofa over which he was leaning.
> "Of course not," said Miss Dunstable; and Frank at once perceived that she spoke in a tone of voice differing much from that half-bantering, half-good-humoured manner that was customary with her. "Of course not: any such idea would be quite out of the question at Courcy Castle ..." [P.218]

The De Courcys, as Miss Dunstable goes on to imply, are the novel's worst humbugs, being at once insolently proud of their blood and quite without compunction or discrimination in diluting it for the sake of money. Theirs, it is made clear, is the influence that taints the Greshams, for Frank and his father and his sister Beatrice, confused as are their own notions, are always uneasy about the "De Courcy notions" of Lady Arabella Gresham and her eldest daughter. Indeed, Trollope must be suspected of making the De Courcys scapegoats for many of the inadequacies of the Greshams, and particularly for their inability to arrive at consistent "notions" about the conflicting claims of money and rank. There is, as I have said, no mistaking these inadequacies: neither the Greshams' confusion about the mystique of blood nor Mary's (which is the same) is in any way unconfounded by the windfall that suddenly transforms her in everyone's eyes, and most significantly in her own, into a fit bride for Frank Gresham. Yet their embarrassment at having to compromise their principles—as they had also been prepared to do for the sake of Miss Dunstable's money—is glossed over, whereas that of the De Courcys, in this or in similar situations, is dwelt upon with relish. The crowning example of Trollope's animus against the De Courcys is the idea of having Lady Amelia, the proudest of them all, steal a plebeian suitor from Augusta Gresham, her most devoted imitator. Although their exchange of letters, in the chapter called "De Courcy Precepts and De Courcy Practice" (chapter 38), is a virtuoso piece of satirical writing, it has too much of the aspect of a coup de grâce, an exultant last swipe at an enemy already mortally wounded.

Its placing in the novel—shortly before Mary receives her windfall—gives it, in addition, the aspect of a calculated diversion from her and the Greshams' moral quandaries, and this impression is strengthened by the fact that, to record Lady Amelia's derogation, the narrative has to leap ahead of itself in an unaccustomed manner.

This is not the only example of satirical exaggeration and one-sidedness. It is paralleled by the treatment of Dr Thorne's arch-enemy Dr Fillgrave, by that of Mr Oriel's extreme high-church devotee Miss Gushing, and even in some respects by that of the Scatcherds. All of these stand, in one form or another, for modern, supposedly progressive notions, but Dr Fillgrave and Miss Gushing in particular are guyed with a brutality and, in the case of Dr Fillgrave, a thoroughness which smacks of personal malice and which often has little to do with their "notions"

Sir Roger Scatcherd is more subtly and sympathetically drawn, but there are signs that Trollope secretly exults in his weaknesses too. It is hard to see any other explanation for the protracted and painful account of his son's disgraceful behaviour when he dines at Greshamsbury (chapter 35): this not only strains credulity, since Sir Louis has after all been educated as a gentleman, but serves no apparent purpose in the novel, since we already know that his education has signally failed in its aim and that, like his father, he will drink himself to death so that Mary can inherit his money. Trollope's disguised hatred of the Scatcherds, however, betrays itself most openly in his sneering references to the stilted eulogies the newspapers will print about Sir Roger after his death (pp.297–98, 306). "No man," he observes, "was vainer of his reputation, and it would have greatly gratified him to know that posterity was about to speak of him in such terms—to speak of him with a voice that would be audible for twenty-four hours." With the pen of Samuel Smiles already active glorifying the heroes of the railway age,[27] the last part of this is surely wishful thinking, its motive all too clear.

On the whole, *Doctor Thorne* is nevertheless one of Trollope's most humane social satires, as well as one of his freshest and most coherent. It is also the most radical in spirit of all the Barset novels, and indeed of all his domestic novels—those that exclude what he calls tragic elements. And in none of the later novels in the series are the county itself, and the high and dry, the "feudal" or "chivalrous" values for which it stands, shown to be in such danger at once from within and without.

In his *Autobiography* (p.109) Trollope professed to have been "surprised by the success of *Doctor Thorne*", which he believed had outsold all his other novels.[28] From its success he inferred, with some

irritation, that a good plot is what will "most raise" or "most condemn" a novel in the public judgment, whereas in his own view the plot was "the most insignificant part of a tale", merely the vehicle for the characters. This view doubtless stemmed in part from his conviction that he himself was incapable of devising and handling complicated plots (*Autobiography*, pp.220, 296, etc.); but it must have been reinforced by the fact that the plot of *Doctor Thorne* had been "drawn out" for him—though one wonders how far—by his brother (*Autobiography*, p.99). Whether it really is a better or more complicated plot than several of his own devising is, I think, questionable; and although Booth,[29] among others, has stressed the melodrama of the story of Mary Thorne's birth and the fairytale flavour of her sudden accession to rank and riches, approximate parallels can be found in a number of Trollope's other novels.[30]

Turning from *Doctor Thorne* to *Framley Parsonage*, however, we are inevitably struck by the comparative looseness of the latter's plot. Trollope himself characterizes it as a mere "hodge-podge", which he is reluctant even to call a plot. The novel was popular, he believed, simply because "the characters were so well handled" and because the "story was thoroughly English": "a little fox-hunting and a little tuft-hunting, some Christian virtue and some Christian cant", "no heroism and no villainy", "much Church, but more love-making" (*Autobiography*, p.124). In outline this is the formula for many of Trollope's domestic novels, including most of those discussed in chapter 3 below, and the popular success of *Framley Parsonage* must be held to have encouraged him in the belief that neither a coherent plot nor a unifying theme was essential. For such a formula implies both a dispersal of interest, to the extent that a number of stories offering different kinds of interest vie more or less equally for attention, and a substitution of the broadly realistic quality of "Englishness"—or "Englishry", as Michael Sadleir calls it[31]—for any more specific unifying idea. The result is that a novel like *Framley Parsonage* does seem to depend less on "plot" and more on "character" than one like *Doctor Thorne*; indeed, it strikingly attests the difficulty, for any novelist, of sustaining interest in characters who have no real part to play either in the story or in the total design of the novel.

Some of the characters who reappear in *Framley Parsonage*, after having been created for specific purposes in earlier Barset novels, are obvious cases in point: the Proudies and Greshams, for example, and Miss Dunstable and Dr Thorne. Though none of these is completely redundant in *Framley Parsonage*, they are clearly allowed to hold more of the stage than their supernumerary role justifies; and even some of the reviewers, notwithstanding the Victorian love of

"characters" for their own sake, suspected that Trollope's imagination must be running out of steam.[32] The new collisions between the Grantlys and the Proudies, on the subject of their respective daughters' matrimonial projects (pp.437–41 and 490–92), are amusing enough and do show the Grantlys in a fresh light, cheerfully allying themselves with a Whig family. But both credulity and interest are strained by the frequent reappearances of, in particular, Mrs Proudie and Miss Dunstable, as part of the frivolous Whig establishment of London and West Barset.

Thus a long episode like that of Harold Smith's lecture (chapter 6), though effectively dramatizing the extent to which the frivolity and shallow cynicism of the "Chaldicotes set" have seduced Mark Robarts from the virtue of old Barset (personified chiefly in Lady Lufton) and even from proper attention to his clerical duties, is obviously included mainly as a showcase for Mrs Proudie in one of her routine roles. As political satire, the lecture itself appears heavy-handed and flippant, like most of the other political satire in *Framley Parsonage*. But however grotesque its banalities and hyperboles, we are hardly prepared for the pointless farce of Mrs Proudie's disruption of it. The Proudies have earlier been brought before us at Chaldicotes in a series of skirmishes with Miss Dunstable and Mrs Harold Smith. Some of these, especially the one climaxed by Miss Dunstable's mischievous compliment to Mrs Proudie, "Well, you've a gay set in the chapter, I must say" (p.61), are pointed and entertaining; and in one the bishop is made to anticipate Mrs Proudie's objection to Mr Smith's lecture (p.31). But much of the entertainment clearly derives from the familiarity of the performance: Miss Dunstable and the Proudies are jumping through the same hoops, repeating precisely the roles and sometimes even the turns of phrase (Miss Dunstable's "Oh—ah!", for instance), that characterized their encounters in *Doctor Thorne*. And similarly Mrs Proudie's terrific eruption at Mr Smith's lecture is on the face of it so maddeningly in character that our first impulse is to cheer from sheer joy of recognition. It is so nice and so typical a comment on her worldliness that she should insist on the power of Christianity to advance the material as well as the spiritual progress of the Solomon Islanders (pp.66–67). When, however, to Christianity she adds "Sabbath-day observance" as a recipe for prosperity ("Let us never forget that these islanders can never prosper unless they keep the Sabbath holy"), the joke is surely being overdone. We already know all about Mrs Proudie's fanatical sabbatarianism, and her further indulgence of it here, so extravagant and out of place, simply accentuates a known eccentricity at the expense of the other, more sensible and practical traits that leaven her absurdities. She is being coarsened into a caricature of herself.

Later Mrs Proudie is used more pointedly to illustrate the sterility of life in the circles frequented by the West Barset Whigs. At her "conversazione" in London (chapter 17), Lord Dumbello and Griselda Grantly conduct an important part of their silent, passionless courtship, and Miss Dunstable engages in raillery so ill-natured that, though familiar enough to the reader, it seems for the first time to reveal itself in its true colours to Trollope. Miss Dunstable, he explains, "was living now very much with people on whom kindness, generosity, and open-heartedness were thrown away" and, as a result, "was gradually becoming irreverent, scornful, and prone to ridicule" (pp.189–90). Mrs Proudie herself must be one of these people, if being subjected to Miss Dunstable's irreverence and scorn is the test. But given Mrs Proudie's eccentricities, her essential dowdiness, and the blight that seems to be cast on all her projects—her daughter's marriage to a widower with three children, a friend of Mr Slope's, is a typical example—the attempt to assimilate her malice and worldly ambition with that of the Whig grandees of West Barset must be judged both pointless and unkind. Certainly, the novel is not equally unkind to Archdeacon Grantly's wife, whose worldly ambitions for her daughter show that high-and-dry Tory Barset is no more proof than low-church Whig Barset against the seductions of London, and no more scrupulous about hobnobbing with the enemy. But Mrs Grantly at least realizes her ambitions and is allowed, into the bargain, to flaunt her triumph before Mrs Proudie (pp.437–41). Indeed, by way of rubbing the Proudies' face finally in the mud, the bishop's daughter is made to stoop to the infamy of having a poison-pen letter sent to Griselda Grantly!

In contrast to Mrs Proudie, Martha Dunstable, who also tends to become more like a caricature of herself the more we see of her, is suddenly plucked back just as she seems about to tumble headlong in the mud. Her closest attachment, it is insisted, has always been to the "old" Barset personified by Frank and Mary Gresham and Dr Thorne. Her relish for fashionable frivolities, such as the puerile baiting of Harold Smith and the endless jokes at the expense of the Proudies, belongs only to the more superficial and impressionable side of her nature. In reality she finds exchanging dull pleasantries with Frank and Mary (pp.79–81) much more congenial, and eventually, for no discernible reason except that she must be rescued from the descent of Avernus somehow, she is made to marry Dr Thorne. But such is the hold the worldly pleasures of London have gained on her that she makes it a condition of the marriage that she be allowed to spend part of the year among them—with or without her husband. This suggests that, even to Trollope's mind, the couple

are less than perfectly matched, and one can't help feeling that her absences in London will be a relief to them both: for to all outward appearances her vitality derives exclusively from her "worldly" social talents. It is evident, however, that Trollope means the marriage to be a happy fulfilment for two characters whom he admits he is very fond of and who represent—though Miss Dunstable in her best qualities only—the values of good sense, simplicity, and respect for (but not worship of) money that the novel prizes most highly.

We also notice that, financially, the marriage is an unequal one. Miss Dunstable is the richest, or one of the richest, women in England; Dr Thorne has only the income from his medical practice. Seen in this light their alliance offers a kind of parallel to the other three that are reported in the last chapter of the novel, all of which are unequal in one way or another: those of Lucy Robarts and Lord Lufton, Griselda Grantly and Lord Dumbello, and Oliva Proudie and Mr Tickler. Perhaps, then, *Framley Parsonage* has some semblance of a coherent plot and of a unifying idea after all? If it has, however, the coherence and unity must be considered tenuous. For the four marriages convey little more than a general, conventional sense of the fluidity of society, with barriers of rank and fortune, and of political and social prejudice, toppling fast. But against this, and in such a way as to cast further doubt on the prominence given to old friends from earlier Barset novels, must be set the contradictory sense—which I believe emerges much more strongly—that at bottom the old Barset is growing increasingly resistant to change, increasingly less fluid. For Lady Lufton, who is old Barset's sturdiest champion in *Framley Parsonage*, is quite free of the "democratic" leanings of Dr Thorne and his niece and is only superficially affected by the "worldliness" of the De Courcys, the Grantlys, and to a lesser extent the Greshams. And although, from time to time, breaches are made in the defence of her citadel, they are nearly all closed by the end of the novel.

The most serious of such breaches is caused by Mark Robarts's entanglement with the "Chaldicotes set"; but the danger of contamination from this source is short-lived. At the time of Harold Smith's lecture, Mark's character does show signs of deterioration; and his later acquiescence in "simony" when he accepts a prebend's stall at Barchester makes it clear that Sowerby is robbing him of his principles as well as his money. With his resignation of the stall, however, he cleanses himself. Not that he will be proof, even now, against minor backslidings: despite Mr Crawley's fervent admonitions, it is unlikely that he will for long devote more of his time to parochial duties and less to following the hunt—without quite participating in it.[33] But there will be no further danger of his being "bought over" by the enemy (cf. p. 201).

Of the other weak spots in Lady Lufton's armoury the worst is her own worldly ambition. This, however, is always rather bashful. It shows up first in her desire to have her son marry Griselda Grantly, and later in her refusal to sanction his marriage to Lucy Robarts. But at heart she is repelled by Griselda's cold worldliness, just as Lord Lufton himself is. Griselda's subsequent engagement to Lord Dumbello, scion of a Whig family whose iniquities are as black as any her imagination can conceive, is a sufficient warning to her of the brittleness of worldly splendour. Once free of the Grantly influence—which exerts itself on the side of worldliness throughout the Barset novels, until near the end of *The Last Chronicle*—there is never any doubt that she will finally accept Lucy. And there is no suggestion that in doing so she will have to compromise her own standards, for Lucy, unlike Mary Thorne, has no stain on her birth and is open to no more substantial objection than that of being "so uncommonly brown" (p.469). The pretence that her marriage to Lord Lufton would be a misalliance is, as at least one contemporary reviewer protested,[34] an all-too-familiar expedient for stringing out the story rather than a pointer to any real conflict of principles or of class prejudices. Lucy's eligibility is clear to the reader long before Lady Lufton comes to recognize it. Her appearance and deportment are contrasted favourably, and pointedly, with those of Griselda Grantly; and the spirit and good sense she shows in stipulating that before she will accept Lord Lufton's offer of marriage his mother must endorse it, confirm that her accession will strengthen rather than weaken the defences of the Lufton citadel.

Lucy and Lord Lufton are perhaps the most impressive as well as the most likable of Trollope's lovers. Though he has been foolish in the past and is still a barbarian in his recreations, Lord Lufton courts Lucy, particularly at the outset, with delicacy and with convincing fervour; unlike most of Trollope's young heroes, he is also faithful to her, despite what seems a complete rebuff. And Lucy distinguishes herself among Trollope's heroines by being able to see her lover's faults and to love him without worshipping him as a "god". Her attitudes, and indeed her actual words, often remind us of some of Shakespeare's romantic heroines, notably Viola and Beatrice. When, for example, her sister-in-law asks her whether much harm has been done, either to Lord Lufton or to herself, by his attentions to her, she replies: "Oh! by God's mercy, very little. As for me, I shall get over it in three or four years I don't doubt—that's if I can get ass's milk and change of air." (p.231) And her later confession of her love to her sister-in-law perfectly captures the slightly hysterical humour, embracing mockery of self, of lover, and of love itself, that is one of the characteristic notes of the Shakespearean heroine:

"I don't care for my heart. I'd let it go—with this young popinjay lord or any one else, so that I could read, and talk, and walk, and sleep, and eat, without always feeling that I was wrong here—here—here— and she pressed her hand vehemently against her side. "What is it that I feel, Fanny? Why am I so weak in body that I cannot take exercise? Why cannot I keep my mind on a book for one moment? Why can I not write two sentences together? Why should every mouthful that I eat stick in my throat? Oh, Fanny, is it his legs, think you, or is it his title?" [Pp.284–85]

Later again, when Fanny wonders that she does not languish under Lady Lufton's disapproval, she is as emphatic as Benedick that, whatever else may make her look pale, love will not: 'I ought to be pale, ought I not? and very thin, and to go mad by degrees? I have not the least intention of doing anything of the kind ... " (p.385).[35] Other Trollopian girls—Mary Thorne and Lily Dale, for instance— strike many of the same attitudes, but Lucy is unique in loving with her eyes fully open yet not unworthily. And although, as she is the first to admit, a man who "devotes all his energies to riding after a fox or killing poor birds" can hardly be a "hero" (p.283), she and Lord Lufton on the whole seem a good deal better matched, morally and intellectually, and a good deal more likely to raise old Barset in the world's, and the reader's, estimation than Mr and Mrs Frank Gresham.

Lord Lufton, like Mark Robarts, is fleeced by Sowerby, the down-at-heels owner of Chaldicotes, and we may take it that he will in future be less complacent about exposing old Barset to the "Whig" danger by hobnobbing with the enemy, by "jeers and sneers at the old county doings", and by heresies such as his remark that as far as he is concerned "Mr. Bright may sit for the county, if he pleases" (p.13). But in any case the political threat to old Barset now seems remote. Happenings at Westminster do on occasions affect the fortunes of Mark Robarts, of Sowerby, and of Archdeacon Grantly. But in general the tiresome machinations of Harold Smith and Supplehouse and, needless to add, of Tom Towers and the *Jupiter* now relate to a sphere of action apparently too far from old Barset to influence it much, or even to offer suggestive parallels: there is, for example, a degree of politicking in the "alliance" of Lady Lufton and Mrs Grantly, but the implicit reminders of politicking at Westminster are at best broad and predictable. And even though the West Barset Whigs, headed by the Duke of Omnium, are sharply contrasted with Lady Lufton's circle in their manners, their sexual mores, and their lust for money (the Duke's "squeezing" of poor Sowerby), there is no suggestion that in parliament their behaviour is distinguishable from that of their enemies. On the contrary, the satirical presentation of Tories as "giants" and Whigs as "gods" has the aim and the effect—characteristic of Trollope's political

novels—of playing down the differences between them. The differences that matter in the main plot of the novel are moral ones, and it is clear that these cut across party differences far more than Lady Lufton acknowledges. Arch-Tories like the Greshams visit Gatherum Castle, and the gaieties of Chaldicotes and Gatherum seduce the Grantlys no less than the worldly Whigs. Lady Lufton's real enemies are fashionable frivolity and money-hunger rather than a political creed.

That old Barset continues to hold its own against them is demonstrated most dramatically at the famous moment when Lady Lufton outfaces the Duke on his home ground, that of London, which is her enemies' capital as West Barset is their country seat:

> Circumstances had so turned out that he had absolutely been pressed close against Lady Lufton, and she, when she heard the voice, and was made positively acquainted with the fact of the great man's presence by Miss Dunstable's words, turned round quickly, but still with much feminine dignity, removing her dress from the contact. In doing this she was brought absolutely face to face with the duke, so that each could not but look full at the other. "I beg your pardon," said the duke. They were the only words that had ever passed between them, nor have they spoken to each other since; but simple as they were, accompanied by the little by-play of the speakers, they gave rise to a considerable amount of ferment in the fashionable world. Lady Lufton, as she retreated back on to Dr. Easyman, curtsied low; she curtsied low and slowly, and with a haughty arrangement of her drapery that was all her own; but the curtsy, though it was eloquent, did not say half so much,—did not reprobate the habitual iniquities of the duke with a voice nearly as potent, as that which was expressed in the gradual fall of her eye and the gradual pressure of her lips. When she commenced her curtsy she was looking full in her foe's face. By the time that she had completed it her eyes were turned upon the ground, but there was an ineffable amount of scorn expressed in the lines of her mouth. She spoke no word, and retreated, as modest virtue and feminine weakness must ever retreat, before barefaced vice and virile power; but nevertheless she was held by all the world to have had the best of the encounter. [Pp.314-15]

It is ominous, however, that even after being publicly snubbed in this fashion the duke retains "a slight smile of derision": his smile can be felt as a portent of the supplanting—in the political or Palliser novels, which followed on from the Barsetshire chronicles—of the old Barset by the fashionable world, essentially a London world, of which the duke is leader.

Framley Parsonage thus continues the process by which the boundaries of Barset are broadened to include new social groups, and it is the first of the Barset novels to devote nearly as much attention to the activities of these groups outside Barset as inside. But at the same time, while West Barset is becoming less and less self-contained, the eastern half of the county, Lady Lufton's half, is con-

tracting and consolidating, becoming more exclusive and intransigent. *Framley Parsonage*, in this respect, looks ahead to the remaining two novels in the series, as indeed it also does in the extent to which it takes us outside Barset altogether. And in addition it introduces us to Mr Crawley, who is to prove the last and staunchest champion of the old Barset and who, significantly, is able to awe even Lady Lufton by his strictness and fervour.

The Small House at Allington seems to me the least successful and least interesting of the Barset novels, and I do not propose to discuss it at length. Trollope himself thought highly of it (*Autobiography*, pp.150, 154–55), but was reluctant to include it among the Barset novels—ostensibly because so little of its action took place in Barset or had to do with Barset identities. But its two chief characters, Johnny Eames and Lily Dale, do appear again, prominently, in *The Last Chronicle*, and a number of others—the De Courcys, for example, and Lord and Lady Dumbello—have already played an important part in earlier novels in the series; Allington, moreover, though not actually in Barset, is in "the next county" (p.152).

Where *The Small House* differs crucially from the other Barset novels is partly in the character and pursuits of the *jeune premier*, Johnny Eames, and partly in the quality of life at Allington. Eames, unlike his counterparts in the other novels, is essentially a townsman. It is in London that he lives and works and is seen at his liveliest; in Allington, though he was brought up there, he is now only a visitor. His chief interest there, his chief attachment to the country, is Lily Dale; but, eager as his love for her is supposed to be, it is seldom allowed to interfere with his London pursuits. This is not to say that he fails to win her solely because of the physical and moral barrier which, in the reader's eyes at least, his London life may seem to erect between them: like most Trollopian heroines Lily is content with brief flurries of attention from her lovers, and there is no suggestion that Johnny's London associations—with such seedy people as Amelia Roper, the Lupexes, and Cradell—automatically make him unfit for Lily. Later, when he dallies with the imbecilic Miss Desmolines in *The Last Chronicle*, Lily does see and spurn the London taint, but at this stage, though one of the chapter headings (chapter 59) assures us that he at last "becomes a man", his immaturity, his "hobbledehoyhood", is clearly meant to plead in his favour.[36] Such as it is, however, his moral bondage to London is probably less injurious to his hopes of winning Lily than his economic bondage. In the absence of more fairy godfathers like Lord De Guest—whom he rescues from the charge of an enraged bull, and who rewards him by settling a small income on him and

securing him accelerated promotion in the public office where he works—Johnny will presumably have to continue to live in London. And if he should marry, he will hardly have the income to shield his wife from vulgar contacts as effectively as the Dales, despite their tiny income, are shielded at Allington. No doubt a girl brought up in a "small house" would not demand Bayswater and a view of the park, as Lady Alexandrina De Courcy does (I: 130–32); but how at home, how truly herself, would the "pearl" of Allington be in the "neat suburban villa" that Johnny presumably would have to choose for her? The novel does not pose such a question directly, but it becomes pertinent when we ask ourselves why Eames, almost alone among Trollope's young men, is denied the hand of the woman he loves.

Up to a point the answer is plain enough: the Dales, we are told, "were ever constant" (I:420), and Lily is one of those Trollopian heroines who worship their lovers as gods and who can never transfer their affections. Having once given her heart to Adolphus Crosbie she cannot fully regain it. Even his perfidy cannot release her; indeed, convincing and appealing as her love is during the period of courtship—despite a few hollow rhetorical flourishes[37]— her greatest moments are those in which she clings to and nurtures it after she has been jilted. It is only gradually that the brave, even laughing face she puts on her grief—not unlike that which Mary Thorne and Lucy Robarts use to dissemble their love—becomes an instrument of emotional blackmail, enabling her to dominate and, from the height of her great experience, patronize her mother, her sister, and of course poor Johnny. This is no doubt what Trollope had in mind when he called her a "female prig" (*Autobiography*, p.154). Eventually she achieves an authority too precious to be surrendered to any husband, be he Eames or even the repentant and now free Crosbie who offers himself to her again in *The Last Chronicle*. She is the most notable exception to Trollope's doctrine that for a woman marriage must be the happiest destiny.

Prig or not, however, she is also a heroine for whom he professes great affection and for whom one would normally predict a happy marriage with complete assurance: "dear Lily Dale—for my reader must know that she is to be very dear, and that my story will be nothing to him if he do not love Lily Dale." (I:17) Yet the two men who do love her are both found unworthy, though neither Eames's faults of callowness and halfhearted philandering nor even Crosbie's treacherous worldly ambition would deter an ordinary Trollopian heroine from loving and marrying them. The real objection, I believe, to either Crosbie or Eames as a husband for Lily is that they belong at heart to a different and incompatible world.

Superficially, the difference is indicated by, for example, the "pollution" Lily's name is said to suffer on the lips of an Amelia Roper (I:135), Crosbie's obviously sincere feeling that the "primitive and rural" life of Allington is morally better than the ceremonious nastiness of Courcy Castle (I:249, etc.), and the authorial assertion that at Courcy "every word that [Crosbie] had heard, and every word that he had spoken, had tended to destroy all that was good and true within him, and to foster all that was selfish and false" (I:309–10). But the enormities of Courcy Castle are by now old hat, and the vulgarities of lower middle-class London are as predictably extreme in Mrs Roper's boarding-house as in kindred settings in Trollope's earlier London novels. (In particular, Eames's experience of them recalls that of Charley Tudor in *The Three Clerks*.) More eloquent testimony of the nature and extent of the gap between Allington and the worlds of London and West Barset is the manner in which the Allingtonians themselves feel it. Mrs Dale, for example, "cannot imagine Lily living in London", feels that if she does she will be "separated" from them not by "the distance" but by "the manner of life", and has to be reassured by her daughter Bell that "men in London are happy with their wives as well as men in the country" (I:252–53). Again, to Squire Dale—in one of Trollope's subtlest confrontations between town and country—the shoulder-shrugging attitude of the London clubman Mr Pratt, not condoning but not outraged by Crosbie's perfidy to Lily, is utterly incomprehensible (I:347–50): it accords with his feeling that "the world is changed" (I:376), a feeling that is shared in varying degrees by all the older generation at Allington—Mrs Dale and the De Guests, as well as the squire. But it is also half-shared by Trollope himself. For not only the squire but he too brands Crosbie a "reptile", a species of "vermin" (I:377–78)—though at other times he can movingly reveal how human and understandable Crosbie's worldly weaknesses are and how painful his remorse.

Johnny Eames, like Crosbie, is a civil servant, subject to the temptations—and the expenses—of London life. And his philandering with Amelia Roper, though less gross than Crosbie's treachery towards Lily, offers an obvious parallel. Yet Eames is allowed not only to go on trifling with Amelia, without compunction and with no more than a hint of authorial disapproval, but to win applause by giving Crosbie a punitive drubbing. This, moreover, is only the lightest part of Crosbie's punishment, the heaviest being the coolness and diminished respect of his friends and the horrors of day-to-day existence with Lady Alexandrina. Eames, on the other hand, besides resuming his silly philandering (in *The Last Chronicle*), is also—and in view of his trivial tastes quite improbably[38]—

rewarded with respect and professional success. If Eames (like Charley Tudor) was to some extent a self-portrait,[39] Trollope's leniency towards him is hardly surprising. But the severity of the punishment visited on Crosbie certainly is. As Mr Pratt observes, Crosbie is "not the first man who has behaved badly to a lady" (I:349), and it is hard to see why a world not normally censorious should turn against him so completely. The reason, surely, is that Trollope is unconsciously aligning himself with Allington, and fulfilling its wishes, by making of Crosbie a scapegoat for the sins of the alien world he represents in Allington's eyes.

Lily, in analogous fashion, also takes on the appearance of a symbol, epitomizing in her rejection by Crosbie and of Eames the self-sufficiency and moral authority of Allington. Indeed, insofar as Allington can be equated with the more traditional part of the "next county"—Barset—*The Small House* can be seen as showing the old Barset withdrawing still further into itself, remaining pure and intact in the modern world not unlike Lily herself. (It is worth noting that both Lily's christian name and her sobriquet—"*pearl* of Allington"—have appropriate connotations of purity and spirituality, as her surname has of seclusion.) In the novel, however, Trollope's imagination is clearly busier elsewhere: in the clubs and offices, and alas the boarding-houses, of London. Apart from the small house itself, Allington is not a lively place, as Barset normally is. Squire Dale is no one's idea of good company, and life at Guestwick, the seat of Lord De Guest, is admitted to be "very dull" (II:323, 325): a Mark Robarts, one imagines, would certainly prefer Courcy Castle. Barset does come to life again at times in *The Last Chronicle*, but only by dint of a recapitulation of old themes from which no new ones can emerge.

Among the Barset novels, *The Last Chronicle* is unique because of its length and panoramic scope and because of the near-tragic stature of its central character. "Taking it as a whole", Trollope considered it "the best novel I have written". The foundation of the main plot, he admitted, was shaky: "I cannot quite make myself believe that even such a man as Mr. Crawley could have forgotten how he got [the cheque]." But certain of the characters—notably Crawley, whose mind he claimed to have portrayed "with great accuracy and great delicacy", but also Mrs Proudie, Mr Harding, and the archdeacon—were "very real"; and there was a "true savour of English country life all through the book" (*Autobiography*, pp.236–37). Many of the reviewers, however, rightly complained that characters appeared to have been "dragged in" from the earlier chronicles simply to eke out the length of the novel and to "wind up" the series.[40]

The reintroduction of half the cast of *The Small House at Allington* is particularly difficult to justify. Lily Dale perhaps deserves a place, as a repository of the values of old Barset, in a final reunion of Barset identities. But in the broader context of *The Last Chronicle* even her preoccupations inevitably diminish in importance: compared to those of Crawley and his friends and enemies, they come to appear merely private and personal, no longer a matter of urgent public concern, with possible consequences for a whole way of life. The change, however, is more than one of perspective. It is also linked to the appearance Lily gives of having become frozen in an attitude, so that the latest phase of her story cannot end differently from the earlier. On the front that she defends, Barset has already proved itself secure; whereas on that which Crawley holds, it does at least appear exposed. Her stubborn pride and moral authority do, nevertheless, remind us at times of Crawley's, and to this extent her presence serves a purpose in *The Last Chronicle*. But clearly she could have been present without, in effect, reliving the whole of her past and without, as Booth puts it,[41] "dragging in by the heels" most of her former and several of her new associates, and even, for good measure, a group of *their* associates. Clearly, too, whatever value we set on her pride is scarcely comparable with that we set on Crawley's. When, for example, she offers to love Eames "as a brother" or as a "friend"—even though, unlike Trollope, she believes him "light of heart" (I:365–66; II:370–71, 375, 383)—her moral pretensions look very like humbug. And the picture of her as a Barsetshire Hester Prynne, appropriating to herself the letters *O.M.* (for Old Maid) as Hester does the letter *A* borders on the ludicrous: "she had written them in her book, making each letter a capital, and round them she had drawn a scroll, ornamented after her own fashion, and she had added the date in quaintly formed figures" (II:13).[42] But although lacking Crawley's—and Hester Prynne's—tragic stature, Lily does epitomize some of the same aspects of old Barset as Crawley, and in something like the same extreme form. As well as being characters in their own right, both are symptoms of the barely tenable exclusiveness, the withdrawal into self, the inviolable conviction of self-sufficiency that characterize old Barset in the last two novels of the series.

In *The Last Chronicle*, Crawley's pride, and to a certain extent Lily's, is set beside the strictly worldly pride of Archdeacon Grantly and contrasted, implicitly, with the humility of Mr Harding. It is also measured against the "ordinary" human pride of such typical Barset identities as Mark Robarts, Dean Arabin, Lady Lufton, and Henry Grantly. The overall effect is to show Crawley not simply as a figure of near-tragic intensity dwarfing his neighbours but also as

the embodiment, in exaggerated form, of many of the distinctive qualities of these neighbours. Thus, while there is no parallel in any of the Barset novels to his conscious conception of himself as enacting a heroic role—that of a hero of Greek tragedy or of the primitive church—there are abundant parallels for many of the attitudes that go to make up this conception. When, for example, we learn that he takes "a certain manly delight in warfare against authority" (I:134), and when, by way of demonstration, we see him putting down a Mr Thumble (chapter 13) or a Mrs Proudie (chapter 18), we instinctively rank him among the champions of old Barset, calling to mind, say, Dr Thorne's tilts with Lady Arabella Gresham and Lady Lufton's famous triumph over the Duke of Omnium. But when, in his exultation at having worsted Thumble, he calls for his daughter in order to "commence the Seven against Thebes with her" (I:135); when, in anticipation of his conflict with Dr Proudie, we see him reading the "awful tragedy" of Oedipus "almost with joyous rapture" (I:179); when he sees himself as a Samson, "eyeless in Gaza, at the mill with slaves" (II:232–33), we glimpse an imaginative capacity far above that of Dr Thorne and Lady Lufton. There is doubtless an alloy of pettiness in his pride, as for instance in his jealousy of Arabin: "It was not sufficient for him to remember that he knew Hebrew, but he must remember also that the dean did not." (II:220) And some of his triumphs are hollow: Thumble, for example, is crushed by Mark Robarts just as easily as by Crawley ("Mr. Robarts gave a look at Mr. Thumble, and Mr. Thumble retired into his shoes" [II:132]); and the comparatively mild Dr Tempest also subdues Mrs Proudie (II:38–44). But what other Trollopian cleric could rebuke a Lady Lufton with impunity (*Framley Parsonage*, pp.163–64) or be thought, without incongruity, "almost a saint" by his own wife (I:422)?

Admittedly, what R.H. Hutton said of Crawley's "intellectual power", that it is "indicated rather than delineated",[43] applies also to his "saintliness" and to most of his "tragic" qualities. Like most of Trollope's tragic characters, he is on the whole more impressive as described than as dramatically represented. Hutton complained that we don't see enough of his "imagination", and it is true that the precise quality of his emotions has too often to be inferred from rough summaries and from his deportment in brief and widely spaced crises. Yet the impression we thus gain of him is at least consistent, both within its own limits and in its suggestion of depths and subtleties beyond these limits. "I think," the narrator observes at one point (I:422), "that at this time nobody saw clearly the working of his mind,—not even his wife, who studied it very closely"; he then shows how accurate Mrs Crawley's observation of her husband

has been in every respect but one: "It did not occur to her that he could see her insight into him. ... she did not dream that this was precisely his own idea of his own state and of his own position." "Precisely" is no doubt an exaggeration, but the passage, like others, does make the point that a complex character's self-consciousness will never be the same as an outside observer's consciousness of him—no matter how practised or privileged that observer. And since we are also told that it was Crawley's "fault" that he was "imbued too strongly with self-consciousness" (II:220), we are sufficiently warned of the likely inadequacy even of Trollope's insight into his private feelings.

The "dramatic" portrayal of Crawley, through his speech and actions, shows greater signs of strain. When he is pictured stalking or trudging along the muddy lane between Hogglestock and Barchester (I:182, 192–94), or sitting out in the rain bewailing his plight (II:216–21), the externals of his position help to sharpen the description of his state of mind. There are also times when his speech is both individual and expressive: for example, in the scene already referred to where he speaks of Milton's Samson and other blind heroes (II:232–33), in his famous reproof to Mrs Proudie ("Madam, you should not interfere in these matters ... The distaff were more fitting for you" [I:192]), and in his letters. At other times, however, there is an air of facile affectation about his speech that Trollope cannot have intended. Crawley can, for example, use biblical archaisms with devastating effect, as when he chides Mrs Proudie, and we can believe that they come naturally to him in moments of excitement or embarrassment: the scene where Toogood informs him that his innocence has been proved is one example (II:352). But his use of such expressions as "methinks" and "it seemeth to me" and "lo", sometimes in the ordinary course of conversation, is altogether too fitful to sound natural, too remote from the austere modern style that he generally uses, and even from the mannered, but by no means primitive or quaint, Johnsonese that he slips into at times. The conclusion of his farewell sermon to his parishioners (II:307), one of his most eloquent passages, is entirely free of biblicality; and the otiosity of his more sententious moments seems quite in character: "When I hear jocose proverbs spoken as to men, such as that in this house the gray mare is the better horse, or that in that house the wife wears that garment which is supposed to denote virile command ... " (II:301). From this kind of stateliness, which becomes toned down when he is speaking to, say, a Dan Morris or a Giles Hoggett (I:121–24; II:221–22), or when he is consciously striving for factual precision (as in his long expository letter to Arabin [II:234–39]), it is an impossibly far cry to his biblical archaisms.

As I hope to show in later chapters, Trollope nearly always found it difficult to achieve a suitably solemn idiom for characters of tragic stature, and Crawley is no exception. But to say this is not to question that in his own surroundings Crawley is a towering figure. At the end of the novel Trollope repeats what has become his standard apology for the failings of his typical clergymen: "Had I written an epic about clergymen, I would have taken St. Paul for my model; but describing, as I have endeavoured to do, such clergymen as I see around me, I could not venture to be transcendental." (II:452) In fact, however, Crawley does approach the transcendental, measuring himself, in his own mind, not only against Simeon Stylites (I:424) but also against Saint Paul himself: "St. Paul, indeed, was called upon to bear stripes, was flung into prison, encountered terrible dangers. But Mr. Crawley—so he told himself,—could have encountered all that without flinching." (I:118)

Yet, although we can believe that Crawley is making no idle boast here, Trollope does not, at the end of the novel, place him among the Saint Pauls—in a separate category from other, non-transcendental clergymen like the archdeacon, Mark Robarts, and Mr Harding. The reason is presumably that by this time, having abandoned the brickmakers of Hoggle End and accepted the living of Saint Ewold's (worth £350 a year), Crawley stands, as he himself puts it, on "more equal grounds" with such a man as the archdeacon. They are, as the archdeacon cosily tells him, "both gentlemen"; to which Crawley responds: "Sir, from the bottom of my heart I agree with you." (II:446-47) The chapter in which this bathetic rapprochement occurs is entitled "Mr. Crawley Is Conquered"; and along with the titles of two earlier chapters, "Mr Robarts on His Embassy" (chapter 21) and "Lady Lufton's Proposition" (chapter 50), it reminds us that for most of the novel old Barset feels hardly more friendly towards him than does the bishop. In particular, the social injustice of which he is a grim embodiment is less easily ignored than that of, say, the Hoggle End brickmakers. To Mark Robarts, anxious though he is to help, it is largely a sign of bad taste on Crawley's part: "There were many clergymen in the county with incomes as small as that which had fallen to the lot of Mr. Crawley, but they managed to get on without displaying their sores as Mr. Crawley displayed his." (I:211) To Archdeacon Grantly, on the other hand, it is an essential part of the picturesque "beauty" of the church that such meagre lots should "fall" to certain of its ministers: "The archdeacon ... loved the temporalities of the Church as temporalities. The Church was beautiful to him because one man by interest might have a thousand a year, while another man equally good, but without interest, could only

have a hundred. And he liked the men who had the interest a great deal better than the men who had it not." (II:439–40) Trollope himself, if we can judge from his *Clergymen of the Church of England*, deplored such "picturesque anomalies" and felt that the church should "cleanse" itself of them.[44] But in the novel he seems quite content to have Robarts and Grantly conquer Crawley, thus achieving, at the cost of £350 a year, old Barset's last great victory.

On artistic grounds such an outcome is indefensible: it is an incongruous anticlimax to the almost tragic passion that Crawley has achieved in the novel as a whole. But in another sense it was inevitable, a predictable confirmation of Trollope's growing attachment to old Barset and his growing reluctance to subject it to real and sustained challenge, whether from within (as in the case of Crawley) or from without. What *The Last Chronicle* demonstrates, especially if we contrast it with the fine "tragic" novel written shortly afterwards—*He Knew He Was Right*—is that tragedy, and indeed social injustice, are simply outside old Barset's terms of reference. It is a society that has hardened, in Trollope's imagination, into a tableau-like stasis which no force can for long disturb.

The comfortable assimilation of Crawley is only one symptom of this. It is also evident in the repetition by most of the leading characters of patterns of thought and behaviour that they have already perfected in earlier novels, in the sense we now receive of London as a quite remote and separate sphere, no longer capable of decisively influencing events in Barset, and most markedly in the weakening of the Proudie influence over the diocese of Barchester. That Crawley and his affairs should be the means by which Mrs Proudie's authority is overthrown and her life brought to an end—both figuratively and literally—is largely fortuitous, since although he is a high churchman it is hardly by his own wish that he acts with and for the high-church party. But even before her final overthrow it is clear that she and her husband have made little—astonishingly little—headway in the diocese. For not only are they shown to be, in many ways, at the mercy of men of lesser authority—the dean, the archdeacon, and Dr Tempest, for example—but when it comes to nominating members of the commission to inquire into Crawley's case they can muster only two low churchmen, and these of obviously inferior talents.

Conceivably, the death of Mrs Proudie, which has little direct bearing on the main story, is meant to be balanced by that of Mr Harding, whose parish of St Ewold's,[45] and perhaps whose spiritual mantle as well, Crawley inherits. But in a temporal sense Mrs Proudie is clearly a more drastic loss to her party than Mr Harding is to his. There is, moreover, a hint that, despite the loss of Mr

Harding, the high-church party in fact makes spiritual as well as temporal gains during the course of the novel. Crawley himself may be a doubtful gain in the eyes of the archdeacon and Mark Robarts, but his moral force and above all his virility (the qualities in which Mr Harding had been so deficient) must strengthen their party. And about the spiritual power of his daughter there can be no doubt: Grace Crawley conquers the archdeacon's pride (II:164–69) as effectively as the archdeacon conquers her father's, and though Mrs Grantly suspects that she has done it chiefly by having a pretty face (II:172–73) she also appears to have cast something like a religious spell over him.

In calling her Grace (the child of Josiah and Mary), we may take it that her father saw the religious significance of the name. And her grace and the grace she brings to others are repeatedly set against the *dis*grace of her family's poverty and of her father's semi-outcast position as a suspected thief. At the beginning of the novel, immediately after we have been told that his family's poverty is "a living disgrace" to Crawley, we are introduced to Grace, "the prettiest girl in that part of the world", who has made her fortune "in the teeth, as it were, of the prevailing ill-fortune of her family" (I:7), by as her father puts it "finding grace" in Henry Grantly's sight (II:256). Grace herself, however, isn't sure "whether she [is] in paradise or in purgatory" as a result of Henry's love (I:310). It is her constant fear that she may bring "disgrace" upon him, and this finds an echo in Crawley's anxiety lest Henry may have "ventured into . . . jeopardy" by supporting him (II:250). Grace, in her father's view, is "pure as the light of day" and, but for being affected by the "stain" of his "disgrace", would be fit to "grace the house of the best gentleman in England": "She shall grace mine," Henry replies (II:254–55). In the circumstances, it is not surprising that even the worldly archdeacon feels it would be "sacrilege" to doubt her word (II:168), and that his wife twits him with believing Grace "all the graces rolled into one" (II:392).

Further evidence that the archdeacon's worldliness has been softened—though not absolutely dissolved—is offered by his response to the death of Mr Harding. At the funeral his religious spirit of reconciliation reaches out even to the bishop:

> The bishop was there, looking old and worn,—almost as though he were unconscious of what he was doing. Since his wife's death no one had seen him out of the palace or of the palace grounds till that day. But there he was,—and they made way for him into the procession behind the two ladies,—and the archdeacon, when he saw it, resolved that there should be peace in his heart, if peace might be possible. [II:424]

"All passion spent," Mr Crawley might have added. Mr Harding's

funeral brings the Barsetshire series to a close on an unusually solemn note and with an assurance to the reader that, though shrunken and less lively than before, old Barset will now stand firm against "the sick hurry, the divided aims" of the modern world.

NOTES

1. For a discussion of some of the conflicting claims, see Michael Sadleir, *Trollope: a Commentary*, rev. ed. (London: Constable, 1945), pp.158–64, and R.B. Martin, *Enter Rumour: Four Early Victorian Scandals* (London: Faber, 1962), pp.180–81. One cannot accept Sadleir's conclusion that Barchester must be Winchester simply because Trollope is supposed to have told his friend Professor Freeman so; from Freeman's own account it sounds very much as if Trollope were merely trying to humour him. However, the architectural and topographical resemblances that Martin notes between Barchester and Winchester are very striking.
2. The fullest account of the Rochester case is Ralph Arnold's *The Whiston Matter* (London: Hart-Davis, 1961), which discusses some of the parallels between this case and that of Hiram's Hospital and commends Trollope both for his realism and his fairness. On the Winchester case, see Martin, *Enter Rumour*, pp.137–84. Martin seems to me to demonstrate conclusively that this was the chief model for the Hiram's Hospital case.
3. At one point in *Phineas Redux* (I:206), a letter is dated "Feb. 8, 1870", but this was probably a slip on Trollope's part as he was writing in 1870. The chronology and relationship to history of the Palliser novels are discussed briefly in appendix 2 below.
4. This matter is examined in Frank E. Robbins, "Chronology and History in Trollope's Barset and Parliamentary Novels", *Nineteenth Century Fiction*, 5 (March 1951): 303–16. In concluding that the "series really has two chronologies, its own ... and that of actual history", and that these two are "constantly in conflict", Robbins seems to me to make too much of the discrepancies that he finds.
5. Cf. Charles Reade: "Domestic, you are aware, is Latin for tame. Ex. domestic fowl, domestic drama, story of domestic interest or chronicle of small beer" (*Love Me Little, Love Me Long*, new ed., 1868, p.72n). In the 1860s, as Reade's definition suggests, "domestic" was the usual antonym of "sensational".
6. Mr Harding makes another memorable appearance in chap. 16 of *The Small House at Allington*, when he is thrown into contact with Crosbie, who is on his way to Courcy Castle to betray Lily Dale. The point of the scene is admirably brought out in A.O.J. Cockshut, *Anthony Trollope: a Critical Study* (London: Collins, 1955), pp.152–53.
7. *Athenaeum*, 27 January 1855, pp. 107–8. The reviewer was H. St. John.
8. *Eclectic Review*, 9 (March 1855): 360.
9. "Trollope Revisited", *Essays and Studies* 6 (1920): 52. A similar view is expressed in *Westminster Review* 67 (January 1885): 94n.
10. *Hard Times* had not begun to appear when Trollope wrote *The Warden*, so he probably had *Bleak House* especially in mind here.
11. Sadleir, *Commentary*, p.389. I dissent from Sadleir's view that by the time he wrote *Orley Farm* Trollope had outlived this weakness. See chap.4 below.
12. Chap.3 of *The New Zealander*, "The Press", is of particular relevance to *The Warden*. The work was not published until 1972 (ed. N. John Hall, Oxford: Clarendon Press).
13. *Commentary*, pp.168–69.
14. See chap.4 below.
15. See, e.g., [H. St John], *Athenaeum*, 30 May 1857, pp. 689–90; [Meredith], *Westminster Review* 12 (October 1857): 595; and *Saturday Review* 3 (30 May 1857):504. My attributions of reviews in the *Athenaeum* are taken from the marked files of the journal in the office of the *New Statesman*. In *Trollope: the*

Critical Heritage, ed. D. Smalley (London: Routledge and Kegan Paul, 1969), Meredith is not identified as the author of the review in the *Westminster Review*, but his authorship of it is established by Gordon S. Haight, "George Meredith and the *Westminster Review*", *Modern Language Review* 53 (January 1958): 1–16.

16. *The House of Fiction*, pp.101–2.
17. It has been suggested, persuasively, that the inspiration for the Thornes' *fête champêtre* came from the celebrated medieval tournament staged by the Earl of Eglinton in 1839. See Martin, *Enter Rumour*, chap.2, especially pp.86–87.
18. Trollope himself seemed to share the archdeacon's view of the happy lot of the modern dean: see his *Clergymen of the Church of England* (1866), chap.3.
19. There is a succinct analysis of the ecclesiastical spectrum at this time in the Rev. W.J. Conybeare's *Church Parties* (London: Longman, 1854), reprinted from the *Edinburgh Review* 200 (October 1853).
20. See, e.g., W. David Shaw, "Moral Drama in Barchester Towers", *Nineteenth Century Fiction* 19 (June 1964): 45–54 (especially pp.52–53).
21. See *Letters*, pp.25–26, 30–31, and Sadleir, *Commentary*, pp.169–75.
22. See, e.g., George Meredith's review of the novel, already mentioned, and Elizabeth Barrett Browning's report (quoted in T.A. Trollope, *What I Remember* [London, 1887] 2: 188) of her own and her husband's admiration for Trollope's "three clever novels" (presumably *The Warden*, *Barchester Towers*, and *The Three Clerks*): of *The Three Clerks*, she exclaims "What a thoroughly *man's* book it is!", and she would clearly ascribe the same quality to the other novels named. The phrase "a man's book" seems to have been an accepted euphemism for one containing strong meat: thus, for the *Saturday Review*, Meredith's own novel *The Ordeal of Richard Feverel* was on this account "entirely a man's book" (8 [9 July 1859]: 48).
23. The "Venetian constitution" to which Disraeli referred so often and with such contempt in the early chapters of *Sybil* obviously meant something quite different to Trollope, as a Whig.
24. Trollope's apology, at the beginning of chap.2, for "beginning a novel with two long dull chapters full of description" is in this instance unnecessary.
25. The same observation of Dr Johnson is also invoked tellingly at the beginning of *The Prime Minister*.
26. Miss Dunstable has forgotten the unfortunate young heir of Redclyffe—in Charlotte M. Yonge's novel—who caught "malaria" from his cousin while on his honeymoon in northern Italy and died one of the most edifying of all fictional deaths.
27. Smiles's *Life of George Stephenson* appeared in 1857, just before Trollope began *Doctor Thorne*. As suggested below (chap.3), his *Lives of the Engineers* (1862) possibly influenced one of Trollope's heroes, Harry Clavering, in his choice of a profession. For an account of Smiles which places him in the same milieu as Trollope, see Asa Briggs, *Victorian People* (London: Odham, 1954).
28. *Doctor Thorne*'s popularity is shown by the fact that it was reissued no fewer than twenty-nine times in Trollope's own lifetime. The comparable figures for other Barset novels are: *The Warden*, twelve; *Barchester Towers*, twelve; *Framley Parsonage*, fourteen; *The Small House at Allington*, eleven; *The Last Chronicle*, seven. See Lance O. Tingay's very useful "Trollope's Popularity; a Statistical Approach", *Nineteenth Century Fiction* 11 (December 1956): 223–29.
29. Bradford A. Booth, *Anthony Trollope*, pp.45–46.
30. For example, *Lady Anna*, *Is He Popenjoy?*, *Marion Fay*, and *Mr. Scarborough's Family*. Notable beneficiaries of windfalls include Harry Clavering (*The Claverings*) and Walter Marrable (*The Vicar of Bullhampton*).
31. Sadleir, *Commentary*, p.398 and elsewhere.
32. E.g. *Saturday Review* 11 (4 May 1861): 452; *Westminster Review* 20 (July 1861): 283.
33. We learn in a later novel, *The Claverings* (p.18), that the proscription of hunting had been one of Bishop Proudie's reforms; so Mark's implicit resistance to it hardly tells against him.
34. *Westminster Review* 20 (July 1861): 283.
35. There is also a pointed reference to Viola's "patience on a monument" speech on p.229 of *Framley Parsonage*.

36. Sir Henry Taylor's *Philip van Artevelde* is again quoted to explain his callowness (as it had been to explain Frank Gresham's).

37. E.g., "Then listen to me again, once more, my heart's own darling, my love, my husband, my lord! If I cannot be to you at once like Ruth, and never cease from coming after you, my thoughts to you shall be like those of Ruth:—if aught but death part thee and me, may God do so to me and more also" (I:203).

38. This point was made by a number of reviewers; see, e.g., [R.H. Hutton], *Spectator* 37 (9 April 1864): 421–23; *Athenaeum*, 26 March 1864: pp.437–38; *Victoria Magazine* 3 (May 1864): 93–94; [A. Innis Shand], *Edinburgh Review* 146 (October 1877): 477–78.

39. See Sadleir, *Commentary*, pp.119–27.

40. The most eloquent attack on the novel in these terms was by J. Herbert Stack, "Mr. Anthony Trollope's Novels", *Fortnightly Review* 5 (February 1869): 192.

41. Booth, *Anthony Trollope*, p.58.

42. Hawthorne's criticism of Trollope's novels, written in 1860, is quoted by Trollope in his Autobiography, pp.124–25. Trollope states that at the time he already knew Hawthorne's works.

43. *Spectator* 40 (13 July 1867): 778.

44. See especially pp.28–30 and 87–88, and chap.8.

45. Ronald Knox, in his "Introduction to the Barsetshire Novels", *The Warden* (the Oxford Trollope edn.), p.xix, points out that in fact it was only by virtue of a lapse of memory on Trollope's part (cf. *Barchester Towers*, p.506) that Mr Harding himself obtained St Ewold's.

3 "Fiction shorn of all romance"

Sending a copy of his *Rachel Ray* (1863) to George Eliot, Trollope observed: "You know that my novels are not sensational. In *Rachel Ray* I have attempted to confine myself absolutely to the commonest details of commonplace life among the most ordinary people, allowing myself no incident that would be even remarkable in every day life. I have shorn my fiction of all romance."[1] These words were written at the time when the outcry against the so-called sensation novel was at its loudest. The appearance, in quick succession, of *The Woman in White* (1860), *East Lynne* (1861), *Lady Audley's Secret* (1862), and Collins's *No Name* and Charles Reade's *Hard Cash* (1863) provoked an angry debate that continued, with gradually abating zeal, throughout the 1860s and 1870s.[2] Trollope himself, not surprisingly, was one of the darlings of the anti-sensationalists, and what he says to the author of *Scenes of Clerical Life* seems to betoken his complacent acceptance of the role. But although he asserts baldly that his novels are not sensational, he can hardly mean to imply that all, or even most, of them exclude "romance" quite so rigorously as does *Rachel Ray*. For in point of fact no more than a dozen or so conform, even approximately, to the definition he gives of "fiction shorn of all romance".

In a sense, as I have already suggested, Trollope shears nearly all of his fiction of romance, regardless of its subject-matter. Nothing delights him more than to expose the prosaic underside of glamour and mystery. He shows little interest in what is unintelligible in human nature or inscrutable in the workings of providence. He never tires of disclaiming any wish to excite or mystify the reader unnecessarily. One of his favourite subjects is the discovery by romantically idealistic young men and women of the attractions of mundane reality. Yet it is also clear that he makes a distinction between unromantic subjects and unromantic treatment. As we have seen (chapter 1 above), he was aware that there was a certain sensational interest in the plot of *Orley Farm*, as in that of most great novels;[3] and in his letter to George Eliot, immediately after the

passage I have quoted, he hastens to stress the humbleness of his endeavours compared to hers: "I do not know what you who have dared to handle great names & historic times will think of this. But you must not suppose that I think the little people are equal as subjects to the great names."

Perhaps this was partly a sop to the author of *Romola*, or perhaps it sprang from Trollope's recognition that, try as he might with more ambitious subjects, his true field was "commonplace life". But the most likely explanation of his persistence with the "little people"— in the 1860s particularly—is simply that he saw in them a challenge to his skill and imagination, less formidable perhaps than that of "dealing with tragic elements", but still capable of stimulating him.

Such a challenge was implicit in the success he achieved with *Framley Parsonage* and *The Small House at Allington*. But above all he must have been flattered by the critical applause for *Rachel Ray*, which was widely hailed as a corrective to morbid sensationalism, and as an example of how much interest a really skilful novelist could generate without it.[4] The reception of some of the novels that followed it, however, must have made him ask himself just how completely he could shear his fiction of romance without alienating both critics and public. *Miss Mackenzie* and *The Belton Estate*, perhaps the least eventful novels he ever wrote, were generally found too unsensational by far; and whether for this reason or because the allure of romance at last became too strong, Trollope made no further attempts in the same line for several years. (*The Claverings*, though published after, was written before *The Belton Estate*.)

Of the attempts he had already made, and those he was to make subsequently, perhaps the most remarkable characteristic is the sameness of their plot materials. They are all love-stories. In all except *Rachel Ray* the central situation is that of a man or woman vacillating between two lovers (or sometimes more), one rather homely, the other seemingly more glamorous; and in all except *An Old Man's Love* and perhaps *The American Senator* the homelier lover is finally successful. The obstacle to true love, almost invariably, is either excessive romanticism or excessive prudence, sometimes on the lovers' own part, sometimes on that of their friends and relatives. True love is never deterred by disparity of fortune, but neither does it overleap the major, and in the end always perceptible, barrier between gentlefolk and non-gentlefolk. Love that does attempt to do so, by looking either too high or too low in the social scale, is usually shown to be romantically deluded.

The pattern, in outline, is largely conventional, and though it

does accommodate many of the "commonest details of commonplace life", it also, in most of the novels, includes glimpses of a more exotic or, as Trollope would say, "romantic" life. Once again, *Rachel Ray* and *An Old Man's Love* are exceptions. These are perhaps the "quietest", the homeliest, of all his novels.

Rachel Ray, however, displays something of his usual variety of incident and characters even within the confines of an almost completely uneventful and, in the most literal sense, domestic story. Nearly all the main action takes place in the privacy of two humble households, that of a small-town brewer and that of a lawyer's widow with "considerably less" than £200 a year. But in addition to what Trollope calls the "Domestic Politics" of these two households (chapter 22), the novel also sketches in the clerical and commercial as well as the strictly political "politics" of the town. We witness the public and private activities associated with an election campaign, meet all the gentry at the dinner-table of the local squire, attend a banquet at the Dragon and a meeting of the evangelical Dorcas society, and even pass a short time in Farmer Sturt's back parlour. None of Trollope's other novels tells us so much in so short a space about a whole community, and none is so rich in amusing folklore: for example, the Sunday paper that comes out on Fridays (p.291), the rhyming saws of Mrs Sturt, and the grim festivities of the local merchants at the Dragon. No other novel makes us so at home in a middle-class or lower-middle-class household as we are in that of the brewer Mr Tappitt and his family.

For all its realistic detail, however, the novel is by no means free of romantic improbabilities. The opposition to Rachel Ray's marriage to Luke Rowan, which supplies the chief plot-interest, never becomes fully credible; nor does the process by which it is overcome. It may be natural that Luke, who is a Londoner, an outsider, and who has a breezy, opinionated manner (described as Byronic [pp.54–55]),[5] should be regarded with suspicion in Baslehurst. But given his good present income and excellent prospects, it is not sufficiently explained why Rachel's mother, or even her puritanical sister Mrs Prime, should be so predisposed to distrust him. Mrs Ray, it is true, is alleged to be morally timorous and easily led, but she steps out of this character completely when she is called upon to defend Rachel against the aspersions of Mrs Prime (pp.152–53) and of Luke's mother and Mrs Tappitt of the brewery (chapter 15). Equally surprising is Rachel's failure to contest the obviously false proposition that it would be "ruinous" for Luke to marry her against his mother's wishes (p.202). And although it is believable that Tappitt's allegations against Luke—who owns a large share of the brewery and makes Tappitt's own position there uncomfortable—should

have won some credence, one would have thought that his undisguised malice, if not the badness of his beer, would have
precluded a general swing of public opinion in his favour and
against Luke. At any rate, its subsequent swing back towards Luke is
too sudden and timely to appear other than a contrivance on the
novelist's part. But all along it has been evident that the lovers have
so much on their side, including the narrator himself, that the obstacles to their union must be merely illusory and temporary. Powerful agencies are nevertheless required to sweep them aside. Mr and
Mrs Butler Cornbury, the lord and lady of the manor, must
intervene in the lovers' favour, even at the risk of jeopardizing Mr
Cornbury's political interests. And Mrs Cornbury must play the part
of a fairy godmother to Rachel's Cinderella, escorting her to the ball
(given by the Tappitts) where, to the chagrin of the spiteful sisters
(the Tappitt girls), she charms her prince.

Like Cinderella's, Rachel's triumph is that of modest and
neglected gentility over ostentatious vulgarity. It puts the
purseproud Tappitts in their place, and in their resentment, against
both Rachel and Luke, they proceed to demonstrate just how inferior this place is, how laughable are their genteel pretensions. As
usual in Trollope, the gulf between true gentlefolk and mere
pretenders is shown to be comfortingly wide. When assuring us
categorically that the low-church clergyman Mr Prong is "not a
gentleman", Trollope is "by no means prepared to define" what a
gentleman is (pp.77–78); but there can be no mistaking the lack of
gentility in, for example, Mr Tappitt's drunken blustering or his
wife's habit, so amusing to Rachel and Luke (p.206), of addressing
him as "T".[6] At the other extreme the evidence that Rachel and
Luke themselves are gentlefolk is equally unambiguous. It is stated
as an "undoubted fact" that Rachel is a lady (p.191), while Luke's
standing is clarified by the judgment of county society as
represented by Mr and Mrs Cornbury. When the Cornburys invite
him to visit them at Cornbury Grange he is at first embarrassed,
reminding himself that, should he succeed in ousting Tappitt from
the brewery, he will be "simply a tradesman in the town", and
warning Cornbury that "if you ask all your supporters over to the
Grange you'll get rather a mixed lot"; Cornbury's reply, however,
makes it gratifyingly clear that Luke is not being rewarded merely
for his political support: "I suppose I should; but I don't mean to
do that. I shall be very glad, however, to see you;—very glad."
(pp.341–42) Rachel and Luke, we can now be sure, will remain on
the right side of the great gulf.

The fairytale flavour of *Rachel Ray*, the wishful thinking implicit
in its polarization of social classes and in its elevation of hero and

heroine from a seemingly ambiguous to a safe place in the social scale, indicate that there is room for romance of a kind even in the homeliest settings and the least eventful stories. It would seem, in fact, that the homelier the novel's raw materials, the broader, in some respects, is the scope for romance—not the romance of the exotic, but that of make-believe. The illusion of homely life fosters simple habitual responses, brings into play comfortable childish prejudices. Among Trollope's novels, *Rachel Ray* is the extreme example of this phenomenon because, on the whole, it confines itself most rigorously to commonplace people and happenings.

A related and equally interesting aspect of *Rachel Ray* is the unexpected touch of poetic symbolism in the motif of the "arm in the clouds", introduced in chapter 3 and recalled from time to time afterwards. The arm is conjured up by Luke Rowan in the moment of heightened fancy or sensuousness accompanying his first intimate exchange with Rachel:

> "Rachel," said he ... "live as long as you may, never on God's earth will you look on any sight more lovely than that. Ah! do you see the man's arm, as it were; the deep purple cloud, like a huge hand stretched out from some other world to take you? Do you see it?"
> The sound of his voice was very pleasant. His words to her young ears seemed full of poetry and sweet mysterious romance. He spoke to her as no one,—no man or woman,—had ever spoken to her before ..." [P.38]

Later, Rachel finds herself unable to shake off the fancy that the arm in the clouds was Luke's own arm, the symbol of his quasi-mystical hold on her love (p.65). But although the idea behind the scene is an appealing and perceptive one, the scene itself evokes none of the "energy"[7] by which Luke "amazes" Rachel (p.39): on the contrary, his language has the flat formality of a set speech, and his tone sounds drily pedagogic ("do you see the man's arm, as it were"). The scene is an arresting example of the bathos to which Trollope can descend in trying to be poetic (although he uses a similar idea more successfully in his next novel, *Can You Forgive Her?*) In addition, I would suggest, it bears witness to his dread of seeming too prosaic in his depiction of "commonplace life"; and if this is so the fairytale of the arm in the cloud can be traced to the same source as the fairytale element in the novel as a whole.

Miss Mackenzie is much less attractive in its subject-matter than *Rachel Ray*. Its middle-aged hero and heroine, though they become brighter towards the end, are for most of the novel anxious, dispirited, and dowdy. All the characters live at best on the shabby fringes of gentility. Even the baronetcy that John Ball, the hero, inherits at the end of the novel is of recent creation, having been con-

ferred on his father when Lord Mayor of London: the father had been in the "leather business"—albeit "undoubtedly wholesale" (p.2)—and the son still works, without great profit, in the City. Miss Mackenzie, though a lady by birth, lacks both "beauty and cleverness", and her education has not been "of a kind to make up by art for that which nature had not given her" (p.5). Most of her associates are altogether nastier in their vulgarity than the Tappitts, because sleeker, more knowing; and Mr Maguire and Mr Rubb, John Ball's two rivals for her hand, are not only vulgar but unsavoury. The circles in which she moves—Littlebath and the London of Gower and Arundel streets—have none of the suggestion of bucolic, slightly *folklorique* charm that softens even the ugliest details of life in Baslehurst, the setting of *Rachel Ray*. As the novel itself observes, "A moated grange in the country is bad enough for the life of any Mariana, but a moated grange in town is much worse." (p.5)

Rachel Ray deals with a settled and integrated community, unsophisticated, conservative, suspicious of outsiders (Luke Rowan, for example, and Mr Prong, and the Jewish parliamentary candidate Mr Hart). By comparison the world of *Miss Mackenzie* is almost picaresque. The heroine has no home and no sense of belonging anywhere. For most of the novel she is vainly trying to find her own level and function in a society that is fragmentary and topsyturvy, a world in which a baronet's son drudges for a meagre living in the City, an old boy of Merchant Taylors' School (Mr Rubb) works at an undignified and unprosperous trade, and a graduate of Trinity College, Dublin (Mr Maguire) reeks of vulgarity and indulges in the most blackguardly calumnies. The precariousness of a foothold even in shabby-genteel society is everywhere emphasized; and at Arundel Street, where her only companion is her landlady and former servant Mrs Buggins, and where she is tempted to take yet a further "step downwards" (p.328) by accepting the company of Mr Buggins, Miss Mackenzie feels that she has all but lost her foothold. The penalty for losing it would be to find herself permanently exposed to vulgarians even worse than Mr Rubb, Mr Maguire, and Mrs Tom Mackenzie, her brother's wife. (Mr Maguire, with his hideous squint and the utter deformity of character it reflects, is the most grotesque and improbable of all Trollope's low-church clergymen; and Mrs Tom's "fashionable" dinner-party, described at length in chapter 8, exposes the hollowness of lower-middle-class pretensions to gentility even more unkindly than does Mrs Tappitt's ball.)

Margaret Mackenzie, then, is on the brink of a much deeper abyss than Rachel Ray and comes much closer to toppling into it. Yet in the end her escape is just as complete as Rachel's, and in retrospect a

suspicion arises that her danger can never have been as acute as it seemed. For notwithstanding its sordid accessories, *Miss Mackenzie* too has something of a fairytale quality. The social and moral gulf between, on the one hand, the hero and heroine and, on the other, Mr Rubb and Mr Maguire proves after all to be quite as wide as that between Rachel Ray and the Tappitts. As in *Rachel Ray*, it also widens during the course of the novel, the vulgarity of Rubb and Maguire, like that of the Tappitts, becoming progressively more blatant. When, for example, we first meet Rubb, we can share Miss Mackenzie's view that in his "manners and mode of speech" he is "not quite a gentleman", but can still believe in his having been at Merchant Taylors' (pp.37–41). Later, however, when he appears in yellow gloves ("primrose he would have called them"), with his hair "full of perfumed grease" and sitting "on each side of his head in a conscious arrangement of waviness that was detestable";[8] and when he "absolutely offered an arm simultaneously" to Miss Mackenzie and her friend Miss Baker, then shook hands "glove and all" with Miss Todd (pp.139–40), it is hard to believe there can ever have been any question of his being thought a gentleman. Miss Mackenzie does well to blush, but the reader is likely to be as surprised as she at the depth of Rubb's ignorance of polite usages.

This, however, is only one of a number of blows to the reader's credulity. Another is the loss and subsequent discovery of the deed of gift by which old Jonathan Ball had made over to his nephew John most of the money that had come to Miss Mackenzie. The aim of this improbable touch of romance is clear enough: to give John Ball the chance to prove that his interest in the heroine is not mercenary; for which purpose the novel also strips her, unaccountably, not only of the money she has wrongly inherited but of the considerable sum her late brother had added to it by his own exertions. As a result, far from adhering to his brave plan to exclude "love" (*Autobiography*, p.162), Trollope was able to turn his novel into one of the most romantic of love stories, that of King Cophetua and the beggar-maid. But the beggar-maid is only one of the legendary or poetic roles that Miss Mackenzie re-enacts. She is also compared several times to Mariana in the moated grange, and she is repeatedly referred to as a "Griselda".[9] The primary purpose of such comparisons is no doubt ironic: they imply the disparity between poetry and prose, legend and reality, past and present. But a not insignificant side-effect of the irony is to distance those elements in the heroine's situation that the reader is likely to find most affecting and most worrying, to lend them a faint but comforting air of the fantastic. In particular it acts, within the novel as a whole, as a sentimental filter for the intense boredom and frustration Miss Macken-

zie suffers through being starved of love and condemned to ladylike reticence about her plight. The scenes in which she is allowed to pour out her sexual protest without this ironical filtering are as impressive as any of their kind that Trollope ever achieved. When, for example, she bridles at the idea of becoming a "lady's companion" after the loss of her fortune to John Ball she almost reaches the passionate eloquence of a Jane Eyre: "I would sooner take a broom in my hand, and sweep a crossing in London, than lead such a life as that. What! make myself the slave of some old woman, who would think that she had bought the power of tyrannising over me by allowing me to sit in the same room with her?" (p.265). And similarly, when she kisses her reflection in her mirror—in what she later thinks of as a moment of "ecstasy" for which she "despises" herself (p.137)—she is as convincingly sexy as Hetty Sorrel:

> ... as her fingers ran almost involuntarily across her locks, her touch told her that they were soft and silken; and she looked into her own eyes, and saw that they were bright; and her hand touched the outline of her cheek, and she knew that something of the fresh bloom of youth was still there; and her lips parted, and there were her white teeth; and there came a smile and a dimple, and a slight purpose of laughter in her eye, and then a tear. She pulled her scarf tighter across her bosom, feeling her own form, and then she leaned forward and kissed herself in the glass. [p.111][10]

Whimsical references to this woman as a Mariana or a Griselda inevitably seem morally evasive, and the whole flavour of fairytale and romance that is allowed to creep into the novel enforces the suspicion that Trollope is trying to shield himself from the grimmer implications of the old maid's plight.

A similar evasiveness is apparent in his insistence that the desire for marriage of old maids such as Miss Mackenzie and Miss Todd shows a "maniacal tendency" that might easily be mistaken for insanity (p.397). This, it is suggested, is what had driven Miss Mackenzie to tolerate the addresses of oily Mr Rubb (and presumably of monstrous Mr Maguire as well). But the novel—to its credit—never convinces us that her natural sexuality is in fact maniacal, and her bad taste in the matter of suitors appears, in consequence, to be more a reflection of her creator's than something intrinsic to herself. Its effect is to accentuate the unpleasant side of the novel's subject in spite of the touches of fairytale and romance. *Miss Mackenzie* in this respect falls between two stools.

The Belton Estate has been one of the most praised of Trollope's novels, but also one of the most savagely depreciated. Contemporary critics found it disappointing, and the youthful Henry James, who was one of them, denounced it as "essentially, organically, con-

sistently stupid . . . as incapable of disengaging an idea as of drawing
an inference".[11] Michael Sadleir, however, awarded the novel
"three stars", an honour he bestowed on only four others,[12] and
more recently Robert M. Polhemus has succeeded in "disengaging"
a number of "ideas" from it.[13]

Clara Amedroz, though introduced "as not a very young lady",
and as one who "in manners, appearance, and habits was, at any
rate, as old as her age" (p.9), turns out to be not another Griselda
but an attractively strong-minded heroine, stamped in much the
same mould as Mary Thorne, Lucy Robarts, and in some respects
Alice Vavasor (of *Can You Forgive Her?*). But it could hardly be
maintained that the choices which confront her in the novel constitute a drama of ideas. James himself later came to see Trollope's
"great taste for the moral question" as one of his distinctive
qualities.[14] But in *The Belton Estate* he clearly, and I think
justifiably, felt that neither the ethical nor the psychological basis of
the heroine's decisions could provoke any real question in the
reader's mind.

Clara fancies herself in love with and becomes engaged to Captain Aylmer; then, sometime after the engagement has been broken
off, falls truly in love with and marries Will Belton. Her imagined
love for Aylmer is fully explained as a reaction to the gloom of her
life both at home, where she and her father brood over the dissipation and premature death of her only brother, and in the house of
her "aunt" Mrs Winterfield, where the atmosphere is low church
and killjoy. Aylmer, though ostensibly a low churchman himself,
and though cold by nature, lightens the gloom for Clara. He can at
least read poetry and talk about "the world of literature"; he has the
polish of a man accustomed to good society, and as a member of
parliament he knows "the inner world of worlds which governs the
world" (p.69). Later, as she grows more aware of his deficiencies as a
man and a lover, she consoles herself with the "prudence" of marrying a man who combines "propriety of demeanour, decency of outward life, and a competence" (pp.128–29). But given Aylmer's lack
of enthusiasm for the engagement, and her own early perception
that he is without Will's "noble qualities" (p.69), it seems inevitable
that one or other of them will find a pretext for withdrawal. The
pretext is supplied partly by the interference of Aylmer's mother,
but chiefly by Clara's rejection of Aylmer's demand that she give up
her friendship with Mrs Askerton, one of her neighbours.

Mrs Askerton's unhappy past is the one concession the book
makes to romance. Before marrying Colonel Askerton she had lived
with him for three years as his mistress. This had happened in India,
where her first husband was an officer in Askerton's regiment. Mrs

Askerton had been driven to place herself under the colonel's
protection by the first husband's drunken brutality. The story clearly touches on delicate moral issues, but the disagreement it provokes
between Clara and Aylmer turns, in the main, not on these but on a
relatively simple question, that of a bethrothed lover's right to exercise a husband's authority. Technically it is obvious that he has no
such right, and to this extent Clara's position is correct; but in practice, according to Victorian notions, Aylmer would be unwise, even
if more tactful, not to make known his wishes on a matter that will
have to be settled once he and Clara are married. To the reader their
disagreement must appear a symptom of their general incompatibility and their common halfheartedness about the engagement
rather than a substantive difference of principle.

But Trollope, unfortunately, is not content to allow honours
between them to remain even. Lest Clara incur any trace of un-
maidenly odium for falling half in love with one man while engaged
to another, the other must be shown to be not only uncongenial but
unworthy. So his skindeep low churchmanship is revealed as the
mark of a pharisee who casts stones at a defenceless and unlucky
woman (Mrs Askerton). And in the end, like so many of the dis-
carded lovers of Trollope's heroines, he proves his paltriness by making a loveless, ambitious marriage to a woman older than himself
and approved by his mother (though his previous inclination had
been not to marry at all). Clara, on the other hand, stands by the unhappy Mrs Askerton and is supported in her stand by Will. And her
and Will's love for each other is shown as both passionate—Will's
first embrace sending Clara into "convulsions" (pp.293–94)—and
"poetic". Their most memorable encounters occur on a "sacred
spot", a "high rock" approached by a stony path, which is to Clara
the "altar" at which she is made love's sacrificial victim (pp.418–19;
and cf. pp.60–64). As a slight but telltale sign of Will's decisive
superiority to Aylmer it is even noted that his farmhouse is Tudor,
whereas Aylmer Park is classical, with a "portico of Ionic columns"
(pp.37, 212).[15] Every detail corroborates the rightness of Clara's
choice, leaving us convinced, finally, that it was no choice at all, that
only a moral imbecile could have failed to appreciate Will's
superiority.

Even her adhesion to Mrs Askerton, which might have given her a
better chance to show her powers of moral discrimination, is by no
means so daring, or so antithetical to Aylmer's pharisaism, as the
novel perhaps wishes us to feel. No critic, to my knowledge, has
drawn attention to Clara's reservations. Before hearing Mrs
Askerton's story from her own lips, she admits that "with a previous
knowledge of such a story she would probably have avoided any in-

timacy", and under ordinary circumstances her judgment would be the same as Aylmer's: "If, in truth, this woman had left her own hus-band and gone away to live with another man, she had by doing so—at any rate while she was doing so—fallen in such a way as to make herself unfit for the society of an unmarried young woman who meant to keep her name unblemished before the world" (p.226). The clichés and the revealing parenthesis suggest that neither Clara nor her creator (who is evidently in sympathy with her) is at all disposed to question the accepted sexual code; and this is confirmed when, after hearing Mrs Askerton's own account of her past, Clara pledges loyalty to her not on principle but because "car-ried away by impulse" (p.237). In justifying herself to Aylmer subse-quently she still finds it necessary to dwell on the "provocations" that led to Mrs Askerton's sin and on the fact that "it all occurred out in India" (p.239). The comfortable implication—which Aylmer was surely right to challenge, even though for the wrong reason—is that Mrs Askerton's case is altogether exceptional and took place vir-tually under a different set of rules.

The Belton Estate, then, differs from *Rachel Ray* and *Miss Mackenzie* in that the one slight concession it makes to romance has the effect not so much of distracting attention from potentially delicate issues as of lending a spurious air of difficulty and impor-tance to essentially banal and inconsequential ones.

Among the novels I see as more or less conforming to Trollope's definition of "fiction shorn of all romance", the most debatable in-clusion is perhaps *The Claverings*. What chiefly distinguishes it from the others is its use of such seemingly exotic characters as the sinister Count Pateroff and his sister Mme Gordeloup, who is rumoured to be a Russian spy (p.142), the diabolical Lord Ongar, the monstrously callous Sir Hugh Clavering, and the quixotic Lady Ongar. It emerges, however, that none of these are quite as exotic as they seem. Sophie Gordeloup, for instance, though she reveals to the no-nonsense mind of the inveterate clubman Captain Boodle a "new world", one with which he is not "conversant" (p.319), is placed by Sir Hugh Clavering's casual remark that "all the ugly old Frenchwomen in London are Russian spies, according to what peo-ple say" (p.246). And Count Pateroff, Lord Ongar, and Sir Hugh himself—who is thought "peculiar" by some of his relatives (p.232)—all belong to a category which, in Lady Ongar's view, is all too common. To Harry Clavering's exclamation that the count "must be a very devil" and "cannot be a man", she replies:

> "Man or devil, what matters which he be? Which is the worst, Harry, and what is the difference? The Fausts of this day want no

Mephistopheles to teach them guile or to harden their hearts."
  "I do not believe that there are such men. There may be one."
  "One, Harry! What was Lord Ongar? What is your cousin Hugh?
What is this Count Pateroff? Are they not all of the same nature; hard as
stone, desirous simply of indulging their own appetites, utterly without
one generous feeling, incapable even of the idea of caring for any one? Is
it not so?" [P.218]

Lady Ongar's comments occur in the course of one of the novel's
most dramatic scenes, and the tenor of this scene will help to indicate why *The Claverings*, without confining itself to the "most ordinary people", still belongs among Trollope's "domestic" novels.
Lady Ongar contends that the difference between man and devil
hardly matters. Harry, on the contrary, would have it that the count
belongs in effect to a different species. It is Harry, too, who smugly
insists, apropos of Sir Hugh, that "no man has a right to be peculiar.
Every man is bound to accept such usage as is customary in the
world." (p.232) And Harry himself is carefully projected, like most
of Trollope's vacillating jeunes premiers, as a representative young
man, neither hero nor villain (e.g., pp.98, 296–97). But only a few
minutes after calling the count a devil he is acting under a devil's influence himself, making a passionate avowal of love to Lady Ongar
although his troth is plighted to Florence Burton (pp.222–23).
Indeed, until the entry of Mme Gordeloup, with "stealthy, cat-like
steps", the stage seems set for a seduction scene rivalling that
between Richard Feverel and Bella Mount. Seductions, however,
are very rare in Trollope, and when they do occur it is always offstage and usually—as in *The Belton Estate*—overseas.[16] On this occasion, characteristically, the moment of impending crisis is barely
separable from the moment of anticlimax, beautifully conveyed in
the narrator's laconic remark: "Clavering had found himself to be
somewhat awkwardly situated while Madame Gordeloup was ... explaining the causes of her having come unannounced into the
room." The keen emotion of the lover has been succeeded, not by
equally keen disappointment or embarrassment, but by a
"somewhat" awkward bemusement.
  The bathetic outcome of this scene, and of all the similar (if less
torrid) scenes that occur in other Trollope novels, may seem to lend
weight to James's complaint—in respect of another novel—that "for
Mr. Trollope anything is preferable to a sensation; an incident is
ever preferable to an event".[17] But Trollope's answer would
doubtless be that in *The Claverings*, despite appearances, he is dealing with the commonest details of commonplace life; and while
many of his other novels show that sensational events can and do
occur among ordinary people leading otherwise commonplace lives,
it is obviously his conviction that more often than not they don't.

The Claverings is consistently anti-tragic, anti-sensational in its vision of life; few other Trollopian novels are so rich in both tragic and sensational possibilities, yet so convincingly "commonplace" in their outcome, and by the same token few are so rich in seemingly exceptional but actually—in the context of the book as a whole—quite ordinary people.

The one exception is Lord Ongar, who has little to distinguish him from the wicked lord of fairytale, and who is a stock Trollopian character, belonging to the same family as Lord Lovel (*Lady Anna*) and Lord Brotherton (*Is He Popenjoy?*). Like theirs, his villainy is perpetrated on the congenial soil of Italy, the homeland of Iago and Bosola, Montoni and Count Fosco; and both its precise nature and its motive are shrouded in a sinister romantic mist. For Trollope's purposes it is enough that the reader should be aware that Lady Ongar has been savagely punished for making a mercenary marriage, and should sympathize with her but also take warning. Once she has returned to England as a wealthy widow there is nothing at all romantic about her position, beset as she is by gossip, greedy suitors, and a former lover (Harry Clavering) who cannot choose between her and his new lover. Her eventual attempt to renounce her fortune, which appears quixotic, and which her sister considers "mad" (pp.480–81), is shown to be not so much a noble gesture of repentance or a masochistic act of self-immolation as a commonsense transaction by which she hopes to purchase peace of mind. That it does not signify any radical change in her nature—such as the reader might find hard to credit—is shown by her refusal to give Harry up of her own accord, despite the eloquent appeal of his fiancée's sister-in-law (chapter 37), and by her prudence in deciding to retain a comfortable income for herself at the time when she offers to restore the rest of her fortune to her husband's family. In all three instances her motives are represented as above all sensible, neither quixotically generous and self-effacing nor mean and calculating. If she does, nevertheless, become a little larger than life by the end of the book, the implication is that this is chiefly because such thoroughgoing commonsense is far from common.

Lord and perhaps Lady Ongar apart, the novel sustains its illusion of commonplace life with great subtlety. There is, admittedly, no problem in this regard as far as the hero and heroine are concerned. When Harry retreats, at the last minute, from the cauldron of unholy love, the narrator convincingly reassures us that if the devil is in him, he is yet no devil: "He had drifted into treachery unawares, ... not because he was wicked, but because he was weak" (p.221). He is unremarkable both in his virtues and his vices; indeed, for a man who is a fellow of his college at Cambridge, but who chooses to work

first as a teacher in a state-assisted school, then as a trainee engineer, his attitudes are disappointingly ordinary. Though he bravely admits that if he came to think much about religion he might have doubts (p.17), he nevertheless says his prayers at night (p.159); and despite his manly determination to "earn my own bread" (p.42) and to emulate the engineering feats of "such men as Locke, and Stephenson, and Brassey" (p.21),[18] both he and the author seem well satisfied when a happy accident carries off the two men who stand between him and the heirship to the family estate. R.H. Hutton objected that his inner life, and the nature of the difference between his feelings towards Florence and his feelings towards Lady Ongar, are left "absolutely to [our] imagination";[19] but the perspective in which the novel as a whole places him suggests, I think, that both his shallowness and Florence's colourlessness are in their own natures rather than in Trollope's portrayal of them. Otherwise it is unlikely that the novel would have virtually passed over both their courtship—which everyone except Harry himself had anticipated—and their final reunion. Theirs is essentially a conventional relationship, functioning as a norm against which others more complex and unpredictable may be measured.

One of these, of course, is Harry's own relationship with Lady Ongar, in which it is clear that his passions are more strongly engaged than they have ever been in his courtship of Florence. But even here it is hinted that their strength is not matched by their depth: "As he went [to call on Lady Ongar] he bethought himself that these Wallikers and the like had had no such events in life as had befallen him! They laughed at him about Florence Burton, little guessing that it had been his lot to love and to be loved by such a one as Julia Brabazon had been,—such a one as Lady Ongar was now" (p.66). The romance, the "poetry" of his and Lady Ongar's situation clearly appeals to Harry—as it would to any ordinary young man. Nor is he altogether indifferent to her money, although his refusal to allow it to override the claims of honour and of humanity is what finally establishes him as merely "weak", not "wicked" like Lord Ongar, Sir Hugh, and the count. From the point of view of conventional morality, he is rightly held up for admiration when he returns to Florence, and it is fitting that he should be rewarded by a windfall at the end of the novel. But the novel is not simply a conventional defence of love-matches and warning against mercenary ones. It also asks more teasing questions about the values of innocence and experience, of security and danger. Lady Ongar, for example, clearly interests both Trollope and Harry more than does Florence, who is reluctant to "leave papa's house where I am sure of my bread and butter, till I'm sure of it in another" (p.34):

Lady Ongar is at least prepared to take risks and can even tempt Harry to take them. And, without denying that Harry is right to resist the temptation—being the man he is, and having committed himself to Florence as a result—we can still feel that in the novel's view Lady Ongar is too good for him, rather than he for her. She puts his character to the test, just as, in a sense, his chosen profession does, and in both cases the test proves too stern.

From this point of view, then, conventional decency and prudence are represented as a necessary refuge for timid and commonplace people. Not, however, in a cynical spirit: for the timid and commonplace people are after all the pleasantest. Yet the novel leaves us in no doubt that poverty and struggle are the conditions of vitality, whereas prosperity, security, and conventional respectability are apt to be debilitating. Harry's lymphatic father is the most eloquent example, but by the end of the novel we can hardly feel confident that Harry himself, and even Mr Saul, that most devoted of curates, won't take after him. Another sad example is Lady Clavering, who, like her sister Lady Ongar, has married for money and who has had her spirit crushed by a bullying husband. Sir Hugh is one of the men Lady Ongar describes as "hard as stone", but he is not entirely to blame for his wife's plight. "Peculiar" though he is, he is no monster. His callousness, rudeness, and parsimony are, in part at least, a response to the conventional dullness of life at Clavering Park ("everybody always seems to me to be dreadfully dull here" [p.113]) and especially to the insipidity of his wife, who he knows, or believes he knows, married him for the same reason as her sister married Lord Ongar. The scene between husband and wife when they first meet after the death of their only son is as grim and affecting as any in the Victorian novel. But although it reveals Sir Hugh's selfishness and half-unconscious cruelty in a horrifying light, it also goes close to making him as much an object of sympathy as the bereaved mother. He at least is living with the brutal truth and is aware that there is no altering it; she has conventional consolations almost within reach:

> "When did he die?" asked the father.
> "It was past four I think." Then there was again silence, and Lady Clavering went up to her husband and stood close by his shoulder. At last she ventured to put her hand upon him. With all her own misery heavy upon her, she was chiefly thinking at this moment how she might soothe him. She laid her hand upon his shoulder, and by degrees she moved it softly to his breast. Then he raised his own hand and with it moved hers from his person. He did it gently;—but what was the use of such nonsense as that?
> "The Lord giveth," said the wife, "and the Lord taketh away." Hearing this Sir Hugh made with his head a gesture of impatience. "Blessed be the name of the Lord," continued Lady Clavering. Her voice was low

and almost trembling, and she repeated the words as though they were a task which she had set herself.

"That's all very well in its way," said he, "but what's the special use of it now? I hate twaddle ... If that is enough for you, let it be so. But don't talk to me of it. I don't like it. It doesn't suit me. I had only one, and he has gone. It is always the way." He spoke of the child as having been his—not his and hers. She felt this, and understood the want of affection which it conveyed; but she said nothing of it. [P.209]

Later, it becomes evident that there is selfishness on both sides, the wife's being epitomized by her grotesque appropriation of the marital bedchamber for her son's corpse. We can even see in Sir Hugh's harsh realism and distaste for his wife's sentimental clichés not only a timid fear of emotion, a lack of any emotional vocabulary, but also a tonic, if drastic, corrective to self-indulgent emotionalism. There is a similar ambivalence about the scene in which he and his wife part for what proves to be the last time (pp.374–75). According to all precedents, our sympathy should be almost wholly with the wife, the "poor fool" who rose at dawn to "peep out between the curtains" at the husband who was only too glad to be "escaping from her", and then "took herself to bed again and cried herself to sleep".[20] But in their last conversation the husband's patient exasperation rings truer than her demonstrative sorrow, which appears slightly ludicrous, perhaps even affected. It is for him rather than for her that we feel as, with his bed-candle in his hand, he "submitted himself" to the "inevitable embrace": "His position with the candle was awkward, and he wished that it might be over."

"Awkward": we are reminded of the bathetic sequel to Harry's passionate embrace of Lady Ongar. In a sense, indeed, the whole novel is about the "awkwardness" of strong emotion, the folly and futility of extravagant gestures in the light of prosaic fact. At one point even Lady Ongar is betrayed into striking an attitude, as she threatens to throw herself off a cliff into the sea to escape Count Pateroff's persecution; his reply is unanswerable: "Ah! That is what we call poetry. Poetry is very pretty, and in saying this as you do, you make yourself divine. But to be dashed over the cliffs and broken on the rocks;—in prose it is not so well." (p.287) The count and his sister, like that other "foreign" adventuress the Signora, know the difference between prose and poetry exactly, even if they know little else; and it is because of this that they are able to make such fools of timid souls like Harry, Archie, and his friend Captain Boodle, who dare to venture into unfamiliar territory with only their conventional armour to protect them. Mme Gordeloup's final denunciation of the English, for all its malicious bias, has very much the effect of a punchline putting all the Claverings—the "peculiar" Sir Hugh included—in their proper prosaic place:

"They are beasts and fools, and as awkward as bulls,—yes, as bulls. I hate them. I hate them all. Men, women, children,—they are all alike. Look at the street out there. Though it is summer, I shiver when I look out at its blackness. It is the ugliest nation! And they understand nothing. Oh, how I hate them!"

"They are not without merit. They have got money."

"Money,—yes. They have got money; and they are so stupid, you may take it from under their eyes. They will not see you. But of their own hearts, they will give you nothing. You see that black building,—the workhouse. I call it Little England. It is just the same. The naked, hungry, poor wretches lie at the door, and the great fat beadles swell about like turkey-cocks inside." [P.483]

Dickens, one imagines, would have appreciated the tribute.

After this, and with the mocking phrase "awkward as bulls"—which the novel has shown to be so just—ringing in our ears, the wedding bells of Harry and Florence, Mr Saul and Fanny at the end of the novel inevitably sound hollow.

The Claverings was well received by contemporary critics; but only Hutton, whom Trollope rightly regarded as "the most observant" of them, as well as "generally the most eulogistic" (*Autobiography*, p.176), saw its greatness. He believed that it had "a higher moral, and a more perfect artistic unity ... than any of Mr. Trollope's previous tales".[21] The only modern critic who seems to me to do the novel anything like justice is Sadleir,[22] but even he devotes more space to *The Belton Estate*.[23]

Ralph the Heir, written five years after *The Claverings*, is best known for its election scenes and, to a lesser extent, for its characterization of Sir Thomas Underwood, the elderly, brooding lawyer, and Mr Neefit, the breeches-maker who nearly succeeds in buying an aristocratic husband for his daughter. The novel as a whole, however, is more interesting than any of its parts. Not only is it, as the ever-perceptive Hutton observed,[24] one of Trollope's best-constructed works; it is also, in conception, one of his most adventurous—though, as I shall suggest, the execution is not always worthy of the conception. The plot, according to the *Athenaeum*, is "of that domestic character which Mr. Trollope has so often illustrated".[25] But it introduces some notable, and welcome, changes. For once the jeune premier, who is presented in the usual Trollopian fashion as neither better nor worse than most young men of his class, falls from grace altogether by the end of the novel. For once a likable young lady draws back, by her own efforts, from the "abyss of constancy" (as the *Saturday Review* called it)[26] to an unworthy lover. For once a young woman ignorant of most of the politer forms of speech (Polly Neefit) is credited with better sense and better feeling than most of her social superiors.

Essentially, the novel is a study of the clash between individual selfishness and social and moral law. For selfish reasons, Sir Thomas Underwood, Squire Newton, and Mr Neefit all neglect or rebel against the duties and restrictions laid upon them by custom—and perhaps by a higher authority still. Sir Thomas fails both as father and guardian because of his dedication, apparently selfless but in fact self-indulgent, to the idea of a vast work of scholarship. Squire Newton tries to circumvent the law of inheritance, and in effect the marriage law, so that his property may pass to his illegitimate son; his motives, too, are ostensibly selfless—love of his son and the wish to secure him "natural" justice—but are in reality dominated by the selfish need to assuage his own guilt. Neefit's ambitions, similarly, purport to be all for his daughter rather than for himself, but to gratify them he is prepared to sacrifice both her happiness and the very class distinctions which alone give point to them. The selfishness of all three men is seen, in a cruder form, in the central character Ralph the heir who is, in fact, directly encouraged in his selfish courses by the Squire and by Neefit (who wishes to marry him to his daughter), and not restrained in them, as he should have been, by his guardian Sir Thomas.

In its conclusions *Ralph the Heir* is conservative. Not entirely with approval, it recognizes that old ways, traditional habits of thought, have unexpected stamina. The sharpest illustrations emerge from Sir Thomas's fruitless efforts to fight an honest election campaign at Percycross and the genuinely moral distaste they produce among men accustomed to the idea that loyal voters deserve to be financially rewarded. Similar attitudes underlie the relief of Squire Newton's tenants when it is found that the legal heir, of whom none of them have heard any good, has not after all been supplanted by the squire's illegitimate son, whom they all like and respect. They also underlie Polly Neefit's music-hall eloquence on the virtues of keeping one's station (II: 302-4)—an unselfconscious parroting of working-class folklore that makes nonsense of her father's ambitions—and the old-fashioned, bourgeois respectability that masquerades as fire-eating radicalism in Ontario Moggs. It seems altogether appropriate to the general conservatism of the novel that once the heroine—Sir Thomas's daughter Clarissa—has got over her infatuation for the unworthy Ralph Newton, she should give herself to his brother, a high-church country parson with a passion for repairing old churches.

The novel's conservatism is not only social and political but also ethical. Much more than is usual in Trollope, we are made to sense the workings of a grim and inflexible moral law, which also operates, though less convincingly, in *Sir Harry Hotspur of Humblethwaite*,

written immediately before *Ralph the Heir*, and in *An Eye for an Eye*, written a year later. Squire Newton has applied to him, appositely, the words of Edgar in *King Lear*: "The gods are just, and of our pleasant vices make instruments to scourge us" (I:273); and the accident that kills him is brought about by his exultation at having, as he supposes, undone the evils resulting from the birth of his son out of wedlock. It is, he believes, "all settled" (chapter 31) that his property will pass to his son rather than his nephew, but his son's cautious "Ain't we counting our chickens before they are hatched?" (I:345) proves prophetic. After the squire's death the harsh, inescapable moral of his failure is drawn by the family butler: "It ain't come to much surely, and I don't suppose it do come to much mostly when folks go wrong." (II:70) The same thought, in different language, is with Sir Thomas as he listens at night to the sad, thin, fitful notes of a flute and hears in them a threnody for his selfish, wasted life: "So idle as he had been in thinking, so inconclusive, so frail, so subject to gusts of wind, so incapable of following his subject to the end, why had he dared to leave that Sunday-keeping, church-going, domestic, decent life, which would have become one of so ordinary calibre as himself?" (II:286)[27]

At the end it is made clear, too, that Ralph (the heir) will have occasion, in the course of a miserable married life, to revise his rosy opinion of the "divine Providence" that "looked after him in a special way" (II:90). Ralph, like Lizzie Eustace—the heroine of the novel Trollope began a few months after completing *Ralph the Heir*—suffers from a "want of reality in his character" (II:229). For him, as for Johnny Eames, trifling with the feelings of "such a pleasant armful" as Polly Neefit is a "lark" (I:70, 258); he snatches a kiss from the heroine, Clarissa Underwood, without any notion that she may take it as a sign of uncommon affection; he is an eager and facile believer in the "doctrine" that "young ladies are all wanting to get married" and that "few can dare to refuse any man who is justified in proposing to them" (I:334).[28] Yet Ralph is no less personable, and only marginally shabbier, than a Johnny Eames, a Harry Clavering, or even a Frank Gresham, and the nemesis that claims him—in the guise of the De Courcy–like Eardham family into which he marries—is unexpectedly grim. It appears even more so when we note that his favourite recreation, hunting, was also Trollope's own and that some of his hunters even have the same names (Banker, Buff) as Trollope's.[29] But in *Ralph the Heir*—though in no other Trollope novel—hunting is regarded largely as a vice, not only leading Ralph into extravagance, idleness, and some dissipation but also supplying Squire Newton with a symbolically appropriate means of self-destruction. Like Sir Thomas's Baconian

studies, it is a form of self-indulgence, a distraction from more challenging tasks; and since both hunting and Bacon were interests that
Trollope himself shared,[30] we may suspect that a measure of self-
reproof underlies the unusually severe punishments that he visits on
Ralph, Squire Newton, and Sir Thomas (whose punishment is his
awakening to the futility of his past life).

I have stated that in *Ralph the Heir* the execution is not always
equal to the conception. This is particularly true of the portrayal of
Neefit, which, although it appealed to the original reviewers,[31]
clearly fails to serve its purpose within the total design of the novel.
Neefit should act both as a comic touchstone for "straight"
characters like Squire Newton and Sir Thomas and as an embodiment of the vulgarity that threatens to submerge Ralph. But by allowing him to hold the stage long after he has fulfilled both these
purposes, retaining him simply as a source of comic business that
grows more and more grotesque, Trollope obscures his subtler function in the novel. A further weakness lies in the portrayal of the
Underwood family. Sir Thomas himself has some highly interesting
and unusual facets of character—his shyness and self-doubt, his
religious scepticism, even his self-preoccupation—but too often
these are belied, forgotten, or at best only half-realized, in his actual
deportment. In particular a deeper, less intermittent exploration of
his nature is needed to clarify the motive for his political ambition
and the moral and psychological basis of his relationship with his
daughters. The feelings that persuaded him to stand for parliament
do not appear nearly strong enough to counteract his love of privacy,
his deep reticence. And his aversion to close contact with his
daughters, which looks very like a form of sexual revulsion, seems
almost impossible to reconcile with the tact, poise, and savoir-faire
he shows in most eventualities—including those in which he is
managing the daughters' own affairs.

By the time *Ralph the Heir* appeared in book form (1871), Trollope
had begun to lose his popular and critical following;[32] but *Ralph the
Heir* itself was on the whole warmly welcomed by the original
reviewers, much more so than most of the novels that immediately
preceded it. For some reviewers it marked Trollope's return to an
earlier, and gentler, manner that he had abandoned in recent novels
such as *The Claverings*, *Phineas Finn*, *He Knew He Was Right*, *The
Vicar of Bullhampton*, and *Sir Harry Hotspur*.[33] There was a
widespread feeling at this time that Trollope had begun to show an
unhealthy predilection for "disagreeable" subjects. In truth,
however, this predilection was not of recent growth. It had been
noted by reviewers from time to time throughout his career; and if it

failed to bulk large in their mind in retrospect, the reason was probably that they thought of him primarily as the creator of Barset, in which a traditional and on the whole "agreeable" way of life was celebrated. The critics nevertheless had good grounds for feeling that *Ralph the Heir* was something of a throwback; because it was not only his first attempt for several years at "fiction shorn of all romance", but was also destined to be one of his last.

In all but a few of his remaining novels romance, in the form of mystery, crime, or violent passion, is given much freer rein than in any of the novels I have considered in this chapter. Nearly all of the later novels are, in Trollope's terms, both realistic and sensational, whereas among the works written in the 1850s and the first half of the 1860s the essentially domestic slightly outnumber the sensational. The handful of domestic novels that came after *Ralph the Heir*, at long intervals, for the most part lack the energy and originality of the more sensational works that appeared during the same period.[34]

Is He Popenjoy? is the one notable exception. Here, up to a point, Trollope achieves as happy and compact a blending of the essence of his domestic "stream" with that of his problem novels and novels of public life as can be found in any of his later works. Brothershire, the setting of the opening and closing sections of the story, is unmistakably the "brother shire" of the "dear county" of Barset. Its capital Brotherton is a small cathedral city, presided over, like Barchester, by a meek lowchurch bishop whose right hand is an unctuous, sycophantic chaplain at loggerheads with the generally high, or high-and-dry, clergy of the cathedral chapter. Dean Lovelace, the heroine's father, is rich, wordly, and pugnacious, in the same mould as Archdeacon Grantly (though, unlike Grantly, he is low-born, being the son of a livery stable keeper and retaining "a smell of the stable" [I:232][35]). When he succeeds in marrying his daughter Mary to Lord George Germain, his worldliness brings him into conflict with his son-in-law's family, who, though high-church tories, are ascetic in outlook and do their best to douse Mary's high spirits. Thus far, the story and setting are Trollopian-domestic, "fiction shorn of all romance". But the Dean has stipulated that Mary and George are to spend half the year in London, and there both begin to live more publicly and more dangerously.

Mary becomes involved with rampant feminists and enjoys waltzing and other innocent "fun" with Jack De Baron. George compromises himself by flirting, tremulously, with Adelaide Houghton. Though he is jealous of Jack and disapproves of waltzing, George feels he cannot interfere without seeming to distrust Mary, and his chance of doing so is lost when Mary accidentally learns of his own

indiscreet behaviour. It is not until after he has dropped Adelaide (temporarily) and scandalmongers have inflamed his jealousy that he acts decisively, plucking Mary from Jack's clutches in the midst of a ball where, under the Dean's chaperonage, they are waltzing gaily, conspicuously, and, as George thinks, too familiarly.[36] After this public humiliation Mary refuses to allow George to remove her to the safe obscurity of Brotherton lest her retreat be taken as an admission of guilt. Instead she remains in London with her father, and the young couple are separated for some months.

By this stage what seemed to begin as a typically low-key domestic tale has developed into a tense moral drama, close to tragedy and fraught with implications of general social crisis. So long as George and Mary remain in Brothershire their difficulties appear merely personal and accidental, the effect partly of contrasting temperaments, partly of lack of conjugal privacy. But once they go to London their marriage becomes part of an environment in which feminists (crudely caricatured, as they always are in Trollope)[37] are raising doubts about the whole social status of women, in which other marriages where (as in George's and Mary's) there is money on one side and less tangible assets on the other are shown to be under strain, and in which indigent young people are seen reducing marriage to a mere matter of money, either the one way of escaping poverty or the one sure way of perpetuating it. One of the features of this environment, as the Dean observes, is that "People in society now do give themselves strange liberty; women ... more than men" (I:153). In such a context George and Mary's difficulties not only become exacerbated but take on a more representative significance: besides illustrating some of the permanent barriers to understanding between the sexes, and between stuffy men and lively women in particular, they appear as symptoms of a widening gap between town and country, between new manners and old, between the new woman and the old man, between a quasi-demotic impulse towards spontaneity and fun and aristocratic high horse. As in *He Knew He Was Right*, Trollope's deepest and most tragic study of marital discord, the problems of one married couple are set against a background of general controversy and uncertainty about sex and marriage.

In the dénouement, however, all the tensions that have built up between husband and wife, all the portents of sexual strife and corruption in society at large, are magically, and bathetically, waved away. First Mary announces herself pregnant. Then the two people who stand between George and the family title die. George naturally cannot remain estranged from the mother of his heir, a future marquis. Once she becomes both a marchioness and a mother, Mary for-

tunately doesn't need to be told that waltzing and feminism must cease. Intoxicated by the joy of their happy ending, Trollope forgets that at the beginning of the novel the Brotherton estates had not yielded the family an income "equal to their rank" (I:4). Suddenly, and without explanation, they become worth over £40,000 a year (II:250).

This fairytale ending belies Mary's conviction that "all would be tragedy" if she married anyone other than the hero of her girlish imagination, who was "not at all like Lord Germain" (I:15). It also disposes fittingly of the fairytale ogre, Lord George's brother, whose plot to pass off his probably illegitimate Italian son as his heir supplies the element of romance in the novel,[38] and who later provokes the one incident of violence, when the Dean hurls him into a fireplace for calling Mary a slut (chapter 41). (It is hinted that his conduct offstage is even more disgraceful, that he scours the fleshpots of the Haymarket each night in company with his servant and that he has spies in his pay both at Brotherton and in London.) In the end he too is reduced simply to a wicked sprite whom George and Mary's good fairies cause to vanish. All signs of evil, of social corruption, of personal incompatibility disappear to produce an ending "made up of sweetmeats and sugarplums"—like that of *Barchester Towers*. But the falsity and bathos of such an ending is an accurate measure of how far the mood of Trollope's "problem" novels and novels of public life diverges from that of his more purely domestic ones.

NOTES

1. *Letters*, p.138. George Eliot's reply, full of praise for *Rachel Ray*, can be found in Gordon S. Haight's collection of her *Letters* (London: Oxford University Press, 1956) 4 : 110.
2. The history of the sensation novel and its critics has yet to be written. W.C. Phillips's *Dickens, Reade, and Collins: Sensation Novelists* (New York: Columbia University Press, 1919) is a pioneering work that is still useful and stimulating, but it suffers from being largely devoted to the most reputable of the sensationalists. The bêtes noires of most of the sensation novel's enemies were Collins, Mrs Henry Wood, and Miss M.E. Braddon (author of *Lady Audley's Secret, Aurora Floyd*, etc.): most critics felt that the work of Dickens, many that that of Reade, and some that even that of Collins belonged to a higher order of art. I shall be referring subsequently to some of the more important contributions to the debate on the sensation novel. See also my pamphlet, *Some Mid-Victorian Thrillers: the Sensation Novel, Its Friends and Its Foes* (Brisbane: University of Queensland Press, 1971).
3. He also had misgivings about the public outcry against sensationalism and thought of expressing them in an article in the *Cornhill*. See Sadleir, *Commentary*, p.258, and *Letters*, p.159.
4. See especially the reviews in the *Athenaeum*, 17 October 1863, p.493, and the *Times*, 25 December 1863, p.4.

5. Byron is also credited with having had a bad influence on the philandering Johnny Eames (*The Small House at Allington* I:188) and, by implication, on Mrs
   Dobbs Broughton (*The Last Chronicle of Barset* I: 415; II: 88, 93, 206). His most
   believable votary, however, is Lizzie Eustace; see discussion of *The Eustace Diamonds* below.
6. Mrs Quiverful, in *Barchester Towers*, has the same unladylike habit. There, too, it
   invites ridicule, and the ridicule jars unpleasantly with the sympathy that Mrs
   Quiverful attracts at other times.
7. Henry James is also fond of attributing "energy" to his male lovers—e.g., to Lord
   Warburton and Casper Goodwood in *Portrait of a Lady*—often, as in the case of
   Warburton, with no more apparent justification than Trollope has here.
8. Perhaps, like Matthew Arnold, Mr Rubb fell under the sway of a French barber
   on one of his frequent visits to Paris (cf. p.39).
9. Trollope's working calendar for the novel (Bodleian MS., Don.c.9, I, 134) shows
   in fact that it was originally to have been called "The Modern Griselda".
   Somebody probably reminded Trollope that Maria Edgeworth had already used
   the title for one of her tales—the sort of tale that Mary Lovelace in *Is He Popenjoy?* (II:123), and presumably Trollope himself, found "sickening".
10. Robert M. Polhemus (*The Changing World of Anthony Trollope*, p.113) suggests
    that the scene in *Daniel Deronda* where Gwendolen Harleth kisses her image in
    the mirror may have been suggested by this one; but as I have hinted, it seems to
    me more likely that the influence was the other way round, that Miss Mackenzie
    had read *Adam Bede*.
11. Henry James, *Notes and Reviews* (Cambridge, Mass.: Dunster House, 1921),
    pp.130–31; reprinted from the *Nation*, 4 January 1866.
12. Sadleir, *Commentary*, pp.392–93.
13. Polhemus, *Changing World of Anthony Trollope*, pp.124–28.
14. Henry James, "Anthony Trollope", in *The House of Fiction*, p.94.
15. Cf. the contrast, in *Doctor Thorne*, between Greshamsbury and Courcy Castle,
    discussed above. On the moral significance of architecture in *The Belton Estate*,
    and in Trollope's novels generally, see Sadleir, *Commentary*, pp.191–93.
16. Other seductions (using the word loosely) occur in Ireland (*The Macdermots of
    Ballycloran, An Eye for an Eye*), Australia (*John Caldigate*), and Germany (*Ralph
    the Heir*); the only one to occur in England is in *The Vicar of Bullhampton*.
17. James, *Notes and Reviews*, p.91; reprinted from the *Nation*, 28 September 1865.
18. Harry, one suspects, had read Samuel Smiles's *Lives of the Engineers*, published
    in 1862—two years before *The Claverings* was written. One of the heads of Har-
    ry's firm is Mr Beilby, who has "thrown a single arch over a wider span of water
    than ever was done before" (p.22); the reference is highly topical, since the
    famous Clifton Suspension Bridge, designed by Brunel and, according to the *An-
    nual Register* (1864, "Chronicle", p.168) "the most remarkable suspension bridge
    in the world", was completed in the year the novel was written.
19. *Spectator* 40 (4 May 1867): 498.
20. The scene invites comparison, in a number of respects, with the final parting of
    George Osborne and his wife in *Vanity Fair*. Sir Hugh, however, is older and
    more hardened than George, and would not have relented towards his wife even
    if he had known, like George, that he was going to his death.
21. *Spectator* 40 (4 May 1867): 499.
22. Sadleir, *Commentary*, p.391.
23. It is worth noting that in a sense *The Claverings* is a Barset novel, Clavering Park
    and the church of which Harry's father is rector being in Bishop Proudie's diocese
    (p.18). But to find the denizens of "old" Barset treated with the same detachment
    as the Claverings, we have to go back to *Barchester Towers* and *Doctor Thorne*,
    written years earlier. It is clear that Trollope does not identify the values and the
    fate of the Claverings with those of Barset itself.
24. *Spectator* 44 (15 April 1871): 451.
25. *Athenaeum*, 15 April 1871, p.456.
26. *Saturday Review* 31 (29 April 1871): 538.
27. This may be meant to remind us of the well-known description of the family
    group on their way to church in Tennyson's "The Two Voices", and of some of

the lines that follow it:

> *Like an Æolian harp that wakes*
> *No certain air, but overtakes*
> *For thought with music that it makes:*
> *Such seemed the whisper at my side.*

28. Trollope no doubt hoped that Mrs Lynn Linton's recent article "The Girl of the Period" would be recognized as the source of this "doctrine". I refer again to Mrs Linton's article in my discussion of *The Vicar of Bullhampton* (chap.4 below) and *He Knew He Was Right* (chap.5).

29. *Ralph the Heir* I:325; and cf. *Letters*, p.299.

30. On Trollope's interest in Bacon, see Michael Sadleir, "Trollope and Bacon's Essays", *The Trollopian* I (Summer 1945): 21–34. It is possible, as Professor Booth seems to feel (*Anthony Trollope*, p.118n), that Trollope's "special interest" in Bacon did not develop till some time after he wrote *Ralph the Heir*; but, to the extent that the judgments he was later to pass on Bacon's "philosophy" are implicit in his portrayal of Sir Thomas himself—as I believe they largely are—it seems more likely that he had already read the Essays and formed fairly strong views on them.

The *Times*, for example, felt that it established Trollope as Dickens's successor (17 April 1871, p.6). See also *North American Review* [C.A. Bristed] 112 (April 1871): 434.

32. See Sadleir, *Commentary*, pp.297–301.

33. See especially the *Saturday Review* 31 (29 April 1871): 537, and [C.A. Bristed], *North American Review* 112: 434.

34. *Ayala's Angel*, which is the most likable of them, is notable chiefly for its tranquillity and geniality, its concentration on love affairs which come to happy and respectable fruition with a minimum of tension and bitterness along the way. Both in the main plot and in the two subplots of which the heroes are a painter and sculptor there is a sense of youthful freedom bursting through conventional obstacles. The novel's brightness gives the lie to the myth of Trollope in old age as a sardonic, embittered Timon. So, though less conclusively, because on a smaller scale, does the long short story *The Two Heroines of Plumplington*, in which he returned to Barset as the setting for a pair of simple, happy love stories. And even the posthumously published *An Old Man's Love*, though its tone is sober and elegiac, finally accepts that elderly solicitude and desire are no substitute for youthful passion, however brash and offhand. *The American Senator* conforms in essence to the recipe for a tale of uneventful rural life, with plenty of lovemaking, fox-hunting, and tuft-hunting, "no heroism and no villainy", which Trollope believed he had perfected in *Framley Parsonage*. Arabella Trefoil is one of the most complex and believable of Trollope's predatory husband-hunters; to the reader's relief, she is also let off more lightly in the end than any of the others. The visiting American senator, Elias Gotobed, is too foolish and opinionated, too clearly a guy, to really trouble the minds of his English hosts: as a public man, posing public questions, he is about as challenging as Harold Smith in *Framley Parsonage*. Worse still, the questions he does pose have little or nothing to do with the problems of private and semipublic life that beset the two heroines, Mary Masters and Arabella Trefoil.

35. This probably explains why the *Times* and the *Saturday Review* found him "coarse" and "vulgar" compared with the clerics of Barset: see *Times*, 14 September 1878, p.4; *Saturday Review* 45 (1 June 1878): 695–96.

36. The episode, and indeed the whole relationship between husband and wife, have obvious resemblances to the story of the Pallisers and Burgo Fitzgerald in *Can You Forgive Her?*.

37. On Trollope's feminists see also my discussion of *He Knew He Was Right* in chap.5.

38. Lord Brotherton recalls Lord Ongar, also Lord Lovel, the wicked Italianized nobleman in *Lady Anna* (discussed in chap.5 below). His plot is similar to the one that Mr Scarborough hatches in *Mr. Scarborough's Family* (discussed in chap.7): both turn on the difficulty of verifying the date, or even the occurrence, of a continental marriage.

4 "Tilting at windmills"

Despite his dissatisfaction with *The Warden*,[1] Trollope persevered in the attempt to establish himself as a novelist "with a purpose". In *Barchester Towers* and *Doctor Thorne*, as I have noted, there are isolated outbursts of social protest as bitter as any to be found in his later novels. And in *The Three Clerks* and *The Bertrams*—which belong to the same period as *Barchester Towers* and *Doctor Thorne*—social protest provides one of the mainsprings of the action. Doubtless, as Michael Sadleir observes, much of the protest fails to carry conviction, consists simply in "tilting at windmills of contemporary abuse or misery" and "airing personal distaste for other folks' opinions".[2] But Trollope himself seems to have taken a more flattering view of his efforts. In their moments of heightened emotion, *The Three Clerks* and *The Bertrams* are perhaps the most selfconsciously solemn of his early novels—at any rate of those set in England—and the solemnity derives in large measure from the weight of implied social significance: indeed, apart from the first three Irish novels, *The Macdermots of Ballycloran*, *The Kellys and the O'Kellys*, and *Castle Richmond*, all Trollope's early attempts at the "higher aim" (as he conceived it to be) of "tragedy" were in novels with a purpose.

The appellation "novel with a purpose" had, and still has, unfavourable connotations. It implies that the novelist's didactic or polemical intentions are obtrusive, not fully assimilated to his other purposes. In this sense, as I have tried to show, it can certainly be applied to *The Warden*; it can be applied also to *The Three Clerks*, *The Bertrams*, *Castle Richmond*,[3] *The Vicar of Bullhampton*, and in certain respects to *Orley Farm* and *Can You Forgive Her?* In all of these, I believe, there is an inflated portentousness of which their pronouncements on matters of public debate are partly cause and partly symptom.

The most revealing example is *The Three Clerks*. Here, Trollope tells us, one of his objects was to "lean very heavily" on the "loathed

system of competitive examination" which had been adopted for the Civil Service in 1855, and which remained a subject of controversy for some years afterwards.[4] In addition, the novel contains a denunciation of Sir Robert Peel for his part in undermining "political honesty" and public morality generally (pp. 346–48), and of the legal profession for its bullying of witnesses in court cases (chapter 40). The first edition also included a whole chapter—subsequently removed—defending the Civil Service against its detractors (especially the newspapers) and bemoaning the lack of adequate incentives, in the way of salary and status, for civil servants (II, chapter 12).

In relation to the novel's social purposes, the most important character is Alaric Tudor. His success in an examination accelerates his rise in the Civil Service; his later corruption and disgrace show up both the deficiencies of the competitive examination system, which puts a premium on intellect at the expense of character, and the low standard of public morality, of which the dishonesty of the lawyer Mr Chaffanbrass, who leads Alaric's defence when he is put on trial for breach of trust, provides a further instance. Alaric is contrasted with two other civil servants, his cousin Charley who gains entry into the service, as Trollope himself had done (cf. *Autobiography*, pp. 30–31), despite his want of the basic formal qualifications, and his friend Harry Norman who prefers to forgo promotion rather than compete for it with Alaric by sitting for an examination. Neither Charley nor Harry is as able or diligent as Alaric, but at least they are honest; whereas he, under the influence of a corrupt politician and speculator, Undy Scott, graduates from misuse of his official position for personal profit to fraudulent misappropriation of trust funds. Alaric is nevertheless pictured more as victim than as villain. The ruthlessly competitive spirit of modern life—typified in the examination system—encourages his belief that nothing counts but success. And though his ambitions outrun his honesty, they aren't unworthy in themselves. Both his desire for financial rewards comparable with those to be won in other professions and his aspiration to sit in parliament are among the legitimate ambitions from which Trollope, in his chapter on the Civil Service, had complained that civil servants were unfairly excluded.

On the face of it, Alaric's decline and the social pressures that abet it are serious matters. They at any rate give rise to intense emotion. Even Alaric's chilly, calculating wife transforms herself into the biblical Ruth and declaims like a tragedienne when bidding him farewell on the morning of his trial (pp. 462–63). And public opinion burns with indignation against Undy Scott after Mr Chaffanbrass reveals his evil influence over Alaric: he is expelled from parliament

and from his club even though the law takes no action against him. Previously, Alaric himself has dubbed him "scoundrel" with appropriate melodramatic flourishes (pp. 454–55). And upon Alaric's release from gaol, when he sets off, as a matter of course, to exile in Australia, the emotion is that not simply of a parting but of a deathbed, as if any reunion, either in England or Australia, must remain forever impossible.

Such hectic emotionalism is the rule in *The Three Clerks.* Charley, Harry, and Alaric all gush tears with an absence of restraint unusual in Trollopian young men. Charley's pubescent sweetheart, Katie Woodward, becomes hysterical at the first onset of her love and subsequently, when parted from him, nearly dies of a broken heart: it is stressed that her lungs are sound. On her supposed deathbed she wallows in the pathos of her situation until Charley dissolves into tears and swears that she is his "own, own, own Katie" (p.501). A little later, Gertrude (who is Katie's sister) imposes a similar strain on Trollope's emotional vocabulary as she assures Mrs Woodward that she is her "own, own mother" (p.526). Touches like these attest the justice of Sadleir's assertion that the novel is "derivative—in ultimate resort from Dickens, nearer at hand from such a Dickens imitator as Frank Smedley."[5]

As we should expect, Dickens's influence is particularly noticeable in the novel's treatment of topical social problems. An example is the blaming of Sir Robert Peel for lowering the tone not simply of political life but of public life generally. Just as, in *Bleak House,* Dickens had blamed the ruling political oligarchy for much of the corruption and apathy he saw in society as a whole, so, though in an altogether cruder way, Trollope ascribes to Peel responsibility for the recent spate of crimes involving fraudulent misuse of money:

> It would shock many were we to attribute to him [Peel] the roguery of the Sadleirs and Camerons, of the Robsons and Redpaths of the present day; but could we analyse causes and effects, we might perhaps do so with no injustice. He has taught us a great lesson, that a man who has before him a mighty object may dispense with those old-fashioned rules of truth to his neighbours and honesty to his own principles, which should guide us in ordinary life. [P. 347][6]

In consequence of Peel's "worship of expediency", a "large class of politicians" have come to believe that "political honesty is unnecessary, slow, subversive of a man's interests"; but this is not the worst of it:

> Such a doctrine in politics is to be deplored; but alas! who can confine it to politics? It creeps with gradual, but still with sure and quick motion, into all the doings of our daily life. How shall the man who has taught himself that he may be false in the House of Commons, how shall he be

true in the Treasury chambers? or if false there, how true on the Exchange? and if false there, how shall he longer have any truth within
him?

And thus Alaric Tudor had become a rogue ... [P. 348]

One cannot help feeling that here and elsewhere Trollope comes
close to unconscious parody of one of the crudest devices of the
reformatory novel, that of making "society" wholly to blame for the
individual's misdemeanours.[7]

This is doubly unfortunate in that *The Three Clerks*, like *The
Warden*, was clearly intended as in some respects a rebuke to
Dickens. Trollope began writing it in the spring of 1857, when *Little
Dorrit* was still coming out in monthly numbers, and its first page includes a pointed allusion to Dickens's novel: the Weights and
Measures office, we are told, "is exactly antipodistic of the Cir-
cumlocution Office". It can safely be assumed too that Dickens was
one of the critics of the Civil Service against whom Trollope was in-
veighing in the full chapter he originally devoted to the subject. *The
Three Clerks*, like *The Warden*, is in part an anti-reformatory novel,
directed not only against reformers (such as advocates of competitive examination) but also against reformatory novelists. Among
the parodies of fashionable styles of fiction in which it abounds,
there is an amusing and not completely farfetched one of the reformatory novel. Charley Tudor, reading his latest story to Harry
Norman, has reached the point where his hero is found lying
motionless with a bottle of poison in his hand:

> "Having committed suicide?" asked Norman.
> "No, not at all. The editor says that we must always have a slap at
> some of the iniquities of the times. He gave me three or four to choose
> from; there was the adulteration of food, and the want of education for
> the poor, and street music, and the miscellaneous sale of poisons."
> "And so you chose poisons and killed the knight?"
> "Exactly; at least I didn't kill him, for he comes all right again a bit.
> He had gone out to get something to do him good after a hard night, a
> Seidlitz powder, or something of that sort, and an apothecary's appren-
> tice had given him prussic acid in mistake."
> "And how is it possible he should have come to life after taking prussic
> acid?"
> "Why, there I have a double rap at the trade. The prussic acid is so
> bad of its kind, that it only puts him into a kind of torpor for a week.
> Then we have the trial of the apothecary's boy; that is an excellent
> episode, and gives me a grand hit at the absurdity of our criminal code."
> "Why, Charley, it seems to me that you are hitting at everything."
> "Oh! ah! right and left, that's the game for us authors. The press is the
> only *censor morum* going now—and who so fit! Set a thief to catch a
> thief, you know ... " [PP. 213–14]

Booth points out that in the novel proper Trollope's own style is
sometimes uncomfortably similar to the styles he parodies in Charley

Tudor's little stories—that of the sentimental romance of high life, *Crinoline and Macassar*, for instance.[8] To some extent, I would suggest, this is deliberate. Many of Charley's experiences, including his experiences as an author, are known to have been Trollope's own (cf. *Autobiography*, pp. 30–31, 40–41, etc.); and Trollope is certainly aware that at least some of the eccentricities of Charley's fiction are mirrored in the novel in which Charley himself figures. Thus, when Uncle Bat objects that no human beings ever bore such names as Crinoline and Macassar, Katie observes that "at any rate ... they are as good as Sir Jib Boom and Captain Hardaport", who are characters in *The Three Clerks*, friends of Uncle Bat's (p.240). In general, however, it is clear that Trollope doesn't wish his novel, and especially those parts of it in which he makes his "protest" against Sir Robert Peel, competitive examinations, and the detractors of the Civil Service, to be regarded merely as a jeu d'esprit. If there is a flavour of parody, of pastiche, about the "serious" as well as the comic parts of the book, it is chiefly because his imagination is working at cross purposes. He cannot see, for example, that his delight in the frolics and derelictions of Charley Tudor makes nonsense of his pontifical defence of the Civil Service, or that he is being inconsistent in inviting us to share the cathartic indignation of a supposedly corrupt and complaisant society at the villainies of an Undy Scott (who is described, significantly, as a "Bill Sykes" [sic] in disguise). It is as if Trollope had unconsciously resolved beforehand to run the whole Dickensian gamut of humour, satire, pathos, melodrama, and social purpose regardless of artistic unity.

Nor is Dickens the only unassimilated influence. Charley Tudor, like Johnny Eames after him, recalls none of Dickens's heroes so strongly as he recalls Thackeray's budding young author, Arthur Pendennis,[9] and the novel's parodies of current literary fashions are very much in the Thackerayan manner: it may be significant that Thackeray himself seems to have been more impressed by *The Three Clerks* than by the early Barset novels.[10] Thackeray also lurks uneasily behind Trollope's next and even more inept study of London low-life, *The Struggles of Brown, Jones and Robinson*, written 1857, 1861, which has an equally pronounced and old-fashioned flavour of pastiche.

The Three Clerks was not, however, a complete dead end. Like *The Bertrams*, it showed the way—past the sidetracks of social and political propaganda—to the ironic detachment of the later political novels. In this respect the long and largely superfluous account in *The Three Clerks* of the deliberations of a parliamentary committee appointed to look into proposals for a new bridge across the Thames (chapter 32)[11] can be seen as a portent; so too can the wealth of

knowledgeable reference to recent parliamentary proceedings, some of which significantly influence events in the novel.[12] The best of Trollope's political novels, *Phineas Finn*, is, like *The Three Clerks* and *The Bertrams*, the story of an ambitious and not entirely scrupulous young man's fight for recognition in a harshly competitive world; and it is *The Three Clerks* and *The Bertrams* that first introduce us to this world, the restless rootless world of business and public affairs, through which the more "sensational" stream in Trollope's work generally flows.

In *The Bertrams*, Trollope resumes his attack on some favourite bugbears: the competitive examination system, the dishonesty of the legal profession, and Sir Robert Peel. As in *The Three Clerks* he traces the careers of three young men. One is a Cambridge double-first who, at the cost of his happiness, lets ambition—partly his own, partly his lover's—vitiate his best instincts; one a successful but unprincipled lawyer and politician who overreaches and finally destroys himself;[13] and the third an obscure clergyman who wins through to contentment and a happy marriage despite the painful setback of failing to take a first at Cambridge. The inferences we draw from their respective fates are largely conditioned by the lengthy jeremiad on the brutal competitiveness of modern life with which the novel opens. This preludes the introduction of the jubilant George Bertram, who has just learnt that he is a double-first, and the woeful Arthur Wilkinson, who is steeling himself to send the sad news to his parents that he has taken a mere second, that he is—as Trollope extravagantly puts it—"a wretched victim to unsuccessful competition" (I:9). His plight exemplifies, in Trollope's view, the "cruelty of spirit" underlying the modern idea that "success is the only test of merit" (I:5). But there is a clear promise of consolation for Arthur in Trollope's warning that "competitive examination will produce something that shall look to be strong; that shall be swift, if it be only for a start of twenty yards" (I:5). Arthur, not surprisingly, proves to have more character, a better sense of values, than either George or the dashingly successful Henry Harcourt, the third member of the trio.

The Bertrams is remarkable for its solemn, indeed elegiac, tone—although this is interspersed with long stretches of generally feeble and irrelevant comedy and sub-Thackerayan moralizing. (It is probably the most prolix and discursive of all Trollope's novels). Perhaps the most solemn moments are those in which George Bertram nearly convinces himself, among the holy places in and around Jerusalem, that he has a religious vocation. Whether or not he has, the novel leaves uncertain: the fervour he experiences on the

Mount of Olives (I, chapter 7) may appear to be as much a tourist's as a religious acolyte's, but Trollope rather than George himself may be to blame for the guide-book flavour. What is clear is that George at any rate believes himself to be spiritually uplifted, notwithstanding the characteristically Trollopian note of bathos in, for example, the description of his visit to the Holy Sepulchre: "He remarked to himself that the place was inordinately close ... " (I:128). Equally, there can be no doubt that his decision not to enter the church is strongly influenced by his friends: by his mercenary father, by the cynical Harcourt, and above all by his ambitious lover Caroline Waddington, who tells him that she "looks up" to him as "one whose destiny must be high" and urges him to work "in such a manner that the eyes of the world shall be upon you; that men and women shall talk of you, and newspapers have your name in their columns" (I:213–15). But having submitted to such dissuasion, he feels robbed of the "highest ambition" open to him (I:285), and later he accuses Caroline not only of destroying the "high spirit" he had initially brought to his legal studies by her "intolerance of enthusiasm" (II:32) but also of having led him into religious "apostasy" (II:241). In return, however, she convicts him of "unsteadiness" and "unfitness for the world's battle" (II:49), and this verdict is supported by the narrator's description of him as "of all men the most infirm of purpose" (III:89). His misfortunes, then, illustrate not only the destructive power of worldly ambition, as personified in Harcourt and Caroline, but also the syndrome of the brilliant examinee without the moral stamina necessary for success in life. Arthur Wilkinson, by contrast, is able at the end of the novel to look back on the "melancholy vae victis" he had sung at the time of his failure to take a first-class degree, with the reflection that fate could have given him no greater happiness even if he had "taken the most double of all firsts".

As part of its exposure of the cruelly competitive spirit of modern life, the novel also paints a sombre picture of an ambitious and loveless marriage—that of Caroline to Harcourt—and it is here that Trollope's "purpose" obtrudes most unhappily. George and Arthur can both be seen, without any strain, as restless products of a competitive environment. So too can Caroline and Harcourt up to the time of their marriage. Afterwards, however, the novel slips into the kind of sensationalism that contemporary critics rightly regarded as the weapon of the novel with a purpose. Within six months the cool, engagingly cynical Harcourt has become a tyrannical ogre, who despite his own coldness is uncontrollably incensed by his wife's and is moved to wild jealousy by her preference for another man. And Caroline herself, formerly a model of selfcontrol, is overcome by

such passionate remorse and longing for her lover that she suddenly throws all her characteristic caution and modesty to the winds and provokes her husband with savage and gratuitous spite. After a passionate, but fortunately premature, farewell to her lover—"Go, George—go—go; thou, only love of my heart; my darling; mine that might have been; mine that never can be now—never—never—never"; to which George replies by "imprinting" a "warm kiss upon her brow" (III:107–8)—she is melodramatically denounced by her husband as "brazen-faced harlot! unmitigated harlot!" (III:115). Admittedly, the melodrama of these moments is more or less typical of Trollope's efforts in his earlier novels to portray the frenzy of passion, but its ludicrousness and theatricality are certainly accentuated by the ostentatious moral attached to it: "Ah! young ladies, sweet young ladies, dear embryo mothers of our England as it will be, think not overmuch of your lovers' incomes ... If a wholesome loaf on your tables, and a strong arm round your waists, and a warm heart to lean on cannot make you happy, you are not the girls for whom I take you" (III:104).

Two subsidiary, but equally overstated and tendentious, themes of social protest are the dishonesty of lawyers and the evil influence of Sir Robert Peel and the Conservative party. Harcourt's ruthless worldliness is epitomized by his spectacular success as a lawyer, a success that consists in "turning white into black"; George Bertram's scruples about the morality of such success Harcourt dismisses as "moonshine", proper enough in "a clergyman, or an author, or a painter" but not in a member of "the only profession which, to my mind, is worthy of an educated man's energies" (I:262–63). In politics, where he is equally successful, it goes almost without saying that Harcourt is a follower of Peel. (The action of the novel takes place in the 1840s). What this means Trollope expounds at wearisome length (II:1–11), but the crux of it is that Harcourt condones "apostacy" (sic), the sin which Peel committed in changing his mind over the repeal of the Corn Laws and which the so-called Conservatives—Trollope prefers the name "Tories ... as being without definite meaning"—have been committing ever since. George Bertram, as I pointed out, accused himself of religious apostasy after his loss of faith, and he rightly—as the novel would have us believe—blamed his defection partly on Caroline, who had shown herself an apostate in love. It is therefore fitting that she should wed the political apostate Harcourt and that when, after his suicide, she returns to her first lover, their marriage (a second marriage of apostates) should be "a cold, sad, dreary matter" and should prove childless like the first.[14]

Orley Farm is the most ambitious of Trollope's early attempts at "tragedy", and I shall be considering it in this light in my next chapter. But it was also, ostensibly at least, written with a "purpose". This was noted, disapprovingly, by its original reviewer in the *Saturday Review*,[15] and some modern critics, taking it more seriously, have been able to convince themselves that it incorporates a more or less coherent criticism of society.[16] Trollope's main targets are again the law and lawyers.[17] Nothing, we are told, will "make an English lawyer think that loyalty to truth should come before loyalty to his client" (I:165). The examination of witnesses in court is stigmatized as a "kind of torture ... equally opposed both to truth and civilization" (II:316). How "any gentleman can be willing to use his intellect for the propagation of untruth, and to be paid for so using it" is a moral mystery (II:165). Such charges—already familiar to readers of *The Three Clerks* and *The Bertrams*—are scattered through the novel. They come sometimes from the narrator, sometimes from Felix Graham, the novel's jeune premier, who is himself a budding but already disillusioned lawyer, and sometimes from the German legal reformer Von Bauhr, who is portrayed with strong feeling and who was the subject of one of Millais' illustrations to the first edition of the novel (facing I:136) even though he plays no active part in the story.

The law's shortcomings are demonstrated most notably at Lady Mason's trial. Chiefly because of her counsel Mr Chaffanbrass's bullying of a key witness, Lady Mason is acquitted although he and all her friends know her to be guilty. But while the acquittal is a miscarriage of justice and the law stands condemned accordingly, only the stoniest-hearted reader could forbear to cheer. So strenuously has sympathy been built up for Lady Mason that the thought of her languishing in gaol would be intolerable. Nor to the layman would such a punishment seem truly just, since it was in effect a denial of natural justice—her husband's failure to provide for their son in his will—that led her to commit her crime in the first place. By producing a verdict that both narrator and reader are bound to applaud, the failings of the law in fact prove altogether providential, so that in the circumstances we can be forgiven for wondering why we should be asked to distress ourselves about them. Without them the author could hardly have brought Lady Mason's story to what he admits he regards as the most humane possible solution. His attack on the legal system, then, comes to appear little more than a smokescreen of moral indignation, behind which he works his novel to an end that he fears the fastidious reader may think morally subversive, an end for which he feels constrained to "apologize".[18]

From this point of view it is significant that contemporary and

later critics—and Trollope himself—saw affinities between *Orley Farm* and the sensation novel of the period. These are apparent not only in the central situation—that of a lady threatened with disgrace by exposure of a past misdemeanour—but also in the use that is made of social protest. Trollope adopts two of the favourite tactics of sensational reformatory novelists like Reade and Collins: over-colouring his picture of a social evil in order to facilitate the working out of his plot rather than to examine the evil itself, and making it the occasion for a display of indignation out of keeping with the morality of the novel as a whole. What is worse, he does so without offering even a token demonstration of the ill effects of the "evil" on society at large. The solicitor Mr Furnival, for instance, though wicked enough to offer a bribe to a witness against his client, otherwise behaves quite honourably. He is not a model husband and is fond of port, but these faults are not peculiar to his profession. Judge Staveley, a pillar of the legal system, appears to be of blameless character, and even the attorney Mr Aram, one of its less reputable props, can appreciate the underlying nobility of Lady Mason's character. Moreover, Felix Graham, the champion of legal reform, displays so much more energy in his courtship of Madeline Staveley, the judge's daughter, than he ever shows as a legal reformer that we are hardly convinced of the urgency of his concern. And the novel further undermines its case against the law by making Joseph Mason, the long-suffering victim of injustice, a repulsive and vindictive character—black-browed and blasphemous like most of Trollope's early villains—while Lady Mason, who has for so long deprived him of his own, is gentle, ladylike, and forbearing. Even Mason's lawyers, though convinced of the justice of his case, can't help sympathizing with his opponent; so much so that the solicitor-general, outlining the case against her, publicly drops a tear on behalf of the son who, he supposes, must soon learn of her guilt (II:282). Almost on its own, this tear nullifies the novel's whole denunciation of the legal profession.

The most convincing of Trollope's early "problem novels" is without doubt *Can You Forgive Her?*. Here, though the social pur-pose is still not fully integrated into the total vision, he is at least try-ing to grapple with a problem that really might be of concern to society as a whole. In the main he also avoids the exaggeration and one-sidedness, the undisguised propaganda aim, that renders his protests in earlier novels so shrill and discordant. The novel's "pur-pose", its precise relevance to the topical social problems from which it takes its inspiration, remains largely implicit, never giving rise to emotional or satirical outbursts on the author's part. If it must

still be regarded as a novel with a purpose in the unfavourable sense, it is at any rate more sophisticated in its methods and more consistent in its aims than any of its predecessors. At its best, moreover, unlike any of them except *The Warden*, it transcends any merely didactic or illustrative aim. This is especially so in the story of Lady Glencora Palliser and her husband, which I shall be considering in more detail later (chapter 6). Where the novel's didactic aims obtrude is chiefly in the main plot, of which Alice Vavasor is the central character.

Viewed as a problem novel,[19] *Can You Forgive Her?* is by no means so "discordantly episodic" as, for example, Michael Sadleir felt if to be.[20] Although it has three distinct plots which only converge occasionally, and which offer a rather indigestible mixture of styles, all can be seen as variations on the same theme. The story of Alice Vavasor shows some of the evils that follow when a young lady is left to manage her own affairs and choose her own lover and future husband. That of Lady Glencora shows the evils of the opposite situation, in which a young lady is dragooned into marriage against her will. While in the comic sub-plot we see how even an experienced and seemingly prudent woman will tend to favour a rake as husband. Our attention is directed throughout the novel to the same questions. How much freedom should a woman be allowed in disposing of her own hand? What are the consequences likely to be if she is allowed too much or too little freedom? What is the relationship between passion and prudence in a woman's nature?

At the time when the novel was written such questions were more than usually topical. The agitation for women's rights and the debate over the legal and social status of women had been raging for the best part of a generation; but they became increasingly bitter after the Marriage and Divorce Act of 1857. This, while liberalizing the procedure for obtaining divorce, enshrined the "double standard" by making the wife's adultery a sufficient ground for divorce but not the husband's.[21] By 1864, when *Can You Forgive Her?* was published, the whole institution of marriage, according to one writer, almost seemed to be on trial.[22] Trollope does not approach the problem from the point of view of a reformer; nor is he concerned specifically with the legal rights of women, though he did touch upon these later, in *He knew He Was Right*. But in many respects Alice Vavasor clearly represents his idea of the new woman. She is not a militant feminist like Wallachia Petrie in *He Knew He Was Right*, the members of the "Rights of Women Institute" in *Is He Popenjoy?*, or Miss Altifiorla in *Kept in the Dark*: a feminist heroine would have been intolerable to Trollope. But she is enough of a new woman to be uncertain whether the ordinary social and

domestic duties of a wife will be a sufficient life's work for her and to wish to play a part in public affairs; and her restlessness is a clear symptom of that which was finding stronger expression in the feminist movement.

To some extent Trollope sympathized with this restlessness. Most of his heroines are more independent and opinionated than the average Victorian parent would have liked, and he was not dismayed by the "fast" heroines of Rhoda Broughton's early novels.[23] He disapproved, however, of women who took part in public affairs, as his letters to his young American friend Kate Field show.[24] If we can judge from his novels, he believed that woman's proper place was in the home and that most women, with some reluctance, recognized this themselves.

In *Can You Forgive Her?* his chief aim was to win sympathy for a woman led by her "romantic" propensities, including her craving for "passion" and for a life of action, into unconventional and seemingly unfeminine conduct. We are asked to forgive Alice for jilting the "worthy" John Grey in favour of the "wild" George Vavasor, then returning to Grey. Presumably we are also asked to forgive Lady Glencora, in the other main plot of the novel, for the more serious offence of contemplating adultery with Burgo Fitzgerald. Both she and Alice are women and therefore, in the novel's view, particuarly liable to romantic delusions.

However, while this thesis is demonstrated more or less convincingly in Lady Glencora's case, it doesn't ring true in Alice's. All the evidence of the early part of the book—from her opening interview with her former guardian Lady Macleod onwards—suggests that she is a strong-minded, almost mannishly hardheaded woman. She resents John Grey's proprietorial attitude and half-playful allowance for her foibles, his inability to understand her desire for a more stimulating life than his quiet Cambridgeshire house will offer her. The picture that emerges is of an intelligent and sensitive woman in love, though perhaps not very deeply, with a man who is unaware of her intellectual and emotional needs. In the circumstances we are no more surprised when she decides to break off the engagement than when Clara Amedroz breaks off hers to Frederick Aylmer (in *The Belton Estate*). But her conduct becomes harder to explain, or to forgive, when she engages herself soon afterwards to her cousin George Vavasor, whom she had previously rejected because he had "behaved very badly" to her (I:43). Not only is she not in love with George, but she is supposed to be still in love with Grey. George, however, appeals to the romantic side of her nature. She admires his audacity and ambition. There is an air of mystery about him that she thinks she likes. For a while it is even suggested that he excites her a

little physically. And at the same time, as a rising radical politician, he offers her an outlet for the "political enthusiasm" that is supposed to underlie her dissatisfaction with Grey.

Trollope wishes us to see her surrender to George as the product partly of intellectual ambitions unbecoming a woman, and partly of a misguided desire for passion. Her pride in her intellect will not allow her to listen to her friends when they warn her against George and leads her to think she can play some part in public affairs. She has, we are told, a "vague idea" that there is something for a woman to do "over and beyond, or perhaps altogether beside ... marrying and having two children":

> She was not so far advanced as to think that women should be lawyers and doctors, or to wish that she might have the privilege of the franchise for herself; but she had undoubtedly a hankering after some second-hand political manoeuvring. She would have liked, I think, to have been the wife of the leader of a Radical opposition, in the time when such men were put into prison, and to have kept up for him his seditious correspondence while he lay in the Tower. She would have carried the answers to him inside her stays,—and have made long journeys down into northern parts without any money, if the cause required it. She would have liked to have around her ardent spirits, male or female, who would have talked of "the cause", and have kept alive in her some flame of political fire. [I:136]

In other words even the strongest-minded woman is likely to be absurdly romantic and unpractical in her political notions. But the romanticism imputed to Alice here seems to contradict everything we see and hear of her elsewhere; and her enthusiasm for politics is so tepid that, except on one occasion when she embarrasses the Duke of St Bungay by asking him if, as a would-be radical, he has "voted for the ballot" (I:290), it appears completely dormant, until the renewal of her engagement to George. Clearly Trollope wishes it to appear so silly, so essentially feminine, that the reader will easily forgive it, but he altogether fails to reconcile such callow imaginings with the rest of her character.

Her desire for passion is only slightly less implausible in relation to her character as a whole. It is understandable that she can be in love, after her own fashion, with Grey, yet be dissatisfied with him as a lover, and for a time the attraction that George exercises over her is almost believable. His spell seems real enough, for example, in the early scene where, sitting alone with him on a balcony overlooking the Rhine at Basle, she experiences an emotion "sweet, undefinable, and dangerous": "Alice felt that the air kissed her, that the river sang for her its sweetest song, that the moon shone for her with its softest light,—that light which lends the poetry of half-developed beauty to everything that it touches." When George as-

sures her, with apparent sincerity, that she needs a "brandy diet", whereas Grey can offer her only milk, she finds herself for once agreeing with him:

> The music of the river was still in her ears, and there came upon her a struggle as though she were striving to understand its song. Were the waters also telling her of the mistake she had made in accepting Mr. Grey as her husband? What her cousin was now telling her,—was it not a repetition of words which she had spoken to herself hundreds of times during the last two months? ... Had she not, in truth, rioted upon brandy, till the innocence of milk was unfitted for her? [I:59,65][25]

On the evidence the answer is no; but here, and later when she shivers at the sensuous abandonment of a group of swimmers as they let the swift current of the Rhine rush them along (I:70–71), we sense a faint stirring of passion—even if it is no more than "a struggle as though she were striving" to shake off her inhibitions, and even if she is still prim enough to think of the man she is supposed to have loved as "Mr. Grey".

Away from Basle, however, she shows no sign of sexual passion and no taste for romance. The first time George tries to embrace her after their engagement has been renewed she is overcome with physical disgust and is, we are told, "astounded at the rapidity with which the conviction had forced itself upon her that a marriage with her cousin would be to her almost impossible" (I:475). Trollope, too, is puzzled: "How am I to analyse her mind, and make her thoughts and feelings intelligible to those who may care to trouble themselves with the study?" (I:473) The suggested explanation is that at heart she has remained in love with Grey; but if this is so, and given that she finds him lacking in passion, it is hard to believe that she herself can be passionate. Later, even Trollope admits that her love for Grey is "too thoughtful" and deficient in romance (II:364); and her remark to Jeffrey Palliser that romance "usually means nonsense" (I:356) is fully in character. We can share her cousin Kate's exasperation at her constant harping on delicacy as a means of avoiding unpleasant facts (I:76–77) and even, on occasions, Lady Glencora's view that she is a prude (II:274, 354). The dominant impression the novel gives is that she is sexually inhibited, and if there is any passion, or hankering after passion, in her eventual decision to marry George—as distinct from her longstanding dissatisfaction with Grey—it is well beneath the surface and must be largely unconscious.

Yet Trollope persists in implying that passion is a motive for the decision and that it is connected with her general—and undeniable—wilfulness, her "scorn" for the "prudence" of advisers like Lady Macleod (I:473). Thus the conflict in her mind at the time

when she transfers her troth from the worthy Grey to the wild
George is represented, with some insistence, as "Passion versus
Prudence" (title of chapter 35), and in her temporary preference for
George she is described, retrospectively, as having been "driven by
a frenzy" (II:380). But in fact she never displays anything remotely
approaching passion or frenzy. Her failure to do so is possibly due in
part to Trollope's own limitations. R.H. Hutton, for example,
thought her one of Trollope's "vague" characters and ascribed the
vagueness to his "having studied with much less care that part of a
novelist's art which consists in describing what the critics call 'sub-
jective feeling' than that which consists in giving the little
characteristic traits of outward manner and action".[26] The poetic
symbolism of the Basle scenes—which recalls the symbolic arm in
the clouds in *Rachel Ray*, the novel written immediately before *Can
You Forgive Her?*—may be felt as a more or less desperate expedient to remedy this deficiency.

But Trollope's difficulty is not simply that Alice—in contrast to
Lady Glencora, with whom he succeeds admirably—is too complex
and inhibited a character to be rendered either by "traits of outward
manner and action" or by mere summary of her private thoughts
and emotions in the author's own words. His major problem is to ensure the reader's sympathy for her, but at the same time make her
serve as a moral example, a warning to other young women against
over-reliance on their own judgment and against romantic hankering after passion. To make her political enthusiasm credible in relation to the rest of her character, he would have found it hard not to
present her as, by Victorian standards, unfeminine; hence the
pathetic, and altogether feminine, absurdity of her ideas of political
action. To show her passion for George as a real passion, he would
have had to convict her, in jilting Grey, not merely of having "sinned against the softness of her feminine nature" (II:380), but also—
given that she is supposed to love Grey—of immodesty. "The
noblest jilt that ever yet halted between two minds!" (II:433) Such
is John Grey's fulsome praise for Alice after she has returned to him,
and it acquits her, belatedly, of any suspicion of sensuality, reduces
the charge against her to one of girlish romantic delusion. But how
could one so deluded have diagnosed Lady Glencora's false romanticism so accurately? The inescapable conclusion is that Alice's own
delusions are designed to illustrate a theory about women that simply does not apply to her.

Such a conclusion is borne out by ambiguities and inconsistencies
in the portrayal of George himself. Within the novel he has to serve
two purposes: he must be both a credible object for Alice's affections
and romantic delusions, which are not evil in themselves, and the in-

carnation of the evil they bring upon her. He is her punishment, and assuming that the punishment roughly fits the crime we can deduce from his misconduct something of the underlying causes of her error. Thus when he is revealed as a creature of violent and terrible passions, we can safely infer that these are the stark reality behind Alice's vapid romantic daydreams. It is almost as if, sensing that he had failed to make her romanticism credible in itself, Trollope set out to compensate by showing its consequences as luridly and unambiguously as possible.

But there appear to be two Georges just as there are two Alices. No doubt George has to behave very badly in order to justify Alice in again throwing him over, but in the event his behaviour is far more outrageous than it needs to be simply for this purpose, so outrageous, indeed, that we almost cease to recognize him. Up to the time when he becomes engaged to Alice, the novel takes pains to weigh his bad qualities against his good. Romantic or not, Alice could not be forgiven for engaging herself to a man she knew to be quite unprincipled. After his engagement to her, however, he is gradually but startlingly transformed. At first his violent passion is seen chiefly in the ominous opening of his scar (relic of a tussle in which, as a boy, he had killed a burglar) and in a slight roughness of tone towards Alice. But after she refuses him a congratulatory kiss when he is elected to parliament, he begins to erupt into actual violence (chapter 46). He assaults his faithful sister Kate, breaking her arm, gloats Sweeney Todd–like over various projects of murder, and finally punches, then tries to shoot, John Grey. In the latter stages he becomes a petty Heathcliff. His natural environment is the wild Westmorland fells where his attack on his sister takes place (chapter 56), where three years earlier Alice had told Kate of his bad behaviour to her (I:397), and where more recently she had allowed Kate to persuade her to renew her engagement to him (chapter 31). The fells are the symbolic place for his feral passions, just as Basle is for Alice's romantic delusions and the ruins of Matching Priory for Lady Glencora's.

George shares his angry scar with another of Trollope's wild men, Lord Chiltern (in the "Phineas" novels), and his habit of baring his teeth with Barry Lynch, the villain of *The Kellys and the O'Kellys* (who at least has the excuse of being Irish). As well, the drift of his private thoughts, when they are revealed to us, suggests affinities not only with Sweeney Todd and Heathcliff but with Dickensian villains like Bill Sikes and Carker:

> Wearily and wretchedly he plodded on ... and every step that he took, plodding through the mud, was a new misfortune to him ... [He] stopped on his way from time to time, leaning on the loose walls, and cursing

the misfortune that had brought him to such a pass. He cursed his grandfather, his uncle, his sister, his cousin, and himself. He cursed the place
in which his forefathers had lived, and he cursed the whole county. He
cursed the rain, and the wind, and his town-made boots, which would
not keep out the wet slush. ... He cursed this world, and all worlds
beyond ... [II:217–18]

No doubt the purpose of this and other scenes describing George's
rages is partly sardonic. His curses are presented as a liturgy, and
there is obvious absurdity in their mixing of the trivial and particular
(the town-made shoes) with the grandiose and universal (this world
and all worlds beyond). One contemporary writer, citing George as
an illustration of the fact that violent temper is always ridiculous,
took it for granted that he was meant to be laughed at.[27] The comedy wears thin, however, when we hear him, on a later occasion
(II:256), going through precisely the same performance and we
become aware that there is no perceptible difference between what
are represented as his self-conscious posturings and his genuine
rages.

Hutton complains that Trollope "shrinks less from the imagination of dark thoughts, than from attempting that intensity of *style*
required when dark thoughts come to a focus in dark deeds" [28] Two
revealing examples may be mentioned. One is the scene in which
George, in the act of furiously hurling a chair across his room, is
represented as asking himself, "What should he do? Where should
he go? From what fountain should he attempt to draw such small
draughts of comfort as might support him at the present moment?"
(II:390) The facetious answer supplied by the narrator—"For the
moment, Vavasor tried to find such fountain in a bottle of brandy
which stood near him"—testifies bathetically that it is not George's
consciousness we have been observing at all, that at least one of the
clichés in which his frenzy is supposed to express itself is not his but
Trollope's. In another scene we are told, reassuringly, "not to suppose" that George "had, in truth, resolved to gratify his revenge
[sic] ... by murdering any of those persons whom he hated so
vigorously" (II:253). But when, having changed his plans, he is actually on his way to shoot John Grey, Trollope pretends (as on
several former occasions) to have momentarily lost his entrée into
George's mind: "It was manifest enough that he had some decided
scheme in his head ... " (II:402). In cases like these the attempt at
comic melodrama is as much Trollope's confession of stylistic, and
perhaps imaginative, inadequacy as the pursuit of an appropriate artistic effect. They confirm the general impression that he has lost
control over George's character.

This loss of control reflects his usual uncertainty, especially in his
earlier novels, as to how to represent strong emotion convincingly,

neither too sharply nor too flatly. But the transformation of George from a recognizable human being into a conventional stage villain, an ogre more symbolic than real, is also connnected, un-questionably, with the dubious moral purpose he is made to serve in the novel. Insofar as he is a warning to Alice, and to all young women, against putting too much trust in their own unaided judg-ment and allowing too much scope to romantic illusions, his excesses must be, in some measure at least, a projection of Trollope's own fears, conscious and unconscious, about where the agitation for greater freedom for women might lead to.

Aspects of the "woman question" continued to occupy Trollope in many later novels. *He Knew He Was Right, Is He Popenjoy?*, and *Kept in the Dark*, for example, all deal with marital problems in the context of feminist agitation. But although Trollope has obvious didactic aims in these, as in all his novels, they cannot be stigmatized as novels with a purpose in the sense that such aims ap-pear discordant or irrelevant in the novel as a whole. The most in-teresting of the later novels that do suffer in this way from being written "with a purpose" is *The Vicar of Bullhampton*; and as it happens it, too, was in some respects a conscious contribution to the debate over the woman question.

The novel opens with a preface in which the reader is warned that one of the characters is "a girl whom I will call,—for want of a truer word that shall not in its truth be offensive,—a castaway". But few elements in Trollope's treatment of the subject could have caused any surprise or offence, even to the "young of both sexes". Before Carry Brattle's seduction, by an army lieutenant, "fair she had been, with laughing eyes, and floating curls" (p.36). Her father, as a mat-ter of course, had disowned her and "beaten [the] miscreant to death's door" (p.37). Other lovers succeeded the first. Her good looks have now left her: she has become "a poor, sickly-looking thing," her beauty "obscured by flushes of riotous living [rouge?] and periods of want, by ill-health, harsh usage, and, worst of all, by the sharp agonies of an intermittent conscience" (pp.171–72). Predictably, like the "unfortunate" of *The Bridge of Sighs*—an "old poem" which she happens to have "seed" (p.177; and cf.p.371)— she contemplates suicide. She finds, however, a comforter in the person of the muscular cleric Mr Fenwick, who invokes the un-answerable precedent of Mary Magdalene (e.g., pp.195, 288) to achieve effortless moral triumphs over a canting methodist and an uncharitable lord. Eventually, after her most recent lover has fled in a vain attempt to escape a charge of murder, she is received back into her father's house, a woeful penitent. There, for a time, her mis-

ery is redoubled by the old man's refusal to forgive her, but once he softens she is able to look tranquilly ahead to the long years of expiatory spinsterhood that remain to her. There are, of course, circumstances that go far to extenuate her sin: the usual ones of youth, innocence, and a beauty of which flattery had made her vain (her name, significantly, half-rhymes with Hetty Sorrel's); and the not unfamiliar one of a fond but severe and forbidding father, whose lack of Christian charity—presented as a result of his lack of Christian faith—has turned his son, as well as his daughter, into a partial outlaw. But it is above all her sufferings and her burning sense of shame that plead for her.

Carry is crushed into conventional flatness by the didactic purpose she is made to carry, a purpose which Trollope seems to have felt precluded his picturing her as a creature of flesh and blood, whose sin entailed some pleasure as well as so much pain. Though her story is genuinely moving at times, notably when her father at last forgives her (chapter 66), it places too much emphasis on the pathetic accessories of her situation, not enough on its intrinsic causes or, indeed, on its present private—as opposed to public— response to it. She is presented almost entirely as victim rather than culprit and appears not only chastened by her experiences but chaste by her very nature. She is, besides, so soft and sweet, and is begirt on so many sides by hard and bitter men and women, that she hardly seems a part of her own or the novel's world.

For the novel's world, as at least one of the original reviewers noted—with distaste[29]—is an unusually grim one: not as grim, certainly, as the haut monde and the commercial and political worlds of London into which many of Trollope's novels lead us, but still very grim by comparison with, say, the world of old Barset, which it adjoins geographically and which it might have been expected to resemble in spirit. Within this isolated rural community—on the Avon, seventeen miles from Salisbury (p.1)—we not only hear of seduction and prostitution and witness robbery and murder. We also observe the vicar, Frank Fenwick, waxing "almost bloodthirsty" over his failure to kill, instead of merely maiming, a suspected thief (p.75).[30] We learn that the vicar's wife shares "that partiality for the corporal chastisement of an enemy which is certainly not uncommon to the feminine mind" (p.349). We hear the old miller and his son, Carry's father and brother, "snarling at each other like animals" (as the *Saturday Review* put it). And we see an exemplary young squire inflict, in a fury of disappointed love, the grossest of all possible insults on the heroine (p.458). Yet none of these people appears monstrous or even notably repulsive; on the contrary, like Janet Fenwick with her relish for corporal punishment, and even like

Jacob Brattle, they are pictured as basically normal—in their motives at least. The more "normal" they are, however, the more disjoined does gentle Carry appear from the view of human nature that the rest of the novel presents.

If Carry's story existed in isolation, its faults could be attributed simply, and almost solely, to Trollope's squeamishness. But the sharp contrast between its generally conventional pathos and the rather acrid spirit of the novel as a whole gives it the aspect also of a form of emotional compensation. This is if we recognize that Carry's story and that of the heroine, Mary Lowther, are not juxtaposed arbitrarily but are intended to comment on each other. Because of the vague and emotional presentation of Carry, the nature of the comment is perhaps not as clear as it might be. But the novel's strong appeal for understanding and charity towards Carry unmistakably has much in common with that which it makes on Mary's behalf, after she has jilted one lover and precipitately engaged herself to another. I would suggest, indeed, that the novel unconsciously wishes us to transfer to Mary part of the sympathy it arouses for Carry, and this may account for some of the superfluous pathos that surrounds Carry.

At first glance Mary's story looks like yet another repetition of a plot-formula which, as some reviewers had for years been protesting,[31] Trollope had already worked to death: that of the young woman unable to decide between two lovers. But, compared to her vacillating predecessors, Mary stands out by reason of both the speed with which, having hesitantly rejected one suitor (Harry Gilmore), she capitulates to another (Walter Marrable), and the extent to which the sensuous element in her love is stressed:

> While conscious of her own coldness towards Mr. Gilmore, she had doubted whether she was capable of loving a man, of loving him as Janet Fenwick loved her husband. Now she would not admit to herself that any woman that ever lived adored a man more thoroughly than she adored Walter Marrable. It was sweet to her to see and to remember the motions of his body. When walking by his side she could hardly forbear to touch him with her shoulder. When parting from him it was a regret to her to take her hand from his. And she told herself that all this had come to her in the course of one morning's walk, and wondered at it,—that her heart should be a thing capable of being given away so quickly. [P.137]

We have learnt previously (p.53) that Mary's favourite heroine is Rosalind, "because from the first moment of her passion she knew herself and what she was about, and loved her lover right heartily". The novel also makes a point of contrasting Mary's attitude to love (and in effect her love itself) with the various attitudes taken by other characters in the novel. The Fenwicks, for example, try to convince her that love will come after marriage even if it is lacking

before. Her aunt Miss Marrable, a relic of the eighteenth century, who likes "strong" literature—Fielding, Richardson, Smollett, and even Wycherley (p.62)—characteristically brands as "missish nonsense" Mary's idea that a girl may fall in love "because she couldn't help it" (p.107). And Parson John Marrable takes it for granted that no man or woman will let love interfere with worldly advancement (chapter 21). Mary herself, in the novel's eyes, makes only one mistake, and that is when "for a while, she allowed herself to believe that it would be right for her to marry a man whom she did not love" (p.518). Like Alice Vavasor, she is held to be entirely right in jilting this man once she has seen her mistake.

The novel, however, does not stop short at the simple Trollopian axiom that love is the only proper motive for marriage. It also goes further than most of his novels in suggesting that even for a woman, desire must be a part of love. Most of the suggestions are of course guarded. For instance, the anomaly whereby a girl, unless she is lucky enough to fall in love with her cousin (as Mary does), must not "allow herself the full flow of friendship" with a young man, yet is supposed to be allowed, in her "intercourse" with him, "to forget for awhile conventional restraints" is skirted rather uneasily. But for this tenterhook, we may infer, most young girls would be no more backward than Mary in recognizing their own sexual drives, their eagerness to participate in what the novel blandly styles "God's purposes with his creatures" (pp.93–94). Later, however, Trollope does risk an outright protest at the impossible demands, in the way of delicacy and modesty, made on young girls by "Saturday Reviewers and others":

> When a girl asks herself that question,—what shall she do with her life? it is so natural that she should answer it by saying that she will get married, and give her life to somebody else. It is a woman's one career—let women rebel against the edict as they may; and though there may be word-rebellion here and there, women learn the truth early in their lives. And women know it later in life when they think of their girls; and men know it, too, when they have to deal with their daughters. Girls, too, now acknowledge aloud that they have learned the lesson; and Saturday Reviewers and others blame them for their lack of modesty in doing so,—most unreasonably, most uselessly, and, as far as the influence of such censors may go, most perniciously. Nature prompts the desire, the world acknowledges its ubiquity, circumstances show that it is reasonable, the whole theory of creation requires it; but it is required that the person most concerned should falsely repudiate it, in order that a mock modesty may be maintained, in which no human being can believe! ... The very idea is but a remnant of the tawdry sentimentality of an age in which the mawkish insipidity of the women was the reaction from the vice of that preceding it. [Pp. 259–60]

Lest we should be in any doubt which "Saturday Reviewers" he has

in mind, Trollope mentions, soon afterwards, that Mary's determination not to seem to pursue Walter is partly a result of her having "heard of public censors, of the girl of the period, and of the
forward indelicacy with which women of the age were charged"
(p.262).[32]

Allusions like these make it less surprising that, though none of
the reviewers were disturbed by Carry Brattle and her story, some
took decided exception to Mary Lowther and hers. One who did was
Mrs Oliphant, who only a few years before had hailed Trollope as
the defender of "our English girls" against the libels cast on them by
Charlotte Bronte (in *Jane Eyre* and *Shirley*) and by the sensation
novelists.[33] Now, however, Mrs Oliphant seems afraid that even he
may be beginning to tread in the steps of Miss Braddon and Ouida:

> Why should he have abandoned those earlier, sweeter, charming young
> women, of whose thoughts and ways and fancies his comprehension was
> so wonderful, to toss us about with all the doubts and tribulations of a
> Nora Rowley [in *He Knew He Was Right*] or a Mary Lowther, girls
> whose marriage out of hand to anybody would rejoice the reader, only to
> get rid of their endless fluctuations and rebounds from one to another ...
> we decline to put up with the disagreeable young women who first ac-
> cept one man and then another, and toss, not their hearts perhaps, but
> their hands, their kisses, their proprietorship, from one to another with a
> painful promiscuousness.[34]

Mrs Oliphant would probably have been even more disgusted if
she had sensed the implicit connexion between Mary's erratic, un-
maidenly behaviour and the sin of which Carry's pathetic plight is
the result. If he had dared, Trollope could have made this clearer by
having Carry quote, from that "old poem" she was familiar with,
"Still, for all slips of hers,/One of Eve's family." Though Mary's offences, if such they are, are obviously not comparable in gravity with
Carry's their source is the same. And as the Rev. Mr Fenwick so
rudely hints to Lord Trowbridge—in one of the novel's best-known
moments (p.123)—not only ladies but even peers' daughters are
members of Eve's family, as Carry is:

> " ... were I to suggest to you to turn out your daughters, it would be no
> worse an offence than your suggesting to Mr. Brattle that he should turn
> out his son."
> "My daughters!"
> "Yes, your daughters, my lord."
> "How dare you mention my daughters?" ...
> The Marquis by this time was on his feet, and was calling for
> Packer,—was calling for his carriage and horses,—was calling on the
> very gods to send down their thunder to punish such insolence as this.
> He had never heard of the like in all his experience. His daughters! And
> then there came across his dismayed mind an idea that his daughters had
> been put upon a par with that young murderer, Sam Brattle,—perhaps

> even on a par with something worse than this ... "I never heard of such conduct in all my life," said Lord Trowbridge, walking down to his carriage. "Who can be surprised that there should be murderers and prostitutes in the parish?" [P.123]

Trollope does not flinch, either, from the corollary that all men—including clergymen—are members of Adam's family. For notwithstanding its insistence on the purity of Frank Fenwick's charitable motives in succouring Carry, and the meanness of the aspersions cast on him by pharisaical enemies, the novel does after all admit that he is influenced, perhaps decisively, by her physical attractiveness. "Was it a fault in him," we are asked, "that he was tender to her because of her prettiness, and because he had loved her as a child?" A little later it is conceded that he "treated her not at all as he would have done an ugly young parishioner who had turned thief upon his hands". And finally, when Carry asks why he treats her so kindly, "the Vicar did not tell her that he did it because she was gracious in his eyes, and perhaps was not aware of the fact himself" (pp.281–84).[35] The word "gracious" is, to say the least, unexpected in this context, but it is not altogether discordant with the book's implied plea for a more open and tolerant acknowledgment of the part played by passion, especially sexual passion, even among placid people in rustic retreats.

Regarded as a problem novel—in toto and not merely in part—*The Vicar of Bullhampton* is more coherent and less squeamish than most modern critics have found it. But for the stale, vapid emotionalism of the portrayal of Carry it would deserve a place among the very best of Trollope's novels. As it stands, it is at any rate the most convincing of the novels with a purpose that I have considered in this chapter, the one that comes closest to assimilating its purpose to its total vision.

NOTES

1. See chap.2 above.
2. Sadleir, *Commentary*, p.389.
3. *Castle Richmond* is discussed briefly in chap.8 below. Its "purpose" is to provide an eye-witness account of the Irish famine of the 1840s and, up to a point, to defend the measures taken by the authorities to alleviate the distress caused by the famine.
4. See *Autobiography*, p.96. Opposition to the competitive system was widespread, and even some of its supporters had doubts—similar to Trollope's—about the manner in which it was at first administered. See especially [William Scott], *Saturday Review* 3 (28 February 1857): 194–95; *Blackwood's* 90 (November 1861): 624–65; and [Fitzjames Stephen], *Cornhill* 4 (December 1861): 692–712. One eloquent hater of the system was Dr Opimian in Peacock's *Gryll Grange* (1860).
5. Sadleir, *Commentary*, p.375.

6. At least three of the "rogues" named by Trollope were in the news about the time when he was writing the novel. John Sadleir, an Irish MP, poisoned himself on 17 February 1856 after being exposed as a swindler; Alaric compares himself with Sadleir and recalls the manner of his death on p.454; Sadleir was one of the models for Merdle in *Little Dorrit* and perhaps for Melmotte in *The Way We Live Now* (see chap.7 below). James Sadleir, also an Irish MP, and involved in the same swindle as his brother John, was expelled from parliament on 19 February 1857, an event which the similar fate of Undy Scott was doubtless meant to recall. William James Robson was tried and sent to gaol for twenty years in November 1856 for larceny and forgery by which he robbed his employers of £28,000. Leopold Redpath was transported for life in January 1857 for defrauding the Great Northern Railway of £250,000 by issuing forged stock. On the Sadleirs, see *DNB*, and on Robson and Redpath, *Annual Register*, 1856 and 1857. *The Three Clerks* was begun in the spring of 1857 and finished on 18 August 1857.

7. As, e.g., the injustice of the laws relating to legitimacy is used to largely excuse the monstrous behaviour of Magdalen Vanstone in Wilkie Collins's *No Name*.

8. Booth, *Anthony Trollope*, pp.113–14. In *Crinoline and Macassar* Trollope was parodying what the *Saturday Review* called "kitchen literature", high-life romances designed to stir the imagination of domestics and printed in papers like the *Family Herald*, *London Journal*, *Reynolds's Miscellany*, and *Cassell's Illustrated Paper*. See "Weekly Romance", *Saturday Review* 1 (8 March 1856): 364–66.

9. Pendennis, like Tudor and Eames, was in essentials an acknowledged self-portrait of his creator.

10. See his letter in Trollope's *Autobiography*, pp.118–19, and T.H.S. Escott, *Anthony Trollope* (London: John Lane, 1913), p.117. At least one contemporary critic felt that the novel established Trollope as a potential rival for Thackeray: see *Saturday Review* 4 (5 December 1857): 517. It is worth recalling that Pendennis, like Johnny Eames—and like Luke Rowan in *Rachel Ray*—was a devotee of Byron.

11. Large sections of this chapter were taken over almost verbatim from Trollope's journalistic work *The New Zealander*: see pp. 123–30 of this work and editor's introduction, pp.xxi–xxii.

12. Notably the Fraudulent Trustees Bill, introduced into parliament on 19 May 1857, just about the time when Trollope began the novel: it is the "new bill about trust property" referred to by Undy Scott (p.429), under which Alaric is rendered liable to criminal proceedings. Reference is also made to a bill for admitting Jews to parliament, introduced on 15 May 1857 (p.422), and to the famous Marriage and Divorce Bill, of which the second reading debate began in the Commons on 18 May 1857 (p.534).

13. No doubt his spectacular success and miserable end were to some extent suggested by John Sadleir's—as were aspects of the careers of Alaric Tudor and Undy Scott in *The Three Clerks*.

14. Both weddings are celebrated in Hadley church, Herts, where Trollope's younger sister Emily had been buried in 1836: cf. his autobiographical aside on the occasion of the first of the two weddings ("I have stood in that green churchyard when earth has been laid to earth ...").

15. *Saturday Review* 14 (11 October 1862):444–45.

16. See, e.g., R.M. Adams, "*Orley Farm* and Real Fiction", *Nineteenth Century Fiction* 8 (June 1953): 27–41, and A.O.J. Cockshut, *Anthony Trollope: a Critical Study*, pp.165–68.

17. An amusing critique by a lawyer of the big trial scene in the novel can be found in Sir Francis Newbolt's "Reg. v. Mason", *Nineteenth Century* 95 (February 1924): 227–36. Booth, however, notes that other legal authorities have defended the

novel's accuracy on points of law: see his "Trollope's *Orley Farm*; Artistry Manqué", *Victorian Literature: Modern Essays in Criticism*, ed. Austin Wright (New
York: Oxford University Press, 1961), pp.369–70. Many of Trollope's charges
were anticipated and answered by another lawyer, Fitzjames Stephen, in an article which Trollope would almost certainly have seen and which appeared just
before he wrote the trial scene in *Orley Farm*; but Trollope evidently wasn't convinced. Among other things, Stephen protested at the ignorance of the law shown
by most novelists—an ignorance that Trollope had admitted, for his own part, in
The Bertrams, when declining to quote the "ipsissima verba" of old Mr Bertram's
will. See "The Morality of Advocacy", *Cornhill* 3 (April 1861): 447–59.

18. His authorial apology (II:404) is quoted in the course of my further discussion of
the novel in chap.5.
19. Escott, however, is surely less than fair to Dickens and Mrs Gaskell in asserting
that *Can You Forgive Her?* established Trollope as "the pioneer of the problem
novel" (*Anthony Trollope*, p.209).
20. See Sadleir's introduction to the Oxford edition of the Palliser novels (1948), *Can
You Forgive Her?* I:x
21. It is worth recalling that that stern social critic Charley Tudor had meditated a
scandalous novel, full of adultery, to "show the immorality" of "this Divorce
Bill": see *The Three Clerks*, p.534. Other literary reverberations of the bill are
discussed in Patricia Thomson's *The Victorian Heroine, a Changing Ideal* (London: Oxford University Press, 1956), especially chap.4.
22. [Justin McCarthy], "Novels with a Purpose", *Westminster Review* 26 (July 1864):
40. See also "The Laws of Marriage and Divorce", *Westminster Review* 26 (October 1864): 442–69.
23. See his letter to Miss Broughton, *Letters*, pp.221–22.
24. E.g., *Letters*, pp.261–62, 363.
25. This scene was important enough in Trollope's eyes to be chosen as the subject of
H.K. Browne's frontispiece illustration for the original edition of the novel.
26. *Spectator*, 38 (2 September 1865): 978. This is one of the finest of Hutton's many
fine reviews of Trollope.
27. See "Temper", *Blackwood's* 114 (November 1873): 574. The author of this article
was Ann Mozley.
28. *Spectator* 38 (2 September 1865): 979.
29. *Saturday Review* 29 (14 May 1870): 646.
30. Perhaps Trollope had heard of the similarly bloodthirsty aversion towards thieves
of a famous real-life muscular cleric, Charles Kingsley.
31. Two notable examples are the reviewer of *The Belton Estate* in the *Saturday
Review* 21 (3 February 1866): 140–41, and Mrs Oliphant in her review of *The
Claverings* (cited below).
32. Mrs Lynn Linton's "The Girl of the Period" appeared in the *Saturday Review* 25
(14 March 1868): 339–40; *The Vicar of Bullhampton* was written June–November
1868.
33. See her article "Novels", *Blackwood's* 102 (September 1867): 276–77. The Trollope novel under review was *The Claverings*.
34. *Blackwood's* 107 (May 1870): 647–48.
35. Cockshut surely overlooks this passage when trying to assess what he regards as
Fenwick's too-ready forgiveness of Carry's sin: see Cockshut, *Anthony Trollope*,
pp.118–20.

5 "The higher aim"

As in poetry, so in prose, he who can deal adequately with tragic elements is a greater artist and reaches a higher aim than the writer whose
efforts never carry him above the mild walks of everyday life.
                                                    [*Autobiography*, p.196]

Mixed with the critical acclaim for the early Barset novels was a
widespread suspicion that Trollope was afraid of tragic emotions,
that he was inclined to ignore the "spiritual" in human nature, that
he was not, as the *Saturday Review* put it, "an adept in the
mysterious workings of the human heart".[1] The scenes of pathos and
melodrama in *The Three Clerks* and *The Bertrams* understandably
failed to establish his credentials in this area; and it was not until
Orley Farm, in which he set out to explore the travails of conscience
of Lady Mason and to win sympathy and respect for her in spite of
her crime, that he was generally credited with achieving the higher
aim of tragedy. None of his previous "English" novels—not even
The Warden—had looked so deeply and fixedly into the workings of
a human heart, and none had shown a hero or heroine of high estate
under threat of so pitiful and terrible a fall.

As I have pointed out, both Trollope himself and a number of his
critics saw resemblances between *Orley Farm* and the fashionable
sensation novel. *Orley Farm* was begun in July 1860, when *The
Woman in White* had almost completed its progress through the
pages of *All the Year Round*, and its subject—a lady of high rank
and moral repute threatened with the exposure of a degrading secret
from her past—is one that the sensationalists were soon to appropriate to themselves. As Trollope presents her, however, Lady
Mason is far removed from her guilty sisters in the sensation novel—
from the Lady Audleys and Aurora Floyds, the Magdalen Vanstones
and Charlotte St Johns.[2] Where their secrets inspire them to preter-
natural cunning or hysterical violence, hers for the most part serves
only to strengthen her composure.

The sensationalism and tragic pathos of Lady Mason's secret are
probably cushioned as much by the three limp sub-plots (concerned

with the loves of Madeline Staveley and Sophia Furnival, the domestic troubles of Mr. Furnival, and the drolleries of Mr Moulder and his "commercial" friends) as by Trollope's moderation. Very nearly half the novel is given over to these, though none of them has more than a superficial bearing on the outcome of Lady Mason's story. Their main function, as Sadleir suggests, seems to be to provide the "variety and sectional interest" demanded by part-issue, and to supplement a main plot too "tenuous" for a novel of three-volume length.[3] They are also used at times to retard the dé-nouement of the main plot, for example in the three chapters that divide Lady Mason's arrival in court from the beginning of her trial (chapters 65–67). But their effect, here and elsewhere, is rather to dissipate interest than to stimulate it.

Trollope's comments on the novel in his *Autobiography* (pp. 143–144) show that for once he did attach some importance to suspense. He considered Lady Mason's story one of his best, its only fault being that of "declaring itself, and thus coming to an end too early in the book". The implication is that the reader will be oc-cupied chiefly with the question whether Lady Mason is guilty or not. But although this question is not answered definitely until early in the second volume, a little more than half-way through the novel, the answer has never been really in doubt—as the narrator himself is the first to admit:"I venture to think, I may almost say to hope, that Lady Mason's confession ... will not have taken anybody by sur-prise. If such surprise be felt I must have told my tale badly. I do not like such revulsions of feeling with regard to my characters as sur-prises of this nature must generate." (II:42) This is not the first occasion—nor the last—on which Trollope sins against his doctrine, proclaimed most fully in chapter 15 of *Barchester Towers*, of "full confidence" between author and reader. Indeed, as is the case in both *Orley Farm* and *Barchester Towers* itself, he is most apt to proclaim the doctrine when he is about to pass on information that must already be obvious to the reader, or, as happens in the well-known passage in *The Bertrams* beginning "I abhor a mystery" (chapter 13), when he is about to make disclosures that it would hardly be possible to delay any longer. In other novels, we find, too, that the ostentatious disclosure of one secret does not rule out the preservation of another, more interesting one.[4] *Orley Farm*, however, is one of a group of novels in which, for the sake of a minimal, almost non-existent, gain of suspense, Trollope not only compromises his own position as narrator, and risks forfeiting our trust in his candour, but also restricts himself to a partial and in some ways misleading presentation of his main character.[5]

This self-imposed restriction accounts, I believe, for what some

critics have felt to be a confusion and others an inconsistency in the portrayal of Lady Mason.[6] The narrator himself admits to having modified his view of her during the course of the novel:

> I may, perhaps, be thought to owe an apology to my readers in that I have asked their sympathy for a woman who had so sinned as to have placed her beyond the general sympathy of the world at large. If so, I tender my apology, and perhaps feel that I should confess a fault. But as I have told her story that sympathy has grown upon myself till I have learned to forgive her, and to feel that I too could have regarded her as a friend. [II:404]

Admittedly it is open to question whether these words can be taken at their face value, or whether Trollope is not simply pretending to see Lady Mason as he supposes the reader will see her: his own sympathy for her has never really been in doubt. But his fear that she may have failed to attract the reader's sympathy to the same extent is well founded. The reason, however, is not so much his own earlier moral reservations about her as his refusal to allow the reader full access to her private thoughts, in which her guilt must be revealed, until midway through the book. And as I have suggested, the sole motive for this refusal seems to be his wish to maintain a faint show of mystery.

Trollope's opening description of Lady Mason (I:18–19) implies contradictions in her nature which prevent us from forming an immediately favourable impression: her forehead is high but "somewhat" narrow, her eyes large and well formed but "somewhat" cold, her teeth beautiful but offset by straight, thin lips, her chin too small and sharp, giving her face an expression of meanness, which, however, is partly offset by the beauty of her figure and the repose of her manner. The narrator is careful to make it clear, at the outset, that his own knowledge of her character is limited: thus he only "thinks" that he "may say on her behalf that she had never thought of marrying"(I:19). Later, however, at a crucial moment when she is discovered alone just after her champion, Sir Peregrine Orme, has left her, he is able to tell us something of her unspoken thoughts, and these, if taken at their face value, might seem cold and calculating: "What she wanted from Sir Peregrine was countenance and absolute assistance in the day of trouble,—not advice" (I:47). But our attention is more forcefully drawn to the outward signs of her state of mind: her unsmiling face and her distracted brushing of the hair from her forehead. "She was alone now," we are told, "and could allow her countenance to be a true index of her mind" (I:46). It is in fact a truer index than Trollope's own account of her thoughts, which, as we are always aware, shows only where they lead to, not where they lead from; and he admits as much when, referring us back to the scene much later on

(II:230), he acknowledges that the "idea ... the reader will have conceived of her" will have come rather from Millais' illustration than from the novel's own description.[7]

But even with Millais' help Trollope must have sensed that he was in danger of excluding Lady Mason from the reader's sympathy permanently. His main remedy, in the first half of the novel, was to create around her as favourable a climate of opinion as possible. Not long before she confesses her guilt to Sir Peregrine, the narrator asks: "What was there about the woman that had made all those fond of her that came near her?" (I:260) The answer must be that, however much the "cold external view"[8] we are given of her may suggest the contrary, she is essentially a good woman, worthy of the regard and affection of such estimable people as the Ormes and the Staveleys. If not, she can only be a monstrously efficient hypocrite, and the narrator is able to assure us, even before her confession, that she is not this:

> Lady Mason was rich with female charms, and she used them partly with the innocence of the dove, but partly also with the wisdom of the serpent. But in such use as she did make of these only weapons which Providence had given to her, I do not think that she can be regarded as very culpable ... It was necessary that she should bind men to her cause, men powerful in the world and able to fight her battle with strong arms. She did so bind them with the only chains at her command,—but she had no thought, nay, no suspicion of evil in so doing. [I:348–49]

Such an assurance as this may not completely outweigh the impression we form of her from her own behaviour, but it does at least prompt us to favourable conclusions when we observe how good are her friends and how wicked her enemies. She, we can hardly fail to note, is part of the county establishment whose high personal standards are revealed in the novel's many idyllic pictures of life at Noningsby and The Cleeve. Her enemies Joseph Mason and Dockwrath, on the other hand, are as mean, spiteful, and graceless in their domestic lives as in their persecution of her. Their ugliness, like that of the legal system to whose workings they expose her (see chapter 4 above), is so gross that even her crime is apt to seem beautiful by contrast. And Trollope unconsciously attests this when, at the end of the novel, he projects her as the "shorn lamb" to whom "God will temper the wind" (II:405)—even though the fleece she has lost was in fact Joseph Mason's. But almost from the start, or at least from the time of our first visit to Groby Park, Mason's house, we have been given every inducement to feel that what Lady Mason stands for, as a lady and as an ornament (albeit a shy one) to county society, is of more consequence than any misdemeanour she may have committed.

To place her crime in this mellow perspective, Trollope finds it

necessary to idealize her friends and vilify her enemies in a manner that hardly accords with his usual moderation. But even this is not enough, on its own, to ensure the reader's sympathy. She must also, once she is free to take her friends into her confidence, prove by her own acts and sentiments that she has deserved their loyalty. She must now, in other words, begin to appeal to us directly, and her appeal must be strong enough to compensate for the ambiguity of her former manner.

In the event it is not fully effective. The scene in which she confesses her guilt to Sir Peregrine (II:39–42) is rightly regarded as one of Trollope's finest. It is tense and dramatic, the dialogue economical, the commentary sharp and unobtrusive, the gestures of the actors natural and restrained; every detail helps to convey the strength and the precise quality of Lady Mason's feelings. In most of the emotional scenes that follow, however, she is too apt to express herself in clichés (both verbal and gestural), and, worse still, in clichés that become monotonous through repetition. The first time we see her after her confession her thoughts and feelings have already begun to lose their individuality. Here, for the first time in the novel, Trollope can let us see exactly what kind of woman she is and exactly how deeply she has suffered under the burden of concealment. But instead he continues to concentrate on externals—the sensation of coldness which makes her shiver, the mechanical actions of putting on a shawl, locking a door—and his account of her state of mind is merely figurative and derivative, stressing its common and proverbial aspects, denying it any individuality:

> There are periods in the lives of some of us—I trust but of few—when, with the silent inner voice of suffering, we call on the mountains to fall and crush us, and on the earth to gape open and take us in. When, with an agony of intensity, we wish that our mothers had been barren. In those moments the poorest and the most desolate are objects to us of envy, for their sufferings can be as nothing to our own. Lady Mason, as she crept silently across the hall, saw a servant girl pass down towards the entrance to the kitchen, and would have given all, all that she had in the world, to have changed places with that girl. But no change was possible for her. Neither would the mountains crush her, nor would the earth take her in. There was her burden, and she must bear it to the end. There was the bed which she had made for herself, and she must lie upon it. No escape was possible to her. She had herself mixed the cup, and she must now drink of it to the dregs. [II:49]

Booth drew attention to echoes of Marlowe's *Doctor Faustus* in this passage, and suggested that the novel establishes significant parallels between Faustus and Lady Mason.[9] Polhemus sees in Lady Mason's story "a parallel with the Christian doctrine of the Fall of Man".[10] But although some of Trollope's metaphors seem to hint at such parallels, Lady Mason's sin and its consequences are not truly

comparable, in motivation, in ethical or theological significance, or in imaginative interest, to either Faust's or Eve's. Hers is a minor, essentially private tragedy of vanity and social ambition, not a case of spiritual or intellectual overreaching, and veiled allusions to Marlowe or to the Bible can hardly do more than suggest rough and remote analogies to her situation. Certainly they cannot express the distinctively personal quality, the "silent , inner voice", of her suffering. Nor, it must be added, can the hackneyed, redundant, and secular images with which the passage I have quoted peters out: the burden that she must bear, the bed that she has made and must lie upon, the cup that she has mixed and must drink to the dregs.

No doubt Lady Mason's feelings have been numbed by shock, and her clichés do at least convey this—if rather mechanically. But even after she has had time to adjust to her new situation, the picture we are given of her emotional nature remains surprisingly conventional and tepid when we recall how strong-minded she had previously shown herself. The soft fulsomeness she now displays in her repeated protestations of repentance and gratitude to her friends may be a natural reaction from the guilty reticence she had had to preserve for so long. But there is something cloying, something too girlish for a woman of her age and with her past, in the "dearests" and caresses she showers on Mrs Orme and in the penitential hurling of herself, again and again, at her friends' feet or around their necks. Normally in a Trollope novel such demonstrativeness would lead us to suspect insincerity. Lady Mason, however, is usually just as sweet and selfless, and just as prosy, in her private thoughts. They seem dominated by her conventional longing for death as an escape from shame (II:49,405), her noble resolve not to bring Sir Peregrine's "gray hairs with sorrow to the grave" (I:359–60; and cf. II:8), and her image of herself as Rebekah (II:355,404). Such feelings may, partly by their very universality, help to melt our hearts, but neither they nor her outward demeanour evoke enough of the complexity, the moral ambiguity, that were so tantalizingly hinted at earlier in the novel.

This is not to deny that at times Lady Mason does achieve genuine pathos, especially just before and during her trial. She is, without doubt, a more successful "tragic" study than any Trollope had previously produced. It is significant, though, that she is most interesting and most believable when forced to restrain her emotions, even to the extent of hiding them from the reader. However imperfectly, the novel does suggest something of the terrible boredom and vacuousness of her moral isolation: for this purpose, as a number of his later novels show, Trollope's rather flat style and fondness for conventional metaphors can be most effective. Where

Orley Farm goes wrong is in exaggerating the change in Lady Mason's manner once her moral isolation has been partly broken down. And the effect of exaggeration, as I have been arguing, must be attributed largely to Trollope's needless refusal to let her reveal, openly and from the outset, her true nature and her true reasons for wanting her friends' "countenance" without their advice. But what makes her later effusiveness of manner seem excessive is not only the startling contrast it offers to her former restraint but also the novel's failure to supply her with enough depth, complexity, or variety of feeling to underpin it. Here Trollope's problem is the deep-rooted and permanent one of finding a style and a method by which to dramatize—and not simply describe—his characters' inner lives. And though suspense may have been part of his motive for excluding the reader from Lady Mason's private thoughts for so long, Hutton was probably right in placing the blame also on his desire to postpone or even evade this problem. Trollope can represent, more or less adequately, the inner numbness that succeeds a crisis and the inner vacancy that is the mark of boredom and loneliness, but inner warmth and excitement are nearly always beyond him. His most powerful "tragic" studies are of men and women who project their emotions, who cast themselves—almost deliberately—in theatrical roles which both they and the reader can contemplate from without.

One such study, which I have already discussed, is that of Mr Crawley in *The Last Chronicle of Barset*. Trollope, as I pointed out, mentions that Crawley's main fault is that he is "imbued too strongly with self consciousness", and one of the symptoms of this fault is his habit of seeing himself as re-enacting various heroic roles. His various styles of speech are a further manifestation of this characteristic self-consciousness. It is, however, Louis Trevelyan in *He Knew He Was Right*, a character of much the same type as Crawley, who most impressively shows the tragic possibilities of a self-conscious theatricality. Both Crawley and Trevelyan are men in whom obstinate pride breeds doubts and suspicions that carry them to the brink—perhaps past the brink—of sanity. In both, a fanatical sense of their own dignity and rectitude becomes distorted into something like a persecution mania when their moral authority is questioned. Crawley's aspirations, it is true, are loftier than Trevelyan's, and in so far as he is the victim of circumstances not of his own making—his poverty, for example—he is better placed to arouse pity. Potentially, as he himself feels, he is a Greek tragic hero, whereas Trevelyan is a man of relatively ordinary abilities and ambitions whose tragic plight, though largely of his own making and though finally irreversible, could not have been predicted from his

character and outward circumstances. Trevelyan's most remarkable attribute as a tragic figure is his unremarkableness. From the reader's point of view Trevelyan's great advantage over Crawley is that tragedy overtakes him unawares, surprises him into a new and evolving sense of his own spiritual capacities and of life's possibilities. Crawley, by contrast, has been all his life preparing for tragedy, rehearsing appropriately heroic responses to it. As a result, Trevelyan's story has a momentum and his reactions to changing circumstances an unpredictability that Crawley's (or for that matter Lady Mason's) generally lacks.

He Knew He Was Right is the least "sensational", the least "poetic" or "romantic", of all the novels in which Trollope attempts tragic or near-tragic characterizations. There is no crime and no real villainy. Passions never run so high as to explode into violent acts or even violent words. Even when his "monomania" on the subject of his wife's disobedience is at its worst, Trevelyan comports himself with a restraint that is at once more affecting and more believable than the strained emotionalism of Lady Mason. Such melodrama as the novel contains is comic in intention and effect.

All this is the more surprising in that *He Knew He Was Right* is a "problem novel". It deals, moreover, with problems akin to those which had already led Trollope into sensationalism in *Can You Forgive Her?*; and Trevelyan's insane jealousy, according to nearly all the precedents available to Trollope, should have emerged as a luridly sensational phenomenon. One thinks, for example, of Bertha in *Jane Eyre*, of Miss Haversham ablaze in her musty wedding finery, of such glamorous homocidal maniacs as Lady Audley and Charlotte St John (in Mrs Henry Wood's *St. Martin's Eve*), and of Charles Reade's Griffith Gaunt who, though sane and admirable in other respects, is subject to an insane "foible" of jealousy under whose influence he commits bigamy.

But perhaps the most pertinent comparison is with Mrs Lynn Linton's *Sowing the Wind*, which appeared early in 1867—the year in which Trollope began *He Knew He Was Right*—and which deals with the same problem. Both novels are about husbands who are driven mad by their inability to exact implicit obedience from their wives and by suspicion—half-real, half-pretended—that their wives have been unfaithful to them. There is in both novels a large cast of supporting characters representing a variety of views on marriage and, in particular, on the topical subject of women's rights. Both are at pains to emphasize how easily quite trivial disagreements between husbands and wives can broaden into a total and inappeasable contest for moral authority. In *Sowing the Wind*, however, the husband is so jealous of his authority that he virtually immures

his wife from the start of their marriage; and once she begins to assert her independence, or at least her "separate identity", he overreacts so hysterically as to suggest some inveterate mental malady. Not surprisingly, he later becomes a raving, homicidal lunatic, and in the best sensational tradition it is discovered that insanity runs in his family. But in any case fate is made to heap so many supererogatory indignities upon him that even without his hereditary taint, and even with the most submissive of wives, he would have been hard put to it to preserve his senses. Trollope's Louis Trevelyan, on the other hand, suffers from no hereditary disease, is treated by fate with no special unkindness, and never becomes more than gently and partially mad. Whether or not Trollope had read, or read about, Mrs Linton's novel, his own is the ideal corrective to it, pointing the same moral much more bravely and sharply and without sensationalism or romantic accessories.[11]

Sowing the Wind may have helped to give Trollope the idea for *He Knew He Was Right* and to condition his treatment of the themes of madness and marital conflict. But he was also—as I have suggested elsewhere[12]—taking up a challenge issued to him from another quarter. The reviewer of Mrs Henry Wood's *St. Martin's Eve* in the *Saturday Review*, trying to explain why madness had become so common in the sensation novel of the day, concluded that Mrs Wood and Miss Braddon were unable to "paint jealousy in its extreme forms" because they lacked "the power to create Othello, or the art to paint, as Thackeray or Trollope might have done, the morbid passion in its naturalistic nineteenth-century dress". Hence their airy ascription of their heroines' insane jealousies to hereditary mental illness. This review was written in 1866, and the following year Trollope did attempt to create Othello and to paint the morbid passion in its naturalistic nineteenty-century dress; for as we shall see, he does explicitly liken Louis Trevelyan to Othello.

It would hardly be worth speculating that Mrs Linton and the reviewer in the *Saturday Review* influenced the design and writing of *He Knew He Was Right* were it not that, even by Trollope's own standards, the novel is conspicuously unromantic and anti-romantic. This seems to have struck contemporary reviewers, and struck them unfavourably: the *Dublin Review*, for instance, felt that the "bareness of truth" in the portrayal of Trevelyan was a mistake,[13] the *Westminster Review* sniffed at the novel's modish "realism" ("There is … a demand for this sort of thing")[14], and the *Times*, longing for "something beyond a mere piece of realism", admitted to being tempted to turn to Ouida for relief.[15] No critic, however, seems to have appreciated the complexity and coherence of the novel's design which, as well as Gissingesque "realism" and "bare-

ness of truth", includes and assimilates, at the opposite end of a broad spectrum, the idealized love-story of Dorothy Stanbury and the near-fantasy of the battle between the French sisters for the reluctant hand of Mr Gibson. What makes *He Knew He Was Right* one of the richest of Trollope's novels is precisely the manner in which it balances grim realities with more pleasant ones and measures both against exciting possibilities of romance.

A first step towards appreciating the richness of *He Knew He Was Right* is to recognize how closely its various subplots and centres of interest relate to each other. The most obvious outward sign of this is the manner in which the "perversity", the "desire for mastery", the insistence on "having his own way" which in Louis Trevelyan develop into a mental aberration are reflected, in a milder form, in several of the minor characters: Aunt Stanbury (pp.72, 204), Priscilla Stanbury (pp.136, 151, 204), and even perhaps Charles Glascock (p.765). In comparison with Trevelyan's, the stiffnecked obstinacy of Aunt Stanbury and her niece Priscilla may be little more than an amusing foible—and one that Trollope had studied often before. But it admirably fulfils its function of helping place the marital dissensions of the Trevelyans in perspective. For the most significant fact about Priscilla and her aunt is that they have remained unmarried, Priscilla because she believes herself too self-willed to submit to a husband's authority, and her aunt, one suspects, because her wilfulness frightened off the man she was to have married. Louis and Emily, on the other hand, though not necessarily more obstinate by nature than Priscilla and her aunt, did not recognize in time, as Priscilla did, their own possible unfitness for marriage and especially for marriage to each other. The novel wishes us to see them as essentially "normal" people (or at least no more abnormal than Priscilla and her aunt) whose tragedy is that they are unusually ill matched. Yet, impressively as it dramatizes the collapse of their marriage, it certainly doesn't concentrate exclusively on the difficulties of marriage; on the contrary, its emphasis is on the advantages, the obvious satisfactions that marriage offers to most people.

So, as well as the marriage of the Trevelyans, it presents the courtship of four other couples, at least three of whom are clearly well-matched temperamentally, and the fourth of whom at any rate understand each other. For none of these couples is marriage likely to pose psychological problems comparable to those of the Trevelyans, though all feel some dissatisfaction with prevailing social attitudes to marriage, partly reflecting that which both the Trevelyans come to feel. In particular, courtship and marriage confront the women with difficult moral decisions, and all the novel's heroines either share or can sympathize with the feminine

grievances that Emily Trevelyan voices. None of them, however, anticipate or seem to have reason to anticipate trouble over the question that causes the break between Louis and Emily, that of wifely obedience. Caroline Spalding, although she is an American girl who has been used to having her own way, and although she has been subject to the influence of a mettlesome misogamist, Wallachia Petrie, gladly promises to obey her future husband. She loves him "infinitely the better" for being strong enough to treat her "almost as a child" and assures him: "You must be master ... whether you are right or wrong" (p.765). Dorothy Stanbury, the most idealized of the novel's heroines, is also the most meek and dependent. Arabella French is able to steal Mr Gibson from her sister by showing herself more submissive and will clearly make him a better wife for the same reason. And even Nora Rowley, the most strongminded and "advanced" of the heroines, who asserts that what she is marrying for is "liberty" (p.897), not only refuses to heed her sister Emily's warning against putting herself in any man's power, but regards it as one of the delights of having a lover to hear in his voice "something of the pleasant weight of gentle marital authority" (p.233). Trollope clearly feels that most men are able to exert a natural and unconscious authority over their wives—without, as Mr Outhouse does (p.132), having to invoke Saint Paul—and that most wives are not only willing but eager to acknowledge this authority.

There is, then, no suggestion that the problems of the Trevelyans, however familiar and unsurprising in their origins, are other than exceptional in their outcome. Unlike *Sowing the Wind*, *He Knew He Was Right* could never be construed as a general indictment of marriage or of the laws and customs regulating marital relationships. It is not the kind of problem novel, or novel with a purpose, that exposes social evils and proposes remedies. We can infer, admittedly, that Trollope sympathizes with Emily in some of her protests at the legal disabilities that she and her sex are forced to endure: for instance, the law that gives a husband presumptive right to the custody of his children in the event of a separation,[16] and the legal system which decrees that even a husband who becomes as obviously deranged as Louis does cannot be deprived of his marital authority. We are left in no doubt, either, that Trollope, from the beginning, sides with Emily rather than with Louis and the more conservative members of the older generation (Lady Milborough, Aunt Stanbury, Mr Outhouse) in his judgment of the issues between husband and wife. He clearly shares her opinion that while a husband is technically entitled to "obedience" he cannot expect "submission" (p.99), and he sees, too, that whatever the merits of the case, public opinion always makes the wife suffer more than the husband:

It is all very well for a man to talk about his name and his honour; but it is the woman's honour and the woman's name that are, in truth, placed in jeopardy. Let the woman do what she will, the man can, in truth, show his face in the world;—and, after awhile, does show his face. But the woman may be compelled to veil hers, either by her own fault, or by his. Mrs. Trevelyan was now told that she was to be separated from her husband, and she did not, at any rate, believe that she had done any harm. But, if such separation did come, where could she live, what could she do, what position in the world would she possess? Would not her face be, in truth, veiled as effectually as though she had disgraced herself and her husband? [P.94]

Deplorable as it is, however, this situation presumably struck Trollope—"in truth"—as being in the nature of things; and, lacking any evidence to the contrary, we may well suppose that he was equally fatalistic about the discriminatory laws under which married women suffered.

But he was at least aware that, as things stood, the rights of married women were fewer and more precarious than those of married men, and that single women, especially in their youth, were subject to even more restrictions than married ones. Nora Rowley, for example, considers that to be a woman is "perhaps better than being a dog " (p.39), and even the compliant Dorothy Stanbury can feel herself a "nobody", to be spiritually "cuffed and kicked and starved" like an ownerless dog or cat (pp.481–82). These are only a milder version of the views of the rabid feminist Wallachia Petrie, and they give added point to a scene such as that in which Mr Spalding, the American minister in Italy, quotes Mill in support of his belief in the equality of the sexes (pp.521–22). There is also favourable comment—from the unprejudiced Mr Glascock for example (p.354)—on the degree of freedom that American women enjoy in contrast to their English sisters. On this question, indeed, the novel takes a surprisingly liberal view, if only by implication; for its principal heroine, Nora Rowley, is in many respects a sympathetically drawn replica of Mrs Lynn Linton's rebellious, sensual, husband-hunting Girl of the Period.[17] By way of recording his distaste for Mrs Linton's prim censures, Trollope allows the repulsive Wallachia Petrie to refer to them approvingly (p.758). He also makes no secret of his approval of a heroine who is certainly very anxious to find a husband, who has great difficulty in smothering her regrets at having turned away a wealthy and aristocratic suitor in favour of a poor one, who openly defies her parents when they refuse to consent to her marrying her poor suitor, who shows no embarrassment when he embraces her more or less publicly (p.862),[18] and who rejoices in the prospect of having to set herself up in "bachelor quarters". Contemporary critics—including, as we have already seen, Mrs Oliphant—were predictably outraged.[19]

It is also worth noting, as an indication of the novel's point of view on the woman question, that the fiercest opponent of women's rights and the fiercest critic of the modern young miss is the diehard Aunt Stanbury:

> "They say women are to vote, and become doctors, and if so, there's no knowing what devil's tricks they mayn't do." [P.111]
>
> "When women can't keep themselves from idle talking with strange gentlemen, they are very far gone on the road to the devil. That's my notion. And that was everybody's notion a few years ago. But now, what with divorce bills, and woman's rights, and penny papers, and false hair, and married women being just like giggling girls, and giggling girls knowing just as much as married women, when a woman has been married a year or two she begins to think whether she mayn't have more fun for her money by living apart from her husband." [P.140]

Aunt Stanbury is on the whole sympathetically portrayed, and some of her conservative prejudices (against chignons, for example) are evidently shared by the author. But the most eloquent comment on many of her views, especially those which imply disapproval of girls like Nora Rowley, is her own past: for she too has known "romance", having in her youth actually taken the rebellious step which Nora Rowley merely threatens, that of setting herself up in bachelor quarters (p.61).

In relation to the marital disaster of the Trevelyans, the most important effect of the novel's liberal standpoint on the woman question is to make Emily's hardness and intractability more understandable and a little less repellent than they would otherwise be. But a further effect is to stress the relative normality of the circumstances in which the breach between husband and wife opens and widens. It is shown to be the outcome of an intricate combination of public and private pressures none of which can be thought of, in its context, as significantly different from those to which the Trevelyans' social group as a whole is liable. Louis and Emily are not maltreated and almost driven to crime in consequence, as Lady Mason is, and as, in a sense, Lady Glencora Palliser is in *Can You Forgive Her?*; nor do they have to contend with exceptional villainy, as Alice Vavasor does. In their story, for the first and only time, Trollope achieves the higher aim of tragedy without departing, to any significant extent, from the "mild walks of everyday life" . And while this alone does not make it intrinsically better than his other attempts, it does, I think, enable him to make better use of his own powers.

At the beginning of the novel Louis Trevelyan is introduced as a generous, handsome, well-read man whose only known fault was that he "liked to have his own way" (p.3). The first two years of his marriage have apparently been happy, but at the time when the story opens there have been high words over the visits of Colonel

Osborne, a longstanding but no longer intimate friend of Emily's father. Louis is suspicious of Osborne, who is a notorious michief-maker, but is reluctant to order Emily not to admit him. She profes-ses to be willing to fall in with his wishes so long as he will state un-equivocally that he has no grounds for suspecting her of any im-proper feelings towards Osborne. In her view, what is at stake is her honour; in his, simply his marital authority. It is not till he discovers the existence of a secret between Osborne and his wife that he begins to doubt her as well as him. He then accuses her, in his anger, of "forfeiting [her] reputation as an honest woman" (p.28). This is as near as he ever gets to charging her openly with infidelity. But in truth his chief anxiety is still about his right to be obeyed rather than about her reputation: "He had pointed out to his wife her duty, and she had said she would do her duty as pointed out, on condition that he would beg her pardon for having pointed it out! This he could not and would not do. Let the heavens fall,—and the falling of the heavens in this case was a separation between him and his wife,— but he would not consent to such injustice as that!"(pp.44–45). It takes Trollope only three chapters—the first weekly number of the novel as originally issued—to show how a trivial disagreement grows into a matrimonial crisis.

Up to this point there is no suggestion that either husband or wife is to be regarded as mentally unhinged. The case, as Hugh Stanbury later observes, is essentially one of "incompatibility of temper" (p.133). Louis doesn't really suspect his wife of an improper attach-ment to Osborne, and at heart she knows that he doesn't. But he cannot explain his disapproval of Osborne—which is understan-dable enough in itself, and which is shared by sensible people like Nora and Lady Milborough—except in terms that Emily may con-strue as insulting to her. When, for example, he insists that his and her "honour" is at stake, he is thinking of honour not as an intrinsic quality but simply as a reflection of favourable public opinion. And although he is no doubt aware, even so, that the word will hurt her, there is clearly a degree of wilful misunderstanding in her angry response to it. Similarly, when she proclaims her readiness to "obey" him, she knows that in his or anybody's eyes enforced obedience is in effect disobedience. There is, in short, provocation and an exag-gerated sense of grievance on both sides; but there is no more self-delusion or distortion of issues than one would expect in any conflict between a strong-willed married couple.

The situation, however, continues to deteriorate, chiefly because of the weaknesses in Louis' character that it brings into play. Or-dinarily, we are told, a marriage can withstand "those passing gusts of short-lived and unfounded suspicion to which, as to other acci-

dents, very well-regulated families may occasionally be liable"
(p.87). Many marriages are momentarily troubled by mischief-
making "interlopers" like Osborne, men who are "malicious" but
"not especially vicious" and who are more often actuated by vanity
than by passion (pp.87–88). And even the private detective Bozzle,
who does so much to inflame Louis' suspicions, is no more unscrupulous than any other man in his line of business. Admittedly,
Emily may seem an unusually implacable wife—as, for instance,
when she accuses Louis in front of her sister of believing her to have
a lover (p.52)—but her implacability derives, in some measure at
least, from exasperation at his weakness. Though his troubles are ag-
gravated by external pressures, there is no reason to dissent from the
novel's judgment that their ultimate source is his own nature. His
faults, in the novel's view, are that he is "jealous of authority, fearful
of slights, self-conscious, afraid of the world, and utterly ignorant of
the nature of a woman's mind" (pp.257–58). He is a man "absolutely unfitted by nature to have the custody or guardianship of others";
and although many such men are happily married, others, with less
docile wives and more time on their hands, inevitably bring "endless
trouble" on themselves (p.257). So it is with Louis, in whom of-
fended pride and consciousness of his own weakness slowly
degenerate into morbid self-pity and jealous "mono-mania".

His decline is dramatized and analysed with great subtlety, its
most memorable stages being marked by his two visits—or flights—
to Italy. The first of these takes him, appropriately, to Venice at a
time when, in the novel's view, he has become mad—at any rate "on
the subject of his wife's alleged infidelity" (p.361)—and when his
state of mind approximates that of the Moor of Venice:

> He came to believe everything; and, though he prayed fervently that
> his wife might not be led astray, that she might be saved at any rate from
> utter vice, yet he almost came to hope that it might be otherwise;—not,
> indeed, with the hope of the sane man, who desires that which he tells
> himself to be for his advantage; but with the hope of the insane man,
> who loves to feed his grievance, even though the grief should be his
> death. They who do not understand that a man may be brought to hope
> that which of all things is the most grievous to him, have not observed
> with sufficient closeness the perversity of the human mind. Trevelyan
> would have given all that he had to save his wife; would, even now, have
> cut his tongue out before he would have expressed to anyone,—save to
> Bozzle,—a suspicion that she could in truth have been guilty; was con-
> tinually telling himself that further life would be impossible to him, if
> he, and she, and that child of theirs, should be thus disgraced;—and yet
> he expected it, believed it, and, after a fashion, he almost hoped
> it.[P.364]

Such are the insight and tragic force of Trollope's study of Trevelyan
that the echoes here of Iago's "green-eyed monster" speech and of

Othello's beginning "I think my wife be honest, and think she is not" do not strike us as impertinent. Indeed, soon afterwards Trevelyan himself movingly likens his situation to Othello's, with Bozzle playing the part of Iago. As he broods over his wife's treachery, his refrain is "the pity of it, Iago", and for a moment, trudging backwards and forwards on the piazza of Saint Mark, he sees himself as the original Othello—not merely his nineteenth-century shadow:

> He walked there nearly the whole night, thinking of it, and as he dragged himself off at last to his inn, had almost come to have but one desire,—namely, that he should find her out, that the evidence should be conclusive, that it should be proved, and so brought to an end. Then he would destroy her, and destroy that man,—and afterwards destroy himself, so bitter to him would be his ignominy. He almost revelled in the idea of the tragedy he would make. [P.423]

Even after this there seems on one occasion to be a faint chance that Louis and Emily will be reconciled. This is when, at their first meeting after his return from Italy, he cannot restrain himself from embracing her; but despite this promising beginning the scene ends with Emily telling him, in no very gentle terms, that he is mad: "Alas, Louis ... neither can the law, nor medicine, nor religion, restore to you that fine intellect which foolish suspicions have destroyed" (p.571). Here again the reminder of *Othello* is grimly apposite, even though it is now Emily, not Bozzle, who is made to echo the cruel words of Iago ("Not poppy, nor mandragora,/Nor all the drowsy syrups of the world,/Shall ever medicine thee to that sweet sleep/Which thou ow'dst yesterday").

The great Italian scenes representing the culmination of Trevelyan's "madness" are notable for their resolute understatement and for their brilliant use of atmosphere. There is, in Sadleir's memorable phrase, a "wild affliction" about them, [20] such as Trollope elsewhere achieves only in one or two of the glimpses he gives us of Lady Glencora Palliser in *Can You Forgive Her?* and Lady Laura Kennedy in the "Phineas" novels. Yet they dispense altogether with violent passion. Except when tactlessly provoked, as in his last interview with Emily's father (pp.735–36), Louis rarely loses his self-control; indeed it becomes firmer as his malady worsens. Nor is there any pathos that is not undercut by grim irony, by reminders that Louis himself is its author and its most appreciative audience:

> "Better for me! Nothing can be better for me. All must be worst. It will be better for me, you say; and you ask me to give up the last drop of cold water wherewith I can touch my parched lips. Even in my hell I had so much left to me of a limpid stream, and you tell me that it will be better for me to pour it away ... What matters it whether the fiery furnace

be heated. seven times, or only six;—in either degree the flames are
enough! ..." So saying, Trevelyan walked out of the window, leaving
Mr. Glascock seated in his chair. He walked out of the window and went
down among the olive trees. He did not go far, however, but stood with
his arm around the stem of one of them, playing with the shoots of a vine
with his hand. Mr. Glascock followed him to the window and stood looking at him for a few moments. But Trevelyan did not turn or move.
There he stood gazing at the pale, cloudless, heat-laden, motionless sky,
thinking of his own sorrows, and remembering too, doubtless, with the
vanity of a madman, that he was probably being watched in his reverie.
[Pp.808–9]

In Trevelyan's speech here—with further Shakespearean echoes,
this time of *King Lear*—Trollope shows how effective clichés can be
as the language of self-conscious and almost exhausted emotion. He
also, in the latter part of the passage, makes telling use of the details
of the Italian landscape to mirror the alienation of Trevelyan's mind
from its normal condition. Above all, he maintains a hard detachment, giving us no other view of the scene than that of an external
observer and that of the scarcely less dispassionate Glascock.

By this time Trevelyan's words have altogether ceased to be "true
indicators of his thoughts", and his arguments no longer "express
either his convictions or his desires" (p.743). His withdrawal to
Casalunga ("far house" as well as "long house"?) is also his
withdrawal from his social self, so that when he entertains Charles
Glascock at breakfast his meticulous observance of the civilized
amenities has the effect of a painful pantomime (pp.803–5). All of
his mental energy is now expended on "long unspoken soliloquies"
(p.787) in which his thoughts traverse the same ground again and
again; and Trollope's flat, regular style is ideal for conveying the
sterile monotony of these soliloquies. Right to the end Trevelyan is
shown as capable of consecutive reasoning, at least in his more lucid
moments, and the question whether he is technically insane is left
undecided. The doctor who examines him reminds Emily that "in
one sense all misconduct is proof of insanity" (p.923) and that "a
man ... need not be mad because he is jealous, even though his
jealousy be ever so absurd" (p.900). So when the narrator refers to
Trevelyan as "the maniac" (p.928) it is clear that he is using the
word not in its popular, slightly sensational sense but in the more
limited sense suggested by the doctor, whose diagnosis is that at
worst "his patient's thoughts had been forced to dwell on one subject till they had become distorted, untrue, jaundiced, and perhaps
mono-maniacal" (p.900). This is not the only occasion on which
Trollope insists on the perilous thinness of the dividing line between
sanity and insanity and on which he shows a reluctance—not shared,
unfortunately, by some of his modern critics—to lay down criteria of
psychological "normality" and "abnormality".

The unspectacular quality of Trevelyan's tragedy, and perhaps of most of life's misadventures, is further emphasized by the manner in which Colonel Osborne is portrayed. In the imagination of the ladies of Exeter and Nuncombe Putney and of the Outhouses, he is a "roaring Lion", an "Apollyon" (pp.199, 203, 385). But in reality he is a vain but "not especially a vicious" man (pp.87–88). Probably, as is suggested on other occasions (pp.11, 13, 26 etc.), his true analogue in the animal kingdom is the serpent, the viper, but if so he is only the serpent that lurks in every garden of Eden. Even the "sacrilegious" Hugh Stanbury has heard of "original sin" (p.55); and, by way of pointing to the universal aspect of Trevelyan's marital misfortune, it is ominous that the opening sentence of the novel describes him, before his marriage, as having "all the world before him where to choose"—a boast that he himself repeats, not without a grim appropriateness, almost with his dying breath (p.922).

Oddly enough, it is Bozzle, the cynical realist, who takes the most sensational view of Trevelyan's affairs. To him the exceptional is the normal. He lives in a world where nothing is but what is not. It is his life's work to unravel mysteries and uncover disgraceful secrets where none exist:

> He lived by the crookedness of people, and therefore was convinced that straight doings in the world were quite exceptional. Things dark and dishonest, fights fought and races run that they might be lost, plants and crosses, women false to their husbands, sons false to their fathers, daughters to their mothers, servants to their masters, affairs always secret, dark, foul, and fraudulent, were to him the normal condition of life. [P.268]

Here Trollope is satirizing both Bozzle's sensational view of life and the new fashion among novelists of glamorizing detectives and their work.[21] It is significant that the one potentially exciting incident in the novel—Trevelyan's abduction of his baby son—is arranged by Bozzle with the ingenuity of a born romancer; Trollope's description of it, however, is confined to a single paragraph relating the bare facts, and even its aftermath, when Emily falls into hysterics, is got over as perfunctorily as possible.

The ordinariness of the Trevelyans' story is also thrown into relief by the mock-sensationalism of the novel's comic subplot. Jilted by Mr Gibson in favour of her sister Arabella, Camilla French appears for a time in the guise of the vengeful sensational heroine, secreting a carving-knife under her pillow and later threatening her sister and uncle with a dagger. So violent are her language and behaviour that her family feel sure she is losing her mind and her mother has to watch the pantry to "see that the knives were right" (p.778). Camil-

la herself holds that "no history, no novel of most sensational interest, no wonderful villainy that had ever been wrought into prose or poetry" could equal the wrong done to her (p.691); and her tale includes such appropriately melodramatic chapters as "Mysterious Agencies", "The Lioness Aroused", and "Mrs. French's Carving Knife". But even her "madness", so much more spectacular than Trevelyan's, quickly exhausts itself as she learns to accept the humdrum sadness of her lot.[22]

Sir Harry Hotspur of Humblethwaite is, or ought to be, one of the two saddest of Trollope's novels. (Its plot is virtually the same as that of the other, *Linda Tressel.*) The heroine, Emily Hotspur, dies of a broken heart after having fallen in love with, and been prevented from marrying, her blackguardly cousin George. Her death is a judgment on the aristocratic pride of her father, who, despite his disapproval of George, had allowed him access to her. A marriage between George and Emily would have realized Sir Harry's dearest wish: that the Humblethwaite property (which will pass to Emily) and the Hotspur baronetcy (which will pass to George) should remain together after his death. But at heart he has known all along that it will be his duty to forbid the marriage even if Emily does fall in love with George. What he doesn't foresee is that the blighting of Emily's love will be death to her. His lack of foresight, however, is understandable, for the novel has not succeeded in representing Emily as a girl who might be expected to die of unrequited love.

Emily is one of only two Trollopian heroines who demonstrably die from such a cause (the other being Linda Tressel), but there are no obvious signs that her passion is deeper or more intense than that of most of her sisters. Lily Dale, for example, seems to suffer at least as acutely when she learns that she has loved unworthily; but, far from pining away as Emily does, she gains new strength of character from her suffering. Emily Wharton in *The Prime Minister* rejects the advice of her family and friends and marries a man almost as unworthy as George Hotspur; but his unkindness and her own shame do not kill her or prevent her, after his death, from loving another man. As rendered in the novel, the symptoms of Emily Hotspur's love are those which nearly all of Trollope's girls show:

> A black sheep! No! Of all the flock he should be the least black. It might be that in the energy of his pleasures he had exceeded other men, as he did exceed all other men in everything that he did and said. Who was so clever? who so bright? who so handsome, so full of poetry and of manly grace? How sweet was his voice, how fine his gait, how gracious his smile! And then in his brow there was that look of command which she had ever recognized in her father's face as belonging to his race as a Hotspur,—only added to it was a godlike beauty which her father never could have possessed. [P.81]

In a Trollopian heroine most of this is too much a matter of course to
prepare us for a love-death. So too is the unashamed forthrightness
of Emily's love:

> She had found that he was dearer to her than everything in the world
> besides; that to be near him was a luxury to her; that his voice was music
> to her; that the flame of his eyes was sunlight; that his touch was to her,
> as had never been the touch of any other human being. She could submit
> to him, she who never would submit to any one. She could delight to do
> his bidding, even though it were to bring him his slippers. She had con-
> fessed nothing of this, even to herself, till he had spoken to her on the
> bridge; but then, in a moment, she had known that it was so, and had not
> coyed the truth with him by a single nay. [Pp.137–38]

The mention here of her delight in the flame of George's eyes and in
his touch is Trollope's way of indicating that her love is sensual as
well as spiritual, but there are stronger hints of sensuality in, say,
Lily Dale and Mary Lowther, and in any case it is made clear, during the brief period when George is her acknowledged lover—
though on probation—that her desire for him is far from sweeping
her off her feet:

> " ... No, George; I will not have it."
> "Not give me one kiss?"
> "I gave you one when you came, to show you that in truth I loved you.
> I will give you another when Papa says that everything is right."
> "Not till then?"
> "No, George, not till then. But I shall love you just the same."

The novel gives no support to Sir Harry's view that it is a "disgrace
... that his daughter should have loved a man so unfit to be her
lover" (p.200). Yet, even after George has casually renounced her
and married his former mistress Mrs Morton, she continues to love
him—"in a way which she could not herself understand, loving and
despising him utterly at the same time" (pp.244–45).

In Emily, as in many Trollopian heroines, love is nourished partly
by wilfulness and thrives on parental opposition. When Lady
Altringham tells George that "even in ordinary cases the fathers and
mothers are beaten by the lovers nine times out of ten" (p.67), she is
voicing what to Trollope—and to most novelists—is virtually an axiom. Just as axiomatic, in most Victorian novels, is the young lady's
response to a parental veto on her love: her dress becomes drab, her
voice hollow and her cheeks pale; novels give way to sermons and
healthy idleness to good works; fathers, in particular, are awakened
to their emotional dependence on filial smiles and caresses. Emily,
however, not only exhibits all these conventional symptoms but
proceeds to a real and eventually fatal breakdown of health: "Our
story is over now. They did remain till the scorching July sun had
passed over their heads, and August was upon them; and then—

they had buried her in the small Protestant cemetery at Lugano, and Sir Harry Hotspur was without a child and without an heir." (p.245) Prior to her heartbreak, the novel had stressed that Emily enjoyed unusually robust health (p.17), and in this regard Trollope diverged significantly from his original conception of her: "Tall. Thin; light-haired. Blue-eyed. Rather quiet. Had been sickly; now well."[23] This Emily might have been expected to languish when thwarted in love, but her languishing might have been mistaken for a symptom of in-nate sickliness. For once, it seems, Trollope resolved (as Cockshut puts it)[24] to present "a type of love strange to his generation—a lord of terrible aspect hard as hell and stalwart as the grave". But, if so, it is strange—and unsatisfactory—that there should be so little in the representation of Emily to distinguish her from most of his other heroines and so much to associate her with any number of conven-tional heroines of romance.

One aspect of her character that might have differentiated her from most of her sisters in Trollope's novels, and raised her story to a more tragic pitch, is her religious sense: "It was granted that [George] was as vile as sin could make him. Had not her Saviour come exactly for such as this one, because of His great love for those who were vile; and should not her human love for one enable her to do that which His great heavenly love did always for all men?" (p.229) She believes that though the image of her lover is all "dross" her prayers may yet prevail to make it gold (p.235). This may re-mind us of George's own sense of his "double identity", including angel as well as ape:

> He was able, though steeped in worthlessness, so to make for himself a double identity as to imagine and to personify a being who should really possess fine and manly aspirations with regard to a woman, and to look upon himself,—his second self,—as that being; and to perceive with how withering a contempt such a being would contemplate such another man as was in truth the real George Hotspur ... [Pp.149–50]

But Trollope himself, while apparently sharing Emily's conviction that society is largely to blame for George's vices—which it tolerates and perhaps even encourages—consistently pours cold water on her religious hope of reclaiming him. When she comforts herself with the parable of the prodigal son, Trollope's comment is: " 'Twas thus she argued with herself, thinking that she could see,—whereas, poor child, she was so very blind!" (p.139) Nor has he any faith that her prayers may save George: "Alas, dearest, no; not so could it be done! Not at thy instance, though thy prayers be as pure as the songs of angels ... " (p.174). Later he remarks drily that "to him who utters them prayers of intercession are of avail" (p.233). Although in *The Vicar of Bullhampton*, written immediately before *Sir Harry Hot-*

spur, the New Testament had promised hope for the "magdalene",
Carry Brattle, it promises none for the prodigal son, George Hotspur; and in this perspective we can hardly see Emily's religiosity as
evidence of either strength, depth, or individuality of character.

On the whole the novel fails to demonstrate that Emily could or
should have died of a broken heart, and to this extent it falls short of
anything like a "tragic" effect. It is even questionable whether there
is, as Trollope himself thought (*Autobiography*, p.288), "much of
pathos" in Emily's love-story: the *Saturday Review* was not far from
the truth when it asserted that the book is "not even a sad story,
though the heroine dies for love; for the author's sympathies are not
with the hopes, and the reader's sympathies are never for an instant
engaged by the lady's sorrows".[25] The cause of its failure was suc-
cinctly indicated by R. H. Hutton: "Mr. Trollope can tell you what a
girl of Emily Hotspur's passion of nature would *do*, and how she
would do it, but he cannot tell you really what she feels. He needs an
intensiveness of style to tell us this, on which he never ventures ...
He needed the command of a 'lyrical cry' in addition to the ordinary
resource of a great novelist, and he had it not at his disposal."[26] I
have already pointed to evidence enough of this deficiency in other
novels.[27]

Lady Anna, though one of the least known and most friendless of
Trollope's novels,[28] seems to me among the more interesting and—
especially in comparison with his other "short" novels—the more
accomplished. Its young lovers, one the daughter of a countess and
the other the son of a tailor, are not remarkable in themselves. On
the contrary, considering how excitingly mismatched they are, and
how much of romance lurks in the background of their story, their
feeling for each other is disappointingly ordinary and level-headed.
What is remarkable is the passion with which Lady Anna's mother,
Lady Lovel, opposes their marriage, a passion that finally leads her
to an act of near-tragic desperation.

Lady Lovel's exaggerated pride of rank is the product of her unhappy past. But by a cruel irony it is precisely the romantic
strangeness of her past—and of theirs—that extenuates the young
lovers in the eyes of the world. It is, as no less an authority than the
solicitor-general affirms, a story "replete with marvels and
romance" (p.292): the story of an evil earl who callously disowned
his wife, telling her that he had married her bigamously and advis-
ing her, when she declined to remain with him as his mistress, to try
her luck in a house of ill-fame; of a fatherless, perhaps nameless girl
who must live in Cinderella-like poverty until the fairy godmother
of justice restores her birthright to her; of a proud embittered lady

who must subsist on the charity of a tailor for nineteen years while she strives to prove her marriage legal, and who is restored to wealth and rank only after her husband's squalid death. The earl himself is a worse-than-Byronic villain. Wallowing in his remote Sicilian fleshpots, hoarding his vast fortune, cynically protesting his love for the woman he claims to have won by a trick, letting himself be shot at by one of her outraged relatives, then vanishing again to his mysterious Venusberg, returning to England only on the eve of his death, prematurely aged, halfcrazed, but still with a slatternly Italian mistress to keep him company, he is a Gothic intruder in the world of Trollope's novels—nastier even than Lord Brotherton in *Is He Popenjoy?*. Trollope, perhaps fearing that his villainies might seem too black for a contemporary nobleman, took the unusual precaution of setting them in the past: Thomas Thwaite, the radical tailor who supported the countess in the days of her poverty, had been friendly with the lake poets at a time when they had "not as yet become altogether Tories " (p.32), and the earl himself, who is said to have died "forty years ago" (p.12), might in truth have been an exact contemporary of Byron. Apart from the historical romance *La Vendée*, no other Trollope novel is set so far back in the past, and few contain so much old-fashioned romance.

The romance, however, is all in the background. It simply establishes the conditions in which an intimacy could arise, naturally and without immodesty on the part of the lady,[29] between a tailor's son and an earl's daughter. By the time her right to her title has been proved, Lady Anna has pledged herself to Daniel Thwaite, and the chief concern of the novel as a whole is with the pressures that bear on her, from within as well as from without, to renounce her pledge. Trollope's own attitude, almost as a matter of course, is that her duty to her lover supersedes her duty to her class, and though her loyalty to Daniel occasionally weakens it never seems likely to break. Despite his low birth and militant radicalism, Daniel knows how to behave more or less as a gentleman; his truculence is not mere stupidity, and unlike nearly all specimens of his class in other Trollope novels he is not ignorant of grammar. Towards the end of the novel, after the money he receives from Lady Lovel enables him to leave his tailor's board, there is speculation that he may soon enter parliament and perhaps even the Beaufort Club (pp.489, 401). Nor do his radical principles prevent him, as they do George Eliot's Felix Holt, from accepting Anna's inherited wealth. And although he does finally take himself and his aristocratic wife off to the more democratic society of Australia, it is hinted that he may shortly return to occupy a place in the English governing class.[30]

Altogether, then, the signs for the marriage are not unpropitious,

especially when we recall its romantically sad origins. Lady Lovel, however, becomes progressively fiercer in her opposition to it, graduating from anathemas and threats to long withdrawals into menacing silence and finally to an attempt to shoot Daniel. The novel's most memorable achievement—characteristic of much of Trollope's later writing—is to convey both the comic extravagance and the impressiveness of her passion. It is shown to be the expression not so much of a personal aberration produced by her long banishment from her own caste as of prejudices which are in essence those of society as a whole. When she tells Anna that it would be a crime for her to marry Daniel (p.339), that by such a marriage she would "pollute", "degrade", "disgrace" herself; when she thinks of Daniel, the son of her old friend, as a "foul, sweltering tailor", "reeking from his tailor's board" (pp.386, 392), she is expressing feelings that are general among people of her class. Nor, except in the final stages, is her language more intemperate than theirs. Young Lord Lovel, too, who is Daniel's rival but a fair-minded man, thinks Anna's engagement "frightful", "disgusting", "indelicate", "degrading" (pp.174–75, 185). His uncle and aunt, oldfashioned Tories of the same stamp as Miss Stanbury in *He Knew He Was Right*, blame the solicitor-general's sympathy for Anna and Daniel on his being a Whig and therefore, by definition, a "traitor" (p.57). Serjeant Bluestone and his wife refrain from discussing the engagement in front of their daughters "lest the disgrace of so unnatural a partiality might shock their young minds" (p.230). And even Anna herself for a while feels "degraded" by her engagement (p.241). Although it is admitted that Lady Lovel's final idea of using a pistol to put an end to Daniel's pretensions is "mad" (p.443), her general deportment is understood and even imitated by conventional middle- and upper-class opinion. Indeed, her "hailstorms of passion" (the phrase is used on p.333) are apt to appear most extravagant when most conventional in their lore and language; when, for example, she catechizes Anna: "Do you not constantly pray to God to keep you in that state of life to which it has pleased Him to call you?" (p.227), or when she casts her off with a tragedienne's flourish: "Then go from me, thou ungrateful one, hard of heart, unnatural child, base, cruel, and polluted. Go from me, if it be possible, for ever!" (p.434)

Out of context, such a style may seem to border on farce, but it becomes more credible—in itself and in the response it draws from Anna—when we note that it is used deliberately, tactically, as an impersonal language of authority. On one occasion Lady Lovel is shown dressing herself in black silk instead of her "old brown gown", so that she may appear to her daughter as "a parent rather

than a mother, and every inch a Countess" (p.377); on another, after learning that Anna has renewed her pledge to Daniel, she mechanically launches into a theatrical denunciation ("If it be so I will never speak word to you more ... You shall never again be child of mine") before "remember[ing] her proper cue" and insisting that she doesn't "believe a word of it" (pp.383–84). Anna, though she is shown to be acutely aware of the difference between a "parent" and a "mother" (pp.372–73), though she is aware that it is an impersonal parent rather than her own mother who ritually curses her (pp.385–86), nevertheless responds in the way Lady Lovel wishes: by accepting her change of roles as a mark of exceptional emotional travail.

That it is not this, or at least that her passion is partly wilful and calculated, is suggested not only by the fact that many of her bitter hyperboles are the common, devalued currency of a whole social class or of the stage, but also by the spirit in which she performs her eventual act of violence. It is almost an axiom in Trollope's world that fiercely emotive language seldom means what it says. Even threats of murder, as Camilla French (in *He Knew He Was Right*) and Lucinda Roanoke (in *The Eustace Diamonds*) discover, are not taken seriously until potential murder weapons are brandished. And the brandishing, the final attempt at violence, is usually a much less true indicator of the character's grievances than his own unheeded words had been. To this extent, the worst tragedy for many of Trollope's more passionate characters—in his "English" novels especially—is the impossibility of tragedy: their destiny is silently to act out their sufferings before an imaginary audience—as Louis Trevelyan largely does, as for a time Phineas Finn and John Caldigate do. Neither by dying nor by inflicting death can they enhance their human stature or make themselves better understood. Those who do succeed in making a kind of tragic gesture, as Emily Hotspur is supposed to do by her love-death or Lady Mason by the outpouring of her long-repressed guilt, tend in the process to become different and unrecognizable characters. Most, like Lady Lovel—and presumably like other would-be assassins such as George Vavasor and Robert Kennedy (in *Phineas Redux*)—are prevented from carrying out a tragic act by the very qualities that impel them to attempt it. Their inability to shoot straight, though no doubt lucky and, from Trollope's point of view, convenient, [31] is also a symptom of their mixed motives. They shoot not so much to kill as to make themselves heard, and the pressing of the trigger is apt to seem a mechanical rather than a willed act.

The scene where Lady Lovel shoots at Daniel Thwaite (chapter 43) is the most remarkable example. Here the reader's view is

restricted almost throughout to mechanical details: to Lady Lovel's movements towards and away from the desk where her pistol is hidden, and in particular to each change in the position of the hand— her left hand—which will grasp the pistol. Her mind registers nothing but the practical difficulty of lining up her target so that his face is towards her, so that in his dying moment he will at last be made to recognize and respect her rage. All her calculations are methodical and almost dispassionate. After the shooting she remains unmoved, barely conscious of what she has done (chapter 44). She puts away the pistol "mechanically", then sits quite still. Ironically, her first thought is that having failed in her attempt she may at least escape punishment. Before, she had thought only of the "glory" that would be hers when her willingness to commit murder and hang for it rather than see her daughter disgrace herself became known. Now, as she is aware, Anna will certainly marry Daniel, but her dismay at this is overborne by her "intense" desire to "escape the disgrace of punishment" and to "do something by which she might help to preserve herself" The feelings that prompted her criminal act, feelings that had held sway over her for more than a year, do not outlive the act itself by even a few minutes. She must live with the bathetic truth that her own life is after all more valuable to her than her family honour.

Stated baldly, this will sound a foregone conclusion; but in the novel itself we do not doubt, even retrospectively, that her recourse to the pistol was in her eyes necessary or that the "insanity" of which, according to the narrator, it was evidence (p.443) was but a mild and shortlived variety. And the novel's view of her motives, its heavy stress on the sympathetic response they find in the world around her, is impressively vindicated by what we know of contemporary readers' reactions. None of the original reviews that I have read express any surprise at Lady Lovel's violence, and one even sides with her openly.[32] Trollope's friend Lady Wood took strong exception to the misalliance but not, apparently, to Lady Lovel's means of trying to avert it.[33] And in his *Autobiography* (p.298) Trollope refers to the "horror which was expressed to me at the evil thing I had done, in giving the girl to the tailor", but makes no mention of any horror aroused by Lady Lovel.

The modest success with which Trollope dramatized class prejudice in *Lady Anna* appears all the more admirable when we set it beside the more pretentious *Marion Fay*. There tragic romance is again a response to the problem of bridging a social gap between lovers, but romance and realism jostle each other to a degree unparalleled in any of Trollope's other novels.

Marion Fay tells of a marquis's son who falls in love with a poor quaker girl and of his sister who falls in love with, and marries, a post-office clerk. The circumstances that bring these ill-assorted couples together are instructive. Lord Hampstead, the marquis's son, believes himself a radical. He meets the post-office clerk, George Roden, also a self-styled radical, at a political meeting and they become friends. George falls in love with Lady Frances, Hampstead's sister, during visits to their house. Hampstead also visits George at his mother's house (in Holloway) and there meets and falls in love with Marion Fay, a neighbour of Mrs Roden's. As professed radicals, neither George nor Hampstead is averse to marrying outside his own class, but they naturally meet strong opposition, chiefly from Hampstead's and Lady Frances's stepmother Lady Kingsbury. Though showing no homicidal inclinations herself—as Lady Lovel does—Lady Kingsbury succeeds, perhaps only half-intentionally, in instilling the idea of murdering Hampstead into the mind of the family chaplain Mr Greenwood. Happily, however, Mr Greenwood has second thoughts—if he can be said to have thoughts at all. It has never been clear to him, or to the reader, whether Lady Kingsbury really wants her stepson killed or why, if she does, he should be the killer.[34] Certainly she is vociferous in her expressions of antipathy to such misalliances as Hampstead and Lady Frances contemplate, but there is a doubt whether this antipathy, or her desire that her own son should inherit the family title, is the chief cause of her enmity towards Hampstead. The picture we are given of her class prejudices, as of Lady Lovel's, has a flavour of caricature but, unlike Lady Lovel's, they never force us to take them seriously. It is even open to conjecture that both she and Mr Greenwood are to be viewed primarily as figures of fun.

The main weakness of *Marion Fay*, however, lies in the fairytale romanticism surrounding the two sets of lovers. This is patently contrived to make the threatened misalliances less unpalatable to squeamish readers. Thus we learn at the outset that George Roden, though a post-office clerk, is a gentleman. There is a mystery about his parentage, and heavy hints are thrown out that once it is cleared up he will be found to be not much inferior in rank to Lady Frances. When, at the end of the second volume, he is revealed as the son and rightful heir of an Italian duke, all opposition to their marriage vanishes. The reader is left wondering, though, why George's mother should have kept the truth from him for so long when she might have spared him so much anxiety by confiding in him: perhaps Trollope was tempted to try his hand at a novel in the sensational style, *Mrs Roden's Secret*. But since it is the disclosure of the secret that puts an end to George and Lady Frances's worries, not

anything that they themselves say or do, all the preceding argument about the responsibilities of rank and the sanctity of class distinctions is suddenly made superfluous and inconsequential. At least one reviewer, it is encouraging to find, accused Trollope of timidity in promoting plain George Roden to the aristocracy.[35]

To make the conservative reader accept a marriage between Lord Hampstead and Marion Fay would have been harder. There is no mystery about her parentage, and although she is well-spoken, demure, and ladylike she hardly seems the stuff of which marchionesses are made. Luckily, she feels this herself, and with all his ardour her lover fails to change her mind. But the question is finally settled for them when she dies of consumption, the only Trollopian heroine to fall to this traditional executioner. Lord Hampstead is the most demonstrative of all Trollope's lovers, and at times we may suspect that the strength of his passion is being offered as an implicit apology for his offence in seeking a bride so far below him on the social scale. Certainly, as Marion's death approaches, pathos becomes so overpowering that we almost forget the difference in rank between the two lovers. Once the danger of a misalliance has passed nothing remains but a tragedy of star-crossed love, more than moving enough to obliterate any discomfort we may have felt at the prospect of such an ill-assorted match. What can we say against a love so eloquent as this?

> "It shall be to me during my future life as though when wandering through the green fields in some long-past day, I had met a bright angel from another world; and the angel had stopped to speak to me, and had surrounded me with her glorious wings, and had given me of her heavenly light, and had spoken to me with the music of the spheres, and I had thought that she would stay with me for ever. But there had come a noise of the drums and a sound of the trumpets, and she had flown away from me up to her own abode. To have been so favoured, though it had been but for an hour, should suffice for a man's life. [III:199]

Later, Lord Hampstead does meet his angel from another world. A month after her death Marion appears to him as he watches over her grave: "He looked up into the night, and there, before his eyes, was her figure, beautiful as ever, with all her loveliness of half-developed form, with her soft hair upon her shoulders; and her eyes beamed upon him, and a heavenly smile came across her face, and her lips moved as though she would encourage him..."[III:244] Compared to this an earthly marriage would have been the merest anticlimax, and to reflect that it might also have been subversive of class distinctions would be crude irreverence.

Reading passages like these calls to mind again the remark of R.H. Hutton, Trollope's favourite 'critic, that he lacked a "lyrical

cry". It is, I believe, this lack that we are most conscious of in nearly all Trollope's efforts to represent tragic passions. In general, his most convincing tragic or near-tragic figures are his least eloquent— figures like Louis Trevelyan and at times Lady Glencora Palliser and Lady Laura Kennedy—and there is usually a touch of irony, a faint suggestion of the ridiculous, in the most effective of his big emotional scenes. When he allows his characters to declaim, and when he takes them as solemnly as they take themselves, his and their language is apt to become stiff, impersonal, and strained. *He Knew He Was Right* and (less subtly) *Lady Anna* indicate the style in which he copes best with what he classed as "tragic elements", a style that is also seen from time to time in several of the novels I discuss in my remaining chapters.

NOTES

1. Review of *Framley Parsonage*, *Saturday Review* 11 (4 May 1861): 452.
2. The heroines of *Lady Audley's Secret* (1862) and *Aurora Floyd* (1863)—both by Miss M.E. Braddon—*No Name* (1862) by Wilkie Collins, and *St. Martin's Eve* (1866) by Mrs Henry Wood.
3. Sadleir, *Commentary*, p.388.
4. See, e.g., my account of *The Eustace Diamonds* in chap.7
5. Other instances—discussed below—include *The Macdermots of Ballycloran*, *John Caldigate*, and *Mr. Scarborough's Family*.
6. See, e.g., [R.H. Hutton], *Spectator* 35 (11 October 1862): 1136; and Bradford Booth, "Trollope's *Orley Farm*: Artistry Manqué", *Victorian Literature: Modern Essays in Criticism*, ed. Austin Wright (New York: Oxford University Press, 1961), pp.363–65.
7. Millais' drawing, not a very expressive one, faces I:36 in the first edition of the novel.
8. R.H. Hutton's phrase.
9. Booth, "Trollope's *Orley Farm*", pp.365–67.
10. Robert M. Polhemus, *The Changing World of Anthony Trollope*, p.79.
11. The comparison between the two novels is suggested by Patricia Thomson in her *The Victorian Heroine, a Changing Ideal* (London: Oxford University Press, 1956), but I feel she hardly does justice to Trollope.
12. "Trollope and the Reviewers: Three Notes", *Notes and Queries* 213 (November 1968): 418–20.
13. *Dublin Review* 19 (October 1872): 452.
14. *Westminster Review* 36 (July 1869): 303.
15. The *Times*, 26 August 1869, p.4.
16. See p.581 (*He Knew He Was Right*). The law in question was the Infants Custody Act of 1839.
17. See above, chaps.3 and 4.
18. Lady Mary Palliser submits to the same enormity in *The Duke's Children* (chap. 29) but is less bold about it afterwards than Nora.
19. See, e.g., *Saturday Review* 27 (5 June 1869): 752, and [R.H. Hutton], *Spectator* 42 (12 June 1869): 707. Mrs Oliphant's attack on Nora occurs in her review of *The Vicar of Bullhampton* and is quoted in my discussion of that novel (chap.4 above).
20. Sadleir, *Commentary*, p.393.
21. Trollope's presentation of Bozzle may well have been influenced by his friend Fitzjames Stephen's article, "Detectives in Fiction and in Real Life", *Saturday Review* 17 (11 June 1864): 712–13, a satirical attack on "the romance of the detective".

22. One of Trollope's later novels, *Kept in the Dark*, was described by Sadleir as "*He Knew He Was Right* in tabloid form" (*Commentary*, p.396). But it is nowhere near as interesting and intense, either as a psychological study or as a problem novel. The conflict that nearly wrecks the marriage of its two central characters is caused by an unhappy, and almost too freakish, coincidence rather than by incompatibility of temper, and the portrayal of both husband and wife is sketchy. Cockshut argues, characteristically, that the husband is "obsessed", a "solitary exponent of a fantastic idea" (*Anthony Trollope*, pp.225–28). But his first fury at the news that his wife, like himself, had been engaged to someone else just before she met him seems to strike her and her friends as natural enough; and unlike Trevelyan he soon gets over it and admits that he has been wrong.
23. Bodleian ms. Don.c.9, p.228; quoted in Sadleir, *Commentary*, p.425.
24. *Anthony Trollope*, p.128.
25. *Saturday Review* 30 (10 December 1870): 753–54.
26. *Spectator* 43 (26 November 1870): 1415–16.
27. Hutton considered the "execution" of the novel at fault rather than the "conception". But George Eliot's scathing comments on the conception also command assent: "Men are very fond of glorying that dog-like attachment ... " See *The George Eliot Letters*, ed. Gordon S. Haight (London: Oxford University Press, 1956) V:132.
28. It is not mentioned at all in the full-length studies of Trollope by Hugh Walpole (1928), Beatrice Curtis Brown (1950), Cockshut, and Booth; L.P. and R.P. Stebbins have nothing to say in its favour; and Michael Sadleir (*Commentary*, p.396) considers that it and *Marion Fay*, alone among Trollope's later novels, "belong definitely to the second class".
29. The lady infatuated with a man of lower rank was a common subject of the sensation novel: one thinks, for example, of Lady Audley, of another of M.E. Braddon's heroines Aurora Floyd (who clandestinely marries her father's groom), and of Trollope's own Lady Fitzgerald (in *Castle Richmond*).
30. The novel's final paragraph half-promises a sequel, but this was never written. We do learn, however, that Daniel's travels made him "perhaps a wiser man", and it is amusing to imagine him emulating Trollope's friend Robert Lowe who, after an apprenticeship in Australia, returned to a distinguished political career in England.
31. There is some justice in the *Saturday Review*'s sneering reference to the "inevitable pistol with which [Trollope] cuts short so many complications" (27 [9 May 1874]: 599), though it seems to me less applicable to *Lady Anna* than to *Can You Forgive Her?* and *Phineas Redux*.
32. *Saturday Review* 27 (9 May 1874): 598–99: "This is a sort of thing the reading public will never stand, except in a period of political storm and ferment ... " The reviewer also noted, as a bad sign, the novel's close similarity to *Felix Holt*. He seems to have overlooked, however, that Trollope, like George Eliot, *did* take the precaution of setting his tale in a period of political ferment. Trollope emphasized the social disparity between his hero and heroine more than George Eliot, who wished above all to win sympathy and respect for her radical hero, to disarm class prejudice rather than to affront it. Both novelists, however, seem to have felt that only a highly romantic set of circumstances would suffice to bridge the conventional gap between lady and artisan. An interesting sidelight is that both also had to seek advice to make sure they "got their law right" (the law being their chief source of romantic complications); see Trollope's manuscript outline of *Lady Anna* (Bodleian ms. Don.c.10, p.7), and *The George Eliot Letters* IV: 214–65.
33. *Letters*, p.308.
34. Trollope's choice of a clergyman as would-be murderer struck the *Saturday Review* as evidence of "what a jaded fancy can have recourse to for a new sensation" (54 [8 July 1882]: 64). Perhaps the idea was suggested by Dickens's *Edwin Drood*, in which the presumed murderer, John Jasper, though not ordained, follows a distinctively "clerical" occupation.
35. *Spectator* 55 (19 August 1882): 1089.

⑥ "All the keen interest of a sensational novel"

If it were so arranged that the same persons were always friends, and the same persons were always enemies, as used to be the case among the dear old heathen gods and goddesses;—if Parliament were an Olympus in which Juno and Venus never kissed, the thing would not be nearly so interesting. But in this Olympus partners are changed, the divine bosom, now rabid with hatred against some opposing deity, suddenly becomes replete with love towards its late enemy, and exciting changes occur which give to the whole thing all the keen interest of a sensational novel. No doubt this is greatly lessened for those who come too near the scene of action. [*Can You Forgive Her?* II:12]

The five novels known variously as the Palliser, parliamentary, or political series—*Can You Forgive Her?*, *Phineas Finn*, *Phineas Redux*, *The Prime Minister*, and *The Duke's Children*[1]—are in some respects an extension of the Barset series. Some of their leading characters, notably Plantagenet Palliser (later Duke of Omnium) and his wife Lady Glencora, first appeared in Barset novels, and Barset itself is one of the settings of all the political novels. Their main setting, however, is the political world of London, most of their characters being members of that "special set which dominates all other sets in our English world" (*Phineas Redux* I:439).

Trollope's remark that parliament can offer "all the keen interest of a sensational novel" is not altogether tongue-in-cheek. Nor do the novels themselves altogether bear out his ironic qualification that the interest is "greatly lessened for those who come too near the scene of action". Politics may often dwindle, even in the eyes of the politicians themselves, into a hollow spectacle, a tableau in which the Olympian postures, the passions and excitements are all cynically simulated. Yet its sensational fascination remains: for Trollope himself it was a "visionary weakness" (*Autobiography*, p.255), and for Phineas Finn it is a "fiend" (*Phineas Finn* I:77) or an addiction, harder to cure than addiction to drink or gambling (*Phineas Redux* I:142).

At times, it is true, this fascination may strike us as not only unreasonable but unreal, reflecting not so much Trollope's excitement

with the subject as his fear that readers will not find it exciting enough. Believing that he "could not make a tale pleasing chiefly, or perhaps in any part, by politics", that he must therefore "put in love and intrigue, social incidents, with perhaps a dash of sport, for the sake of my readers" (*Autobiography*, p.273), he provided all the novels with episodes and subplots not overtly relevant to events on the public stage; he clung, in short, to the "hodge-podge" of "thoroughly English" ingredients that had made *Framley Parsonage* so popular. But he also, on occasions, compensated for the sober truth of politics by magnifying the exciting illusion, by crediting politicians and their doings with a prowess, importance, and popular appeal for which the imaginative evidence that we are given seems hardly sufficient.

How sober the truth can be is shown in the first parliamentary scene in the series, when George Vavasor takes his seat for the first time. George's anticipatory excitement is fully shared by the narrator:

> Between those lamps is the entrance to the House of Commons, and none but Members may go that way! It is the only gate before which I have ever stood filled with envy,—sorrowing to think that my steps might never pass under it. There are many portals forbidden to me, as there are many forbidden to all men; and forbidden fruit, they say, is sweet; but my lips have watered after no other fruit but that which grows so high ... [*Can You Forgive Her?* II:53]

From the House of Commons, he goes on to exclaim, "flow the waters of the world's progress,—the fullest fountain of advancing civilisation" (II:54). Yet the debate in progress as George enters the house seems to him "but a dull affair", and it is followed by still deeper bathos as an earnest member, who has waited months for the chance to address the house on his favourite subject, is silenced by a count-out.

Later we find that even the most stirring parliamentary events soon begin to pall for the onlookers. In the great debate on a Conservative measure to disestablish the Church of England (*Phineas Redux*, chapter 33), "men could listen with pleasure" as long as the prime minister would "abuse" the opposition leader. But the part of his speech devoted to the details of the bill is "felt to be dull by the strangers". And at the height of the debate even some of the most vitally concerned onlookers, including "a bishop or two", leave the house rather than postpone their dinner. This, moreover, is during the period when Trollope's parliament, dominated by the "two gladiators" Daubeny and Gresham, is at its most eloquent and turbulent. With their departure, in the last two novels of the series, even the politicians feel that much of the excitement has gone. It is

worth noting, too, that in the eyes of Phineas Finn and Plantagenet Palliser, the two politicians whom we get to know most intimately in the series, the truly heroic days of parliament came to an end earlier still, when Mr Mildmay, the Whig prime minister in *Can You Forgive Her?* and the first half of *Phineas Finn*, departed from the scene. Phineas had felt "reverence" for him (*Phineas Redux* II:334) and Palliser had "almost worshipped" him (*The Duke's Children* II:258–59); but for the reader he is only a shadowy, semi-legendary figure far less vividly and individually drawn than Daubeny and Gresham. Trollope must have sensed that none of the politicians of whom he allows us a nearer view could believably be credited with inspiring such hero-worship.

The sober truth is nevertheless only a part of the truth about Trollope's parliament. Some of its excitement and heroism may, as I have suggested, strike us as factitious, may appear to be a tactical exaggeration of Trollope's to capture the reader's interest. In this category might be included much of the fervid curiosity that the public is supposed to feel about the private lives of politicians, much of the muckraking journalism of Quintus Slide, and much of the fascination that politics is supposed to have for women. At their best, however, the novels do convince us, with some force and subtlety, that the passions and preoccupations of the political scene really are those of society at large, and that values as well as power are at stake in the political arena. Nor can we fail to recognize that some at least of the gods and giants to whom we are first introduced in *Framley Parsonage* (chapters 20, 23) do possess godlike and gigantic qualities in Trollope's eyes. He may facetiously jib at describing their counsels in *Framley Parsonage*, on the grounds that no mere mortal can visit Olympus. He may begin his account of a later cabinet meeting (*Phineas Finn*, chapter 29) by mockingly invoking the muses to assist his "bewildered brain" in telling of "so august an occasion", then let us down with the prosaic information that "at first sight [the cabinet] seemed to be as ordinary gentlemen as you shall meet anywhere about Pall Mall on an afternoon. There was nothing about their outward appearance of the august wiggery of state craft, nothing of the ponderous dignity of ministerial position." But among them are men of whom it would be real sacrilege to speak with disrespect: Mr Mildmay, "the much-honoured grey-haired old Premier", and Mr Gresham, "said to be the greatest orator in Europe". (On other occasions, however, Mr Gresham is characterized as touchy, impetuous, without any reverence for the past, and his speech in the disestablishment debate in *Phineas Redux* is generally thought to have been "too passionate" and "very inferior to the great efforts of the past"—though in the debate on

the ballot in *Phineas Finn*, Trollope's other great parliamentary scene, he "delivered an oration of which men said that it would be known in England as long as there were any words remaining of English eloquence".) Also among those at the cabinet meeting in *Phineas Finn* is the Whig Nestor, the Duke of St Bungay, whom we first met in *Can You Forgive Her?* (chapters 23–24). There Alice Vavasor embarrassed him by asking his views on the ballot, and the malicious poet Mrs Conway Sparkes made him "uneasy" by taunting his stupid wife. But he has been helping form cabinets for thirty-five years and is considered not beneath comparison with his uncle "who was Canning's friend" and his grandfather "whom Burke loved" (*Phineas Finn* I:329).

One means by which Trollope enhances the stature of his leading politicians and the excitement and momentousness of their deeds is to model the history of his imaginary parliament on real-life parliamentary history. Cockshut has defined the relationship between the two as "similarity with difference",[2] and its effect is to make us sense similarities even when we cannot actually recognize any. A symptom of this is the assiduity with which, ever since the novels first appeared, prototypes have been hunted down for most of the politicians. Daubeny has been identified with Disraeli, Gresham with Gladstone, Mildmay with Lord John Russell, Lord Brock with Palmerston, Lord De Terrier with Derby, Turnbull with Bright, Monk with Bright, Monk with Cobden, Palliser with Lord John Russell, the Duke of St Bungay with Lord Lansdowne, and Phineas Finn with John Pope Hennessy, Joe Parkinson, and (incredibly) the swindling Irish MP James Sadleir.[3] There are also, as I shall be noting, important resemblances between Palliser and Gladstone. Naturally some of the likenesses struck the original reviewers of the novels, but there was as much disagreement on the matter among them as among subsequent critics. Trollope himself was not helpful. Apart from protesting that in Turnbull he "intended neither portrait or [sic] caricature" of Bright,[4] he made no public comment on the suggested identifications. Privately, he did later admit that Disraeli and Gladstone had served as models for Daubeny and Gresham, but only in respect of "their particular tenets";[5] no reader, however, could fail to detect likenesses of political style as well.

The relationship between the novels' version of parliamentary history and real-life parliamentary history is at its closest in the first three novels of the series, less close but still discernible in *The Prime Minister*, virtually non-existent in *The Duke's Children* (which is the least "political" of the novels).[6]

Trollope's decision, in most of the novels, to use the real-life political scene as the point of departure for his own entailed dif-

ficulties as well as advantages. There is a gain in terms of surface realism and also, as I have suggested, in terms of excitement and political interest. But inevitably there is at times a corresponding sacrifice of psychological subtlety. This is because Trollope, as a gentleman, could not depict the private lives of characters in some respects modelled on living politicians, or likely to be compared with them, as anything like the private lives of their real-life counterparts. But neither, without detracting from the exciting illusion of proximity to history, could he give them private lives altogether different. He was committed, in short, to portraying them exclusively as public men. So apart from Palliser and (briefly) the Duke of St Bungay, we never see any of the real grandees of his political world—the Mildmays, Greshams, Daubenys, and Monks—in their domestic habitats. The result is that they tend to appear remote, slightly larger than life, even slightly mysterious, compared to the ordinary mortals—including the underlings of politics—with whom we are allowed to rub shoulders. Moreover, their remoteness and the touch of glamour with which it invests them become the measure not only of their imaginative impact on their own world but also of the impact of this world itself on those who, like the reader, like the "public", can never hope to be part of it. They are the extreme examples of that "delight" which the spectacle of politics holds for those who have no desire, or no opportunity, to "peep behind the scenes" (*Can You Forgive Her?* II:12); and it is, by a not unfamiliar paradox, their very closeness to real life that makes them, in the novels, somewhat larger than life. In doing so, however, it sometimes weakens Trollope's own imaginative grasp of life, causing him to mistake the exciting, magnified illusion for the real thing—for the whole of the real thing—and leaving him struggling to regain the safe shores of prose after having struck too far out into the deep seas of poetry.

There is, then, a certain tension between the fully imagined "private" world of the novels and their semi-historical "public" world. It is, moreover, a tension of which Trollope himself is perhaps aware. Certainly the conflicting claims of private and public life are a problem for most of the leading characters in the novels: so much so, indeed, that this problem can be seen as the chief unifying subject of the series. But although the novels dramatize the tension as a moral phenomenon, inherent in political life itself, and although the dramatization generally carries conviction, there are moments when the tension is unmistakably at work not only in the action of the novel but also in the novelist's own uneasy imagination. Significantly, these moments are most frequent in the two *Phineas* novels, where the semi-historical element and the emphasis on public life

and its dominance over private are most pronounced. In the other novels, where the Pallisers are the centre of attention, private life is certainly shown to be vulnerable to the dehumanizing influences, the showiness and often factitious sensations, of public life; but in the end its own values always assert themselves, if rather shakily. Commenting on *Phineas Finn* in his *Autobiography* (pp.271–75), Trollope referred to it as marking the commencement of "a series of semi-political tales"; presumably he placed the earlier *Can You Forgive Her?* in a different category, although it too, like all the novels in which the Pallisers appear, had functioned as a "safety-valve" for the "expression of my political and social convictions" (ibid., p.155). For him, what made *Can You Forgive Her?*, and the series as a whole, memorable was chiefly the "art" with which they showed the development over a long period of the characters of Plantagenet Palliser and his wife. The Pallisers, however, play only a small part in the *Phineas* novels, and their diminished role can be seen as the condition of a reversal of emphasis from private life sometimes shading into public (in *Can You Forgive Her?*, and later in *The Prime Minister* and *The Duke's Children*) to public life of which private is simply an extension (in the *Phineas* novels). The more detailed discussion of the novels that follows will, I hope, show that this reversal of emphasis, though interesting and impressive in some of its results, also created artistic problems that Trollope failed to cope with.

Frederic Harrison considered the *Phineas* novels "undoubtedly the most sensational of Trollope's tales".[7] But *Can You Forgive Her?* and *The Prime Minister* are hardly less sensational—by Trollopian standards at least—and the sensationalism, as I have been suggesting, is due primarily to their imperfect imaginative assimilation of the glamour and excitement of public life to relatively humdrum private life.

Can You Forgive Her? may seem at first glance to belie this generalization in that most of the excitement it offers belongs to private lives (George Vavasor's and Lady Glencora's), while its politicians and their doings are generally rather dull. It is in fact an anti-political novel, an explicit defence of the values of private life against those of public, and this could not be said of any of the later novels in the series, despite the disgust and weariness with politics that they often express. Leaving aside George Vavasor, the "Three Politicians" of whom we see most in *Can You Forgive Her?* are those to whom we are introduced in chapter 24: Mr Palliser, the Duke of St Bungay, and Mr Bott. In describing these, Trollope's tone is chillingly unexcited. Palliser is not only "not a brilliant man"

but is "very dull"; he is "an upright, thin, laborious man, who by his parts alone could have served no political party materially" (I:303). The Duke of St Bungay is a man of great authority behind the scenes, yet "nobody ever knew what he did; nor was there much record of what he said"; his great virtue in the House was that he "never grew either hot or cold in a cause" (I:308–9). The best that can be said for Mr Bott, the middle-aged, middlingly rich, middlingly radical member for St Helens is that he is a "very serviceable man in his own way" despite his ugliness and unctuous toadying (I:311–13). In the background there are greater men—Lord Brock and Finespun and Sidonia—but we do not see and hear these in action as we do the Mildmays, Daubenys, and Greshams of the later novels. Parliament itself we visit only on the day when George Vavasor takes his seat and finds proceedings dull.

But politics is not only shown to be drab and distasteful in itself. It also, in the course of the novel, operates as an active evil, diverting both Alice Vavasor and Plantagenet Palliser from what should be their closest personal attachments—to fiancé and wife respectively. This is the active aspect under which, in the later novels, it becomes for men a "fiend", an addictive drug, and for women a crypto-erotic seducer. But in *Can You Forgive Her?* the only one of its male victims who might seem to be truly possessed by it is George Vavasor, and he is possessed by many other demons as well. Among the women Lady Glencora as yet shows no direct signs of being seduced by it, and its seduction of Alice Vavasor, as I have already pointed out (chapter 4), is hardly convincing. In the *Phineas* novels, by contrast, many of the politicians are personable and zestful. Women like Lady Laura Kennedy can derive both intellectual and emotional stimulus from them, can love the activity because of the actors and the actors because of the activity. But in Lady Laura's circle politics is not an eccentric interest for a woman, as it had been in Alice Vavasor's. Her feeling that a "woman's life is only half a life, as she cannot have a seat in Parliament" (*Phineas Finn* 1:70) is shared by her friend Violet Effingham, who is not at all mannish, but who has a slight hankering to "knock under to Mr. Mill, and go in for women's rights, and look forward to stand for some female borough" (ibid., II:145). Madame Max Goesler, Lady Mabel Grex, and (from *Phineas Finn* on) Lady Glencora also take a lively, if not always very serious, interest in the parliamentary scene. Even allowing that Trollope sometimes appears to exaggerate women's interest in politics as a means of heightening the reader's, the fascination imputed to it in the later novels remains in sharp contrast to its general dullness in *Can You Forgive Her?*.

Yet, notwithstanding its own dullness, it does contribute impor-

tantly to the excitement of other aspects of that novel, not least to
the essentially private drama involving Lady Glencora and her lover
Burgo Fitzgerald. Burgo and Lady Glencora are nearly always in the
public eye and conscious of being so, and for both them and the
reader the consciousness is a source of excitement. Burgo, with his
good looks, his casual generosity (as displayed in the well-known
scene in chapter 29 where he gives half a crown to a street girl who
has accosted him), and his physical and moral recklessness, is a
Byronic exhibitionist. In a public scene such as that in which he
scandalizes the guests assembled for breakfast at Lady Monk's
country house by cursing Palliser for having prudently left Lady
Glencora at home (I:423–24), his romantic wildness is much more
believable than that of the novel's other "wild man", George
Vavasor. And the daredevil fury he displays during the hunt later in
the same day reveals the natural man in him more eloquently than
George's escapades on the Westmorland Fells. His appeal for Lady
Glencora is fully understandable, since she too, unlike her cousin
Alice, believes herself a romantic and is certainly an exhibitionist.

As it expresses itself in private, Lady Glencora's romanticism is
disappointingly conventional:

> She had a little water-coloured drawing called Raphael and Fornarina,
> and she was infantine enough to tell herself that the so-called Raphael
> was like her Burgo—no, not her Burgo, but the Burgo that was not hers.
> At any rate, all the romance of the picture she might have enjoyed had
> they allowed her to dispose as she had wished of her own hand. She
> might have sat in marble balconies, while the vines clustered over her
> head, and he would have been at her knee, hardly speaking to her, but
> making his presence felt by the halo of its divinity. He would have called
> upon her for no hard replies. With him near her she would have enjoyed
> the soft air, and would have sat happy, without trouble, lapped in the
> delight of loving. [II:25]

On its own this would seem almost as "infantine", as silly and
characterless, as the romanticism attributed to Alice. But in the
novels as a whole it appears more an example of Lady Glencora's incapacity for introspection, the poverty of her private mental life,
than a sign of insipidity. Her daydream about Raphael and For-
narina takes place after she has received a letter from Burgo proposing that they elope, a proposal as to which, the narrator observes,
she "could not analyse her own wishes" (II:19). But if she cannot
analyse her feelings in private, she can express them, and express
them with great power, in public—in any situation offering scope
for emotional display. Then she can be, at once or in turn, richly and
originally comic and genuinely pathetic, revealing an emotional
range that probably no other Trollopian character can match.

The clue to Trollope's success with her lies partly in her affinities

with the group of characters I have described as outsiders, a group that also includes the Stanhopes (in *Barchester Towers*), Martha Dunstable (in later Barset novels), Sophie Gordeloup and Count Pateroff (in *The Claverings*), Lizzie Eustace (in *The Eustace Diamonds*), and Mr Scarborough (in *Mr. Scarborough's Family*). Like these she generally has no real private existence. She can think only aloud, perform only in front of an audience—preferably an actual one, but, *faute de mieux*, an imaginary. Nearly all her big scenes, even those which are ostensibly private, domestic, are in effect public confrontations in which her interlocutor is society itself. Like the other outsiders she is marked by what we may call spots of uncommonness, areas in which her feelings and values are not simply unorthodox and irreverent but radically different from those which animate her society as a whole—and, one may add, from those to which Trollope himself is consciously committed. Her tactlessness and huge "vulgarity"—which reach their climax in *The Prime Minister*—are the expression of a spirit almost free from the dictates of custom, and in them Trollope's own imagination finds freedom. In *Can You Forgive Her?* there are already signs of the famous flippancy and demotic raciness of speech that so pain her prim husband, the perfect foil to her liveliness. Even a mild piece of slang like "the long and the short of it" makes him wince (II:109). He is "struck wild with dismay" by her crude sketch of his political ally Mr Bott as "that odious baboon with the red bristles" (II:110). And Alice Vavasor is similarly shocked by Lady Glencora's errors of feeling and language, which Lady Glencora exaggerates for her benefit. For the reader, however, these insistent blazons of nonconformity, these shots at a public that is always in Lady Glencora's sights even when she is in private, are the essence of her vitality.

It is nevertheless her womanly dignity rather than either her raciness or her romanticism that comes to the fore in the finest scenes of *Can You Forgive Her?*. In these there is, for once, nothing histrionic about her expression of her emotions, no playing to a public gallery for applause or disapproval to enhance her own excitement. She is enacting what is in truth the emotional crisis of her life, and it is one that for the most part she must cope with alone— the more so because of the public eye upon her. The outcome of her crisis, as we later see, will decide the pattern not only of her whole future relationship with her husband but also, after her death, of his relationship with his children. Husband and wife will inevitably recall this crisis, silently, during every lesser crisis of their marriage. Lady Glencora emerges from it with a stature, in the reader's eyes, and to some extent in her husband's, that none of her subsequent follies, not even her gradual loss of originality in her follies, can

seriously diminish. The stature is, in some respects at least, that of a heroine, of a woman who has once, for all her weakness and frivolity, stepped out as a champion of her sex and of the sanctity of human relationships.

Sadly, her right to be judged in this light is not acknowledged explicitly by the narrator or by her friends. The official judgment is that of Alice, the novel's nominal heroine, who sees her at the time when she is tolerating Burgo's addresses as a "poor deluded unreasoning creature" (I:357), or that of the narrator, who describes her as a "poor, wretched, overburthened child, to whom the commonest lessons of life had not yet been taught" (II:25). Both Alice and the narrator pity her as a woman cajoled into a loveless marriage and beset by gossips and spies. But both are shocked, nonetheless, that she should even entertain the idea of adultery and credit her, in rejecting it, with no quality more heroic than that of "sanity". For them the true hero is Mr Palliser who can bring himself, despite her errors, to "kill her by his goodness" (II:232) and who finally sows the seed—of a son and heir—that Lady Glencora feels will "make it all right" for her (II:508). It is only in retrospect, within the context of the political series as a whole, that this complacent conclusion is seen to be no conclusion at all and that a fairer, more respectful, less stereotyped view of Lady Glencora emerges.

But even without the advantage of hindsight the ending of *Can You Forgive Her?* is likely to strike us as unsatisfactory. That the reconciliation between Lady Glencora and her husband may prove at best an uneasy one is clearly enough suggested; but Lady Glencora's eager desire for it, coming immediately after her very reluctant dismissal of Burgo and well before her pregnancy, is not adequately accounted for. It is believable only on the assumption that her love for Burgo is no love, merely a mixture of romantic daydream and exhibitionism. But such an assumption is ruled out by the eloquent signs of real sexual passion and of a truly unconventional nature that she gives in her great crisis scenes. These establish her as deserving a better fate than that of the tamed, though not cowed, wife of "worthy" Mr Palliser. (One cannot altogether disagree with Henry James's complaint that such a conclusion is an anticlimax, a "mere begging of the issue", and that it leaves Lady Glencora and Burgo "vulgarly disposed of".[8])

The intensity of Lady Glencora's love for Burgo, and the dignity and power with which she can express it, are most evident in the chapter called "The Last Kiss" (chapter 67), where she finally rejects him. But, as James noted, her and Burgo's story "touches at a hundred points almost upon the tragical".[9] One such point is when Alice, whom Lady Glencora is trying to persuade to transfer her af-

fections from George Vavasor to Jeffrey Palliser, seems to accuse Lady Glencora herself of having similarly transferred hers from Burgo to her husband; Lady Glencora admits her apparent treachery with a moving simplicity that disarms even Alice:

> "It is an unmaidenly thing to do, certainly," said Lady Glencora very slowly, and in her lowest voice. "Nay, it is unwomanly; but one may be driven. One may be so driven that all gentleness of womanhood is driven out of one."
> "Oh, Glencora!"
> "I did not propose that you should do it as a sudden thing."
> "Glencora!"
> "I did do it suddenly. I know it. I did it like a beast that is driven as its owner chooses. I know it. I was a beast. Oh, Alice, if you knew how I hate myself!" [I:329]

She is no less eloquent, in her direct, homely way, in the scene among the Priory ruins at her country house, Matching, where she taunts Alice with her "prudence" and again expresses her own sense of degradation in being married to a man she doesn't love (chapter 27).

At her farewell to Burgo, Alice is again present, counselling prudence, playing her familiar, indispensable role of foil and audience. Alice almost succeeds in persuading Lady Glencora to dismiss him without even a final interview, but after he has turned to go and is on the threshold, Lady Glencora calls him back:

> "Oh my God!" she said, "I am hard,—harder than flint. I am cruel. Burgo!" And he was back with her in a moment, and had taken her by the hand.
> "Glencora," said Alice, "pray,—pray let him go. Mr. Fitzgerald, if you are a man, do not take advantage of her folly."
> "I will speak to him," said Lady Glencora. "I will speak to him, and then he shall leave me." She was holding him by the hand now and turning to him, away from Alice, who had taken her by the arm. "Burgo," she said, repeating his name twice again, with all the passion that she could throw into the word,—"Burgo, no good can come of this. Now, you must leave me. You must go. I shall stay with my husband as I am bound to do. Because I have wronged you, I will not wrong him also. I loved you;—you know I loved you." She still held him by the hand, and was now gazing up into his face, while the tears were streaming from her eyes ...

Before Burgo leaves, she allows him to embrace and kiss her. In reply to Alice's trite comment that, in losing him she has "gained everything", she cries: "The only human being to whom I have ever yet given my whole heart,—the only thing that I have ever really loved, has just gone from me for ever, and you bid me thank God that I have lost him. There is no room for thankfulness in any of it;— either in the love or in the loss. It is all wretchedness from first to last!" (II:341–42)

This is without question the first fully effective "tragic" love scene that Trollope had written, and he never wrote a better one. There is none of the theatricality of language and gesture that mars nearly all the "tragic", and especially the love, scenes in earlier novels like *The Three Clerks*, *The Bertrams*, *Castle Richmond*, and *Orley Farm*, as well as some of those in later novels (*Marion Fay*, for example). The voice and emotions remain unmistakably those of Lady Glencora. Almost alone among Trollope's heroines she is able to give utterance to sexual passion without seeking refuge from her shame and embarrassment in the impersonality of a stylized tragedienne's manner. And she is able to do so largely because in Trollope's eyes she is not cast in a heroic role, is not a woman of either great vices or great virtues and not, in her acts and their consequences, a moral "example" from which the reader needs to be advised to take warning. She is not even capable of intensifying and sophisticating her emotions by prolonged introspection. They issue from her spontaneously, under pressure of the particular situation.

If there is nevertheless a touch of melodrama, of sensationalism, in her love affair with Burgo—as there undoubtedly is—it lies essentially in their own view of themselves, and in other people's view of them, as performers on a semi-public stage. This view is most apparent at the dramatic climax of their story, the ball given by Lady Monk at which Lady Glencora waltzes and whispers with Burgo as he tries to persuade her to elope with him. It is the finest example of Trollope's skill in externalizing Lady Glencora's emotions, allowing her actions and the reactions they produce in onlookers to bespeak her inner excitement and the tension of her situation. It is also the culminating example in the novel of the impact of public life upon private, and in particular of the manner in which the characters' awareness of the public gaze upon them magnifies their, and our, sense of the importance of their private affairs. The ball is a gathering of the ruling class, the political elite, of England. They are present in such numbers as to create a crush which at first forms a physical barrier between Burgo and Lady Glencora and subsequently, when they are together, a screen hiding them occasionally from Lady Glencora's "duennas", Mr Bott and Mrs Marsham. The lovers are able to converse only in snatches, and Lady Glencora is so distracted by the crowd and by the eyes that she feels watching her as to be slow in grasping the full import of Burgo's proposals. When she does she rebuffs them, but promises to allow him to see her again later. Her chief concern, once he begins pressing her, is to be rid of him before his attentions become too obvious to the onlookers. But she cannot upbraid him without creating a scene. When, at one point, she reproaches him "almost passionately", she is in effect cut

short by a further glimpse of Mr Bott's watching eyes (II:129). All her subsequent words are spoken "in the lowest whisper", so low as to be "all-but-unuttered" (II:130). The tête-à-tête is abruptly broken off with the return to the ball of Mr Palliser, who has been summoned by Mrs Marsham.

The scene as a whole is operatic in its manner of half-submerging the lovers, with their urgent, muted private passions, in a busy, swirling crowd, of whom only a few are identified, though many others, it is implied, watch the lovers with varying degrees of curiosity. Lady Glencora and Burgo's furtive excitement, their tremulous whispers, are balanced by the less covert but still guarded excitement, and the "almost hoarse" whispers (II:124), of their watching enemies, Mr Bott and Mrs Marsham. And, as in opera, solo voices are heard occasionally amid the crowd, the voices of other principals (like Lady Monk) or simply those of particular onlookers expressing some of the characteristic responses of the crowd as a whole:

> The Duchess of St. Bungay saw it, and shook her head sorrowing,—for the Duchess was good at heart. Mrs. Conway Sparkes saw it, and drank it down with keen appetite,—as a thirsty man with a longing for wine will drink champagne,—for Mrs. Conway Sparkes was not good at heart. Lady Hartletop saw it, and just raised her eyebrows. It was nothing to her ... Lady Monk saw it, and a frown gathered on her brow. "The fool!" she said to herself. She knew that Burgo would not help his success by drawing down the eyes of all her guests upon his attempt. [II:127–28]

Lady Hartletop, we infer, suspects nothing more between the lovers than a tepid and all-but-silent flirtation like the one between herself and Palliser in *The Small House at Allington*: an altogether public and impersonal relationship not very different from the kind that Palliser appears to have since formed with his wife. And the parallel that is in Lady Hartletop's mind is more pertinent than it seems because for Lady Glencora—and, one assumes, for Burgo too—the ball scene does prove the virtual impossibility of a fully private, a merely personal relationship, in the highly public world—the world of public life—that they both frequent.

The same point is dramatized in the scene where Lady Glencora and her husband breakfast together on the morning after the ball. It begins with Lady Glencora in a characteristically defiant and mocking mood. She is not ashamed of her behaviour at the ball. Nor, in her anger at her husband for having, as she believes, set spies upon her, is she any longer convinced that life as Burgo's mistress would be more shameful or miserable than life as Palliser's wife. At the climax of the scene she passionately declares her love for Burgo, her sense of having failed her husband by giving him no children, and

her wish to release him from a marriage that he must find as distasteful as she does. Up to this point he has kept his composure so well that there had been "something of feeling" in his voice only when denying that he had for a moment thought it necessary to have his wife spied upon. But following Lady Glencora's desperate outburst he puts his arm around her ("softly, slowly, very gradually, as though he were afraid of what he was doing") and three times pronounces: "I do love you." He promises to "give up politics for this season" and take her abroad, with her cousin Alice as her companion. Miraculously (as the reader may feel) she is totally disarmed: "He was killing her by his goodness. She could not speak to him yet; but now, as he mentioned Alice's name, she gently put up her hand and rested it on the back of his." (II:232) It is a moving culmination to what some critics consider one of Trollope's finest scenes.[10] But it is also, once we look beyond the emotion of the moment to what has gone before and what is to follow, a surprisingly abrupt and conclusive surrender on Lady Glencora's part. As with some of the equally moving reconciliation scenes in *Middlemarch* (between Mr Bulstrode and his wife and between Lydgate and his, for example), we are left wondering what either party can possibly *say*—after the first gesture of tenderness—that won't immediately sever the flimsy tissues of understanding established between them. Trollope's artistic instinct, however, enables him at once to evade this problem, to deflect the reader's curiosity away from the surprising implications of the scene that has just occurred, and to foreshadow the likely pattern of the Pallisers' married life now that its continuance seems assured:

> ... she gently put up her hand and rested it on the back of his.
> At that moment there came a knock at the door;—a sharp knock, which was quickly repeated.
> "Come in," said Mr. Palliser, dropping his arm from his wife's waist, and standing away from her a few yards.

The intruder is the Duke of St Bungay, who has come to offer Palliser the chancellorship of the exchequer. And although Palliser refuses the offer, in obedience to his promise to take his wife abroad, the "sharpness" of the knock that announces the duke's arrival, the immediate distance ("a few yards") that it creates between husband and wife, are portents of the effect that public life will continue to have on the marriage. The semi-regal state in which the Pallisers must travel on their trip abroad, and the popular curiosity that it naturally evokes, are further portents.

Subsequently, Lady Glencora will develop a taste for such grandeur and publicity, and for politics itself. She will use her powers of persuasion and intrigue to try to advance the fortunes of

aspiring politicians like Phineas Finn and Ferdinand Lopez (in *The Prime Minister*). As the prime minister's wife she will fight strenuously for a purely ceremonial position in the queen's household, and will embarrass her husband by turning his house into a hotel, where all those who may help to keep him in office are entertained with imperial prodigality and ostentation. Finally, it will be he who sickens of public life: of the treacheries and histrionic pretences of political colleagues like Sir Orlando Drought, the importunities of upstarts like Major Pountney (*The Prime Minister*, chapter 27), the scurrilities of political journalists like Quintus Slide, and even the courtesies of old political friends like the Duke of St Bungay and Phineas Finn. He has never cared for the social side of political life, being no sportsman and having no talent for small talk. Indeed, right from the start he shows that he can be extremely rude and overbearing in his personal relationships, with women particularly. Both Alice Vavasor and Phineas Finn's wife (in *The Duke's Children*) innocently incur his displeasure and are snubbed with a brutality that seems surprising in the man Trollope regarded as "a perfect gentleman" (*Autobiography*, p.310). The great dream of his political career is to inaugurate decimal systems of currency and weights and measures, but it is a dream that most of his political associates treat as a joke, even to his face.[11] In his weariness with affairs of state during the latter stages of his prime ministership, his only private recreation is the long rambles he takes with the dowdy, middle-aged Lady Rosina De Courcy, who is not fashionable and takes no interest in politics. And this at a time when his wife, who has long since become the "most inveterate of politicians", is doing her best to rob him of his private life.

Lady Glencora's transformation into a politician has struck some critics, Bradford Booth for example,[12] as difficult to accept; and it does come as a shock to hear her, during one of her earliest appearances in *Phineas Finn*, opining that "the tendency of all lawmaking and of all governing should be to reduce ... inequalities" (*Phineas Finn* I:155). Fortunately, however, she seldom theorizes in this solemn fashion. Politics for her (and to some extent for Trollope) is a social game, a field for sensational plots and feminine wiles; and by these means she achieves at least one major coup, her successful conspiracy, in *Phineas Finn*, against Phineas's enemy Mr Bonteen. The attraction of politics for her is the excitement it offers, just as it is for some of the male politicians: her cousin Barrington Erle, for example, to whom "a successful plot is as dear ... as to a writer of plays" (*Phineas Redux* II:415). It is clear, moreover, that this excitement is her substitute, her compensation, for the other source of excitement that she has been forced, or has felt herself forced, to

forgo. Politics provides an outlet for the energy, imagination, and self-importance that her marriage fails to satisfy; and, to the extent that she specializes in championing handsome young men like Phineas and Lopez, men of some sexual notoriety, it may even provide a kind of erotic satisfaction. Subconsciously, or perhaps half-consciously, she also uses her political activities as an instrument—one virtually of his own devising—by which to punish her husband for his early neglect of her. In all the circumstances, therefore, her transformation is not merely plausible but a subtle and original piece of characterization. Nor is it entirely surprising. Even in *Can You Forgive Her?*, although she professes that she has trouble remembering what has been happening in parliament and doesn't "really care two pence how it goes" (I:283), Lady Glencora is already reputed to be something of a politician. George Vavasor, at any rate, has heard that Palliser "is led immensely by his wife, and that she is very clever", and the later novels in the series certainly confirm George's belief in the power of petticoat government: "Do you think women nowadays have no bearing upon the politics of the times? Almost as much as men have." (I:272)

Following the fall of his coalition government, Palliser for a time turns his back on public life. When he next appears, at the beginning of *The Duke's Children*, he is a widower whose most urgent problem is the management of his family. But although this novel, unlike its predecessors in the series, is devoted almost exclusively to domestic life, although Palliser's retirement from politics and his wife's death have at last restored his private life to him, his punishment for his early neglect of it is not yet complete. For him, though hardly for the reader, Lady Glencora lives on in her children, who embarrass him publicly and privately as she had done. His son and heir Lord Silverbridge not only takes the opposite side to his politically—in a spirit, apparently, of mere perversity—but also becomes a prey to gambling and low company: both vices for which Lady Glencora had shown some taste.[13] Silverbridge and his younger brother are both sent down from Cambridge for breaches of discipline, and both he and his sister engage themselves, without his consent, to partners whom Palliser considers beneath them: Lord Silverbridge to an American girl, ladylike but of no family, and Lady Mary to a clever young Cornishman who is a staunch Conservative and has little money. In reality they are all proper and goodhearted young people, copies of characters that Trollope had long since learnt by heart. Lord Silverbridge and Lord Gerald become a little reckless under the influence of drink, and Lady Mary once publicly flings herself into her lover's arms in emulation of Nora Rowley. But none of them shows any trace of their mother's energy or originality.

Only to Palliser's nervous fancy could Lady Mary's poor but respectable young man appear as another Burgo Fitzgerald, or Lord Silverbridge's involvement with the shady horse-trainer Major Tifto revive memories of Lady Glencora's championing of such dubious characters as Lizzie Eustace and Ferdinand Lopez. Ironically, the cleverest and least orthodox of his children's friends, Lady Mabel Grex, is the woman he would have his eldest son marry.

From a different point of view, however, Palliser is not mistaken in his diagnosis of his problems with his children. It is not only his fear that they may be following in the steps of Lady Glencora but his own personal prejudices that cause him to oppose his son's and daughter's marriage plans. At heart he objects to their marrying commoners, even though such an objection contradicts all his political principles, the whole creed of a gradual advance towards complete social equality that he so eloquently expounds in chapter 68 of *The Prime Minister*. And he is aware of the contradiction, aware that his public life and his private, as well as encroaching upon each other down the years with painful consequences, may actually have been directed, all along, to conflicting ends. If so, then the fissure, the disjunction between his two lives which Lady Glencora's threatened elopement had revealed to him twenty years before has persisted, and the last laugh—or cry—is hers.

In the two *Phineas* novels, written and published between *Can You Forgive Her?* and *The Prime Minister*, the hero's private life is even more public than that of the Pallisers, and its greater publicness makes it more sensational. Phineas and most of his associates appear to live so completely in the public eye that they have virtually no private existence or private character. Although it is a crucial, and explicit, assumption of the novels that living in the glare of publicity weakens a man's hold on reality, including the reality of his own nature, we are seldom given more than a glimpse of either the hero or any of the other characters in their truly private moments of self-examination. And such glimpses as we are allowed, notably at critical points in Phineas's own tortuous career, generally fail in their purpose of demonstrating an inner reality of character. The side of him that they reveal is neither distinct enough in itself nor compatible enough with the outward show to be measured against it—and against all the falsities, the theatrical and sensational illusions, of public life. The novels themselves thus partake of the very imbalance, the very distortion of vision, which it is one of their main objects to expose. Only Lady Laura Kennedy, whom Trollope rightly considered the "best character" in the novels (*Autobiography*, p.274), appears to have emotional needs that conventional postur-

ings cannot express. And her individuality and depth of character are an artistic as well as a moral reproach to the shallowness of Phineas and most of the other characters.

Except during his brief, cursorily reported visits to his childhood home in Ireland, Phineas is never shown as having interests and personal relationships that are not in some way connected with his political ambitions. In London all of his actions, no matter how "private", are either politically motivated or have political repercussions. Even his relationship with his landlady, Mrs Bunce, becomes more political than domestic: her husband is a radical and a trade unionist, and when he is arrested for his part in a demonstration outside parliament, the treatment he receives stirs Phineas's own dormant radicalism. Similarly, Phineas's London love affairs all affect his political career, and each of them is primarily actuated by his need for a wife with the money and social position to ensure him "that political social success which goes so far towards downright political success" (*Phineas Finn* I:175). His order of priorities is summed up in the remark that he "had two things near his heart,— political promotion and Violet Effingham" (ibid. II:41).

Both the narrator and Phineas's own friends are often critical of his seeming absorption in his career as a public man. Indeed he is presented in a half-ironical light throughout *Phineas Finn*, though in the sequel we are asked to take him more seriously. Violet is particularly caustic about his easy amorousness. "He tried his 'prentice hand on you," she remarks to Lady Laura, "and then he came to me. Let us watch him, and see who'll be the third." (*Phineas Finn* II:83) And even Lady Laura, who loves him, expects no very high standard of honesty from him either in love or in politics. Early in his political career she observes coolly that as a politician he is "indifferent honest,—as yet" (I:93), and in respect of his capacity for love she compares him unfavourably with her brother Lord Chiltern: "I believe that Oswald really loves her [Violet];—and that you do not. His nature is deeper than yours." (II:20) To the narrator he is "our hero", but the designation is half-jocular: "Our hero's friends were, I think, almost more elated by our hero's promotion than was our hero himself" (II:59). Phineas is a watered-down picaresque hero, a latter-day Roderick Random or Tom Jones. He is morally footloose, an adventurer whose "fate" it is to "walk over volcanoes" (I:37). He has few advantages other than good looks and a good address; and as Violet Effingham says he is "a little too much a friend to everybody", he "lacks something in individuality" (II:381). At the beginning of *Phineas Finn* the narrator has to assure us that the hero is "a young man not without sense,—not entirely a windbag" (I:9).

The evidence that he is not is presumably his periodic dissatisfaction with his London life and character. Insofar as this is a moral revulsion, and not simply an expression of personal disappointment, it reaches its peak at the end of *Phineas Finn*, when he resigns from the government on an issue of principle—Irish tenant right[14]—and returns to Ireland and marries Mary Flood Jones, his original sweetheart. Previously, though his liberal principles had made him uneasy about his Whig colleagues' indifference to the unjust treatment of Mr Bunce, he had not allowed them to stand in the way of his political advancement. In Loughshane, his first seat, he had reconciled himself to depending on the patronage of a Conservative (Lord Tulla); in Loughton, his second, he had half-succeeded in converting his disapproval of himself, for accepting the seat as a gift from the Whig grandee Lord Brentford, into disapproval of Lord Brentford for his condescending manner towards him; and he had experienced only minor qualms about accepting the equally valuable favours conferred on him by the mistress of Loughlinter, Lady Laura. Each of his three "Loughs" (locks?) had demanded of him a similar surrender of principle and acceptance of patronage as a condition of his political success. Only with his resignation over Irish tenant-right do both his principles and his native pride fully assert themselves. And his marriage to Mary Flood Jones, whatever doubts we may feel about the strength of his attachment to her, is at least untainted by the mercenariness and ambition of his London love affairs.

It also suggests that he has solved the problem of identity that had perplexed him at each crisis of his London life: the sense of possessing "two identities", one Irish, unfashionable, and in love with Mary Flood Jones; the other English, fashionable, and in love first with Lady Laura, then with Violet Effingham (I:401). When in Ireland he had felt "a falling off in the manner of his life" that made him fear that he "had been in some sort out of his own element in London" (II:286). And when in London he had sometimes felt that his life was a "pretence" and that he himself, a poor Irishman of no particular talents and without any claim to mix with high society, was a "cheat" (II:308; I:311). His return to Ireland at the end of *Phineas Finn* therefore implies both a moral rejection of his "public", London life and a discovery of his "true" self.

By the beginning of *Phineas Redux*, however, Mary has died and Phineas is eager to return to London. And although, when he does so, the former sense of unreality soon comes over him again, its causes are different and its moral significance much more clouded. He is still penniless and therefore essentially a careerist. He soon becomes troubled again by what he sees as the shame and duplicities

of politics. But presumably as a result of Mary's death he no longer
feels that he really belongs to Ireland. Nor, though he equivocates
on the question of church disestablishment, is he forced to compromise any strongly held political convictions as he had been in
Phineas Finn. Problems of identity do again arise, and London again
becomes unreal to him; but in his eyes, and evidently in Trollope's
too, the fault is no longer primarily his own. He has become a victim
of the world in which he has chosen to live, which is also perhaps a
mirror of England as a whole, and even of rootless, friendless
modern man everywhere. But, however acute, his feelings of unreality, of alienation from the hollow public world he inhabits, prove
to be only temporary.

Trollope accused himself of a "blunder" in making his hero Irish.
He did so, he asserted, for no better reason than that he happened to
be in Ireland when he "created the scheme" of the novel. He also
believed that he had been wrong in marrying Phineas to Mary Flood
Jones when he had intended all along that he should return to
London. It does not seem to have struck him that Phineas's
Irishness—and his Irish sweetheart—provide the only element of
resolvable moral conflict in his nature, and that by in effect leaving
them out of the second of the two novels he commits his hero to an
essentially passive and static role. He did appreciate, however, that
the new Phineas could not fill a whole novel, as he had done in
Phineas Finn. Hence the quite lengthy sub-plot in *Phineas Redux*
dealing with Adelaide Palliser's courtship of Gerard Maule and Mr
Spooner's abortive courtship of Adelaide. We are meant, perhaps, to
descry in both Gerard and Spooner unflaterring aspects of Phineas
himself. But it is clear that the sub-plot is included mainly to supply
the domestic interest, the private life, that Phineas's story now lacks
almost completely.

The worst effects of Phineas's shallowness, and of Trollope's
failure to recognize it, are seen in the account of his relationship
with Lady Laura in *Phineas Redux*. This is the only one of Phineas's
love affairs in which any real passion seems to be involved, though it
is Lady Laura who displays most of it. In *Phineas Finn* the oc-
casional signs of her love for Phineas—for example, her jealous fury
when he professed to have been truly in love with Violet Effingham
(II:205–7)—had caused Phineas some embarrassment and made
him look slightly foolish. But having herself made a loveless ambitious marriage she had lost her right to reproach Phineas for
wishing to do the same. She had been, she admitted, weak and
foolish in trying to cling to him. Her weakness had been extenuated,
however, by the evident depth of her attachment to him, which
greatly intensified the punishment that she, like any Trollopian

woman who marries without love, would in any event have incurred.

One of Phineas's first actions after resuming his political and social career in London is to visit her in Dresden, where she has fled from her harshly puritanical husband under her father's protection. At their reunion Lady Laura embraces Phineas and gives "her face to him to kiss". But Phineas is "a man far too generous to take all this as meaning aught that it did not mean,—too generous, and intrinsically too manly". What he "remembers chiefly", and with gratitude, is that "this woman had called herself his sister" (I:114). Later, she insists that Phineas take her as she really is, "as your dearest friend, your sister, your mother, if you will" (I:124). And after a passionate embrace she hastens to reassure him that "it shall never be so again" (I:127). By the time of his departure, though she looks into his face "with an unutterable love" (I:132), they are both satisfied that it is that "of an elder sister,—of a sister very much older than her brother" (I:129).

In *Phineas Finn*, Lady Laura had scoffed at Phineas's request that she love him as a sister (II:18). But her acceptance of it now is not to be interpreted as a conscious change of tactics. Phineas's tautological insistence that she is "a genuine, true-hearted, honest woman" is echoed by the narrator's testimony that she is "a true, genuine woman" (*Phineas Redux* I:114). Trollope is clearly at pains, here and elsewhere, to preserve the reader's sympathy for her, despite her error in marrying without love and despite the ambiguity of her present position. But not at the price of imputing blame to Phineas. He, it appears, is so convinced of the fraternal quality of their relationship that he is stunned when Lady Laura, as her husband nears death, shows signs of hoping for a closer one. He had evidently submitted to her embraces, and made "passionate conversation" with her (I:129), without any idea that he might be committing himself, emotionally or morally, in the event of her becoming free to remarry. When they meet again in London, the intimacies that had seemed comfortable and innocent in Dresden suddenly become distressing and dangerous:

> In her intercourse with him there was a passion the expression of which caused him sorrow and almost dismay. He did not say so even to himself, but he felt that a time might come in which she would resent the coldness of demeanour which it would be imperative upon him to adopt in his intercourse with her. He knew how imprudent he had been to stand there with his arm round her waist. [I:419]

In retrospect, Lady Laura not surprisingly comes to recognize that Phineas had never really loved her. She admits to herself, in words suspiciously like an echo of the narrator's own comforting comment at the time, that at Dresden Phineas "had kissed her, and pressed

her to his heart,—not because he loved her, but because he was
generous" (II:267). By now, however, her husband has died,
Phineas is on trial for his life, and her passion for him at last expresses itself irresistibly and unequivocally. It does so, indeed, with a
conviction and naturalness almost worthy of Lady Glencora, and
certainly a good deal more affecting than the tragic pangs of
Caroline Waddington (in *The Bertrams*) and Lady Ongar (in *The
Claverings*), who also pay the penalty for spurning true love for the
sake of worldly ambition. The best example is the scene that begins
with Lord Chiltern's condemnation of her' for admitting that she
loves Phineas:

> "It will make people think that the things are true which have been
> said."
> "And will they hang him because I love him? I do love him. Violet
> knows how well I have always loved him?" Lord Chiltern turned his
> angry face upon his wife. Lady Chiltern put her arm round her sister-in-
> law's waist, and whispered some words into her ear. "What is that to
> me?" continued the half-frantic woman. "I do love him. I have always
> loved him. I shall love him to the end. He is all my life to me."
> "Shame should prevent your telling it," said Lord Chiltern.
> "I feel no shame. There is no disgrace in love." [II:115]

After Lord Chiltern angrily stalks out, his wife takes up his role of
mouthpiece for the womanly decorum which Lady Laura is defying
and which is the measure of her distraught emotions:

> "If a woman, a married woman,—be oppressed by such a feeling, she
> should lay it down at the bottom of her heart, out of sight, never men-
> tioning it, even to herself."
> "You talk of the heart as though we could control it."
> "The heart will follow the thoughts, and they may be controlled. I am
> not passionate, perhaps, as you are, and I think I can control my heart.
> But my fortune has been kind to me, and I have never been tempted.
> Laura, do not think I am preaching to you."

Violet's psychological theories are sunnily pre-Freudian, but it is
worth recalling that she is supposed to be anything but a prude. She
married the wild and bucolic Lord Chiltern against her friends' advice; and in her single days she had boasted, with some justification,
that she would rather have a "roué" than a "prig who sits all night
in the House, and talks about nothing but church rates and suf-
frage"; her preference was for "men who are improper, and all that
sort of thing" (*Phineas Finn* I:116). She had added, however, that as
a woman "I must take care of myself. The wrong side of a post for a
woman is so very much the wrong side." Earlier in the same scene
she had shrewdly prophesied that whereas she would "never go
beyond genteel comedy" herself, Lady Laura would "some day inspire a grand passion", to be followed by "cutting of throats, and a

mighty hubbub, and a real tragedy" (I:111). The "grand passion" is in fact inspired in the wrong man—Robert Kennedy instead of Phineas—but it is on Lady Laura herself that most of the ensuing hubbub and tragedy fall. And in the scene between her and Violet from which I have been quoting her sense of her tragic destiny emerges movingly:

> "And what have I? To see that man [Phineas] prosper in life, who they tell me is a murderer; that man who is now in a felon's gaol,—whom they will hang for ought we know,—to see him go forward and justify my thoughts of him! that yesterday was all I had. To day I have nothing,— except the shame with which you and Oswald say that I have covered myself ... I would become that man's wife ... at the foot of the gallows;—if he would have me. But he would not have me." [*Phineas Redux* II:118–19]

Lady Laura is right. After his acquittal, and after he has recovered from the shock of being a murder suspect, Phineas proposes to the wealthy Madame Max Goesler and is accepted. Near the end of *Phineas Finn*, Madame Max had proposed to him and been rejected. And although there have since been clear signs that her affection for him has not withered, no scenes have been presented from which we might deduce that Phineas is beginning to reciprocate it. It is suddenly disclosed, however, that he "had fully decided that he would sooner or later ask [Madame Max] to be his wife" and that he "had come to love [her] with excessive affection, day by day, ever since the renewal of their intimacy at Broughton Spinnies" (*Phineas Redux* II:399–400). The excessive affection has never manifested itself previously, either in his speech or in his private thoughts; nor does it shine in his proposal:

> "I have come—"
> "I know why you have come."
> "I doubt that. I have come to tell you that I love you."
> "Oh Phineas;—at last, at last!" And in a moment she was in his arms. [II:427]

Such a business-like settling of Phineas's tangled love affairs simply renders them—and Phineas himself—meaningless and inconsequential. Moreover it reduces Lady Laura's wild and poignant passion, and much of the violence which, directly or indirectly, it has entailed upon Phineas, to little more than an excrescence on the novel as a whole. Lady Laura's love has an emotional reality beside which Phineas's and Madame Max's seems unreal, and the unreality is accentuated when the scene of Phineas's successful proposal is placed immediately after his parting with Lady Laura:

> Then she suddenly turned upon him, throwing her arms round his neck, and burying her face upon his bosom. They were at the moment in

the centre of the park, on the grass beneath the trees, and the moon was bright over their heads. He held her to his breast while she sobbed, and then relaxed his hold as she raised herself to look into his face. After a moment she took his hat from his head with one hand, and with the other swept the hair back from his brow. "Oh, Phineas," she said, "Oh, my darling! My idol that I have worshipped when I should have worshipped my God!" [II:420]

The incongruity between Lady Laura's tragedy and Phineas's happy ending is emphasized even further when she goes on to attribute all her suffering to her initial mistake of marrying for ambition rather than love. For it is obvious that, in Phineas no less than in her, ambition has nearly always been at least as strong a motive as love.

That Phineas, in the end, is not punished for his ambition as Lady Laura is for hers presumably implies partly that he has been punished enough already and partly that he has sinned less deeply. Though he incurs no direct penalty for his offences against Lady Laura, and against love itself, he can be seen as having suffered severe indirect punishments: first by being forced into a duel with Lord Chiltern in defence of his right to court the wealthy Violet Effingham, later by being shot at by Lady Laura's jealous husband and becoming a subject of scandal in consequence. For his more general offence of sacrificing the claims of private life, of personal relationships, to those of public life, he in effect suffers the most drastic penalty of all, that of being put on trial for murder. It is appropriate that all these punishments—if punishments they are— expose or threaten to expose him to violence; for each of them stems from expressions of violence, of violent passion or violent intentions, on his own part. And although he ultimately emerges unscathed from all of them, and appears to put them quickly out of mind, the reader is clearly meant to see them as causing him great distress, in fact greater distress than he deserves.

All the physical violence that Phineas meets with—and it was no doubt because he meets with so much that Frederic Harrison found the *Phineas* novels so sensational—is closely connected with Lady Laura. In his first and happiest encounter, he saves her husband from death at the hands of garrotters (*Phineas Finn*, chapter 30)[15] and is rewarded by the opportune offer of the seat of Loughton, which is virtually in Lady Laura's father's gift. He also receives favourable publicity. But in the long term the incident tells against him by associating him in the public mind both with Lady Laura and with violence. His duel with Lord Chiltern, Lady Laura's brother (chapter 38), has little immediate effect either on his relationship with Lady Laura or on his career and reputation, but it too tells against him later, when he is suspected of a crime of violence. He is forced into it, moreover, in defence of his right to woo a

woman (Violet Effingham) whom he has no chance of winning and for whom his love must be mainly pretence or self-delusion. Lord Chiltern, who shares his sister's passionate nature and who genuinely loves Violet, might almost be acting for Lady Laura herself in wishing to punish Phineas for simulating a passion that he hardly feels at all: Phineas had professed the same passion for her, perhaps with equal insincerity.

It is, however, Robert Kennedy's attempt on his life, closely followed by his angry quarrel with Bonteen just before the latter is murdered, that causes both Phineas and the novelist most trouble. At the time of his senseless duel with Chiltern, Phineas had asked himself: "And if he were shot, what matter was that to any one but himself? Why should the world be so thin-skinned,—so foolishly chary of human life?" (I:432). But he does not ask himself the same question when Kennedy shoots at him or when he is on trial for his life, and the novel, surprisingly, does not bring it up against him. Prima facie, Kennedy would seem to have much more right and reason to shoot at Phineas than Phineas had had to shoot at Chiltern (regardless of provocation). But the novel seems not to acknowledge that Kennedy had a legitimate grievance against his wife, and at least a presumptive one against Phineas himself, until after Kennedy's death. And similarly during and after Phineas's trial for the murder of Bonteen, the reader is apparently expected to share to the full his anger at the way he is misunderstood and his true nature traduced, whereas in truth Phineas's publicly expressed wish that he could "fight" Bonteen (showing how little he has learnt from his previous encounters with violence), and his obviously not undeserved reputation for recklessness, would seem to afford very natural grounds for suspicion—would seem indeed to have provoked the punishment he is now undergoing.

At the time when it occurs, Kennedy's attack on him is seen by the narrator and all concerned as the action of a madman. He is presumed to be suffering from a religious mania that has been exacerbated by his failure to make his wife "obey" him. Such is his madness that he continues to treat Phineas more or less as a friend despite his secret jealousy of him. The murder attempt, in consequence, comes as a complete shock to both Phineas and the reader. As Trollope well knew, the unpredictable crimes of mad people and the bewildered alarm created in their victims were familiar ingredients of the sensation novel, and Kennedy's mad act served his purposes admirably: both by winning sympathy for Phineas and Lady Laura—who obviously needs a generous protector against her homicidal husband—and by supplying a means of removing Kennedy from the scene so that Lady Laura can return to England for

her final, and most affecting, moments with Phineas. In addition it gave Trollope another opportunity to expound his favourite equation of puritanism with madness. Its usefulness to him, however, is too blatant not to jar, particularly when it is dependent on the absurd fiction that Phineas's behaviour with Lady Laura at Dresden would not have given a "sane" husband cause for jealousy. Much later, Lady Laura is made to concede that she had "sinned against" her husband by loving another man better than him (*Phineas Redux* II:324), but by then all the emotion to be got out of her innocent but dangerous relationship with Phineas has been exhausted and the time has come, now that she is free again, to make it clear that she does not really deserve Phineas.

Like most such scenes in Trollope's novels, Kennedy's unsuccessful gunplay is presented semi-comically. Trifling mechanical difficulties hinder violent intentions and, compared to its inward stress, the actual expression of fierce emotion is bathos: " ... the mechanism of the instrument required that some bolt should be loosed before the hammer would fall upon the nipple, and the unhandy wretch for an instant fumbled over the work so that Phineas, still facing his enemy, had time to leap backwards towards the door" (I:250–51). Subsequently, Phineas's chief solicitude is for his hat, which remains at the madman's mercy. But after a time "the door of the room above was opened, and our hero's hat was sent rolling down the stairs". The landlady of the hotel where the affray occurs is very frightened, but, being Scottish, does not forget to remind Phineas as he is about to leave: "The brandy wull be saxpence, sir."

The idea that violence is slightly ridiculous, a bumbling and stagy means of expressing emotion, clearly relates to the emphasis in the *Phineas* novels on pretended violence as the source of most of the excitement of politics. Even the most momentous parliamentary debates, such as those on the ballot and church disestablishment, lose their edge when the participants stop "abusing each other", when they no longer appear to "hate each other" (cf. *Phineas Redux* I:360,423). Daubeny and Gresham are rival "gladiators", each with murder in his heart:

> .. whereas Mr. Daubeny hit always as hard as he knew how to hit, having premeditated each blow, and weighed its results beforehand, having calculated his power even to the effect of a blow repeated on a wound already given, Mr. Gresham struck right and left and straightforward with a readiness engendered by practice, and in his fury might have murdered his antagonist before he was aware that he had drawn blood. [Ibid., I:363]

Against this bloodthirsty backdrop the violence that Phineas and other politicians (Kennedy and Bonteen) have to undergo outside

the House becomes less surprising, especially as it is treated in, if anything, a cooler, more matter-of-fact spirit than the merely histrionic violence of parliament. Thus the duel between Phineas and Chiltern is not described at all; it has "come off on the sly" (*Phineas Finn* II:1) almost before the reader has had time to become concerned as to its possible outcome. Even Phineas himself, once back in London, reflects that "the thing seemed to have been a thing of nothing"—despite his wounded shoulder (II:8). For most of his political friends, notably Laurence Fitzgibbon, who acts as his second, the violence and secrecy of the affair make it deliciously diverting, much in the manner of the backstage drama of politics itself.

When Phineas quarrels with Bonteen, his longest-standing political enemy, and is then put on trial for murdering him, the parallel between the excitement occasioned by a crime of violence and that of politics itself becomes even closer and more telling. On the afternoon after the murder, we are told, "there was not a member who did not feel that something had occurred which added an interest to Parliamentary life" (*Phineas Redux* II:101). Before the trial opens the same scramble for places in court takes place as before the great debate on Mr Daubeny's Disestablishment Bill:

> If a man be the possessor of a decent coat and hat, and can scrape any acquaintance with any one concerned, he may get introduced to that overworked and greatly perplexed official, the under-sheriff, who ... will probably find a seat for him if he persevere to the end. But the seat when obtained must be kept in possession from morning to evening, and the fight must be renewed from day to day. And the benches are hard, and the space is narrow, and you feel that the under-sheriff would prod you with his sword if you ventured to sneeze, or to put to your lips the flask which you have in your pocket. [II:223]

Similarly, at the beginning of the disestablishment debate,

> The Speaker had been harassed for orders. The powers and prowess of every individual member had been put to the test. The galleries were crowded. Ladies' places had been ballotted for with desperate enthusiasm ... Two royal princes and a royal duke were accommodated within the House in an irregular manner. Peers swarmed in the passages, and were too happy to find standing room ... Men ... came to the galleries loaded with sandwiches and flasks ... The very ventilating chambers under the House were filled with courteous listeners,[16] who had all pledged themselves that under no possible provocation would they even cough during the debate. [I:354–55]

Phineas's trial has of course an unusual "glory" because of the "social position of the murdered man and of the murderer" (II:183), and not least because a royal prince had witnessed the quarrel that preceded the murder (II:104). Even the prime minister, Mr

Gresham, is reported to have a theory of his own about the murder
(II:105). And Lady Glencora, now Duchess of Omnium, takes as
much delight in the sensational aspects of the crime as she had
earlier taken in Lizzie Eustace's criminal escapades. Her first
response, splendidly in character, is sympathy for Lady Laura: "Only think of Lady Laura,—with one mad and the other in Newgate!"
(II:80) Later she becomes as enthusiastic a partisan of Phineas as she
had been of Lizzie.

What is most remarkable, however, is not the intensity of public
interest in the trial—an interest which Trollope describes and illustrates with brilliant vividness and economy—but the manner in
which the actual horror of the crime, and of the supposed criminal's
predicament, is almost universally unrecognized. The public imagination is shown, as in so many of Trollope's later novels, to feed
only on easy sensations, averting its gaze from squalid and relatively
prosaic realities. No one laments poor Mr Bonteen. No one's
stomach is turned by the gory details of his murder. Few, even
among Phineas's friends, are particularly appalled at the idea that
he may be the murderer. Public opinion, it is clear, makes little distinction, either morally or simply as a matter of fact, between attitudes of violence and deeds of violence; it in effect sees violence
only as an attitude. And the novel in the main restricts itself to the
public view, not expecting us to care much about the fate of either
the murderer or his victim, and certainly not expecting us to recoil at
the goriness of the crime. In the "public" world of the novel even
violence is merely part of the theatrical spectacle, merely an extension of the melodrama of public life. To a politician, "a successful
plot is as dear ... as to a writer of plays" (II:415), and the public's
easy enjoyment of the suspense, intrigue, and violence of a murder
mystery is an obvious commentary on its enjoyment of politics.

During the trial and immediately after his acquittal, Phineas
himself half-sees the unreality of his situation as epitomizing,
climaxing, the unreality of his public life generally. From an old
Latin grammar-book he remembers the sentence: "No one at an
instant,—of a sudden,—becomes most base" (II:164). Yet many of
his political friends and their wives could believe that he had committed murder, that he "had been a base adventurer unworthy of
their society!" (II:216). When alone for the first time after his acquittal, "he stood up in the middle of the room, stretching forth his
hands, and putting one first to his breast and then to his brow, feeling himself as though doubting his own identity" (II:292). He feels
convinced that he "could never again go into the House of Commons, and sit there, an ordinary man of business, with other ordinary men ... never more enjoy that freedom from self-

consciousness, that inner tranquillity of spirit, which are essential to public utility". Twice, in his thoughts, he applies to himself Elizabeth Barrett Browning's lines:

> The true gods sigh for the cost and pain,—
> For the reed that grows never more again
> As a reed with the reeds in the river. [II:293,296]

His melancholy conclusion is that "no life could any longer be possible to him in London" (II:297).

But his crisis proves as short as it is sharp. He does not return to Ireland or even, as far as we know, contemplate doing so. He does not give up politics, but contents himself with resigning his seat and then re-contesting it. Even before his trial his omission from the government after the scandal over Kennedy's attempt to kill him had renewed his revulsion from the falsity of politics, its perversion of personal relationships. Now, when Mr Gresham offers him a place in the government, he proudly refuses it: "the chicaneries and intrigues of office [have] become distasteful to him", and he doesn't "know which are the falser, the mock courtesies or the mock indignations of statesmen" (II:412). But notwithstanding this new fastidiousness it is hinted, right at the end of the novel, that he will soon take office again. The novelist, moreover, is of the opinion that he should. Otherwise he will not have shown that he has deserved his good fortune in having won such a wealthy and eligible wife as Madame Max.

Such an ending doubtless implies a certain irony at Phineas's expense, a certain deliberate devaluing of him as a human being. But it also virtually negates his and the novel's own insights, denies any significance to those moments of moral illumination—especially at the end of *Phineas Finn* and during and just after his trial—in which he did seem to have achieved a real and valuable sense of the shortcomings of public life. The novel in effect robs Phineas of his "true" private identity in order to ensure his success as a public man. In the other political novels—those in which the Pallisers are the main characters—public success is shown, implicitly, to be incompatible with wholeness of life and full human development. And indeed, as my next chapter will indicate, the enmity of public and private life, of the oversimplified, often sensational external view of a human situation and the more tangled, prosaic internal view, becomes a central theme of Trollope's later novels. It is a theme that enables him to make the best of his considerable talent for semi-comic melodrama, and to achieve something of a "tragic" effect, without betraying the limitations of style and imagination that appear in most of his efforts to treat tragic subjects solemnly. In the *Phineas*

novels, however, the melodrama, the external view, is so pervasive as to practically block the deeper, private view against which, from time to time at least, we are invited to measure it.[17]

NOTES

1. *The Eustace Diamonds* is often included as well; but as it is not primarily concerned either with politics or with the Pallisers, I prefer to discuss it separately (see chap. 7 below).
2. *Anthony Trollope*, p.245.
3. On Sadleir, see chap. 4, note 6 above. On resemblances between Trollope's politicians and real-life ones, see *Saturday Review* 27 (27 March 1869): 432; *Daily Telegraph*, 31 March 1869, p.4; *Spectator* [R.H. Hutton] 42 (20 March 1869): 356; *Contemporary Review* 12 (September 1869): 142; Frederic Harrison, introduction to George Bell ed. of *Phineas Finn* (1911), p.xii; Sadleir, *Commentary*, p.418; R.W. Chapman, "Personal Names in Trollope's Political Novels", *Essays Presented to Sir Humphrey Milford* (London: Oxford University Press, 1948), pp.72–81; Frank E. Robbins, "Chronology and History in Trollope's Barset and Parliamentary Novels", *Nineteenth Century Fiction* 5 (March 1951): 303–16; Cockshut, *Anthony Trollope*, pp.241–49; Blair G. Kenney, "Trollope's Ideal Statesmen: Plantagenet Palliser and Lord John Russell", *Nineteenth Century Fiction* 20 (December 1965): 281–85; and J.R. Dinwiddy, "Who's Who in Trollope's Political Novels", *Nineteenth Century Fiction* 22 (June 1967): 31–46.
4. *Letters*, pp.240–41.
5. Ibid., p.355.
6. For a more detailed discussion of this matter, see appendix 2 below.
7. Introduction to George Bell edition of *Phineas Finn* (1911), p.xvi.
8. Henry James, *Notes and Reviews* (Cambridge, Mass.: Dunster House, 1921), p.90; reprinted from *The Nation*, 28 September 1865.
9. Ibid., p.89.
10. W.G. and J.T. Gerould, for example, list it among the scenes that they believe all admirers of Trollope will "unite" in considering his finest (*A Guide to Trollope* [Princeton: Princeton University Press, 1948], p.vi).
11. See especially chap. 55, "Quints or Semitenths", of *The Eustace Diamonds*. At the end of that novel a somewhat amended Decimal Currency bill is on the brink of being passed by the House. But at the end of *Phineas Redux* a similar measure is still only "on the very eve of success", even though the matter has become contentious enough to have helped bring down the previous (Conservative) government. In real life introduction of decimal currency had been supported by Royal Commissions in 1838 and 1843 and by a select committee of the House of Commons in 1853, but opposed by Royal Commissions in 1857 and 1868: it was never "on the very eve of success", though the introduction of the florin in 1849 was regarded as a first step towards decimalization.
12. Bradford A. Booth, *Anthony Trollope*, p.88.
13. Lady Glencora's surreptitious visit to the casino at Baden Baden in *Can You Forgive Her?* (chap. 75) anticipated that of Gwendolen Harleth in *Daniel Deronda*.
14. When *Phineas Finn* was written (1866–67) agitation for tenant right had been going on for a number of years. But the first of Gladstone's two Land Acts incorporating the principle was not introduced until 1870. In Trollope's parliament tenant right is introduced by Phineas's own party less than two years after his resignation over the issue: see *Phineas Redux* I:5. (*Phineas Redux* was written in 1870–71.)
15. At the time when the novel was written there was a scare about the prevalence of garrotting in London. *Punch* offered its readers a "Patent Antigarotte Collar" (with long metal spikes) as the only guarantee of safety. Trollope later poohpoohed the scare in his article "The Uncontrolled Ruffianism of London" (*Saint*

Pauls I [January 1868]: 419–24), but characteristically he was not above exploiting it to provide his hero with the happy accident he so badly needs. (Similar opportunities for heroism providentially befall Johnny Eames, who rescues Lord De Guest from a raging bull, and Ferdinand Lopez, who rescues Everett Wharton from two other London ruffians in *The Prime Minister*.)

16. Anne Thackeray heard Gladstone's speech in support of Russell's Reform Bill of 1866 under similar circumstances. An entry in her diary reads: "To the House of Commons to hear Gladstone's great speech on redistribution of seats. We stood in a cellar under the floor of the House and all I could see were the two soles of Gladstone's feet above my head, while I heard his wonderful voice coming down like a flood through the ventilator." (*The Letters of Anne Thackeray Ritchie*, ed Hester Ritchie [London: John Murray, 1924], p.129.)

17. The virtual inoperancy of Phineas's private character is paralleled, intermittently, in a number of the other characters. Mr Palliser, for example, "kills a stag" in company with Phineas and other politicians gathered together at Loughlinter, even though it is repeatedly stated elsewhere that he neither hunts nor shoots (*Phineas Finn* I:156; *Phineas Redux* II:314,375). Presumably as a representative public man, introduced at this stage simply as an adjunct to the hero's political career, he has for the moment dropped his private character altogether. Lady Glencora appears to do the same when, as I have noted, she enthuses about "equality" in a solemn, official voice quite unlike her own (*Phineas Finn* I:155). And so, perhaps, does Robert Kennedy, normally a man of no eloquence and little moral perception, when he speaks out authoritatively on the immorality of gambling on one's own physical prowess (*Phineas Finn* I:163). Both he and Lady Glencora seem to be speaking for Trollope himself, or for some impersonal moralist, rather than for themselves; and the same is probably true of Phineas and Lady Laura when, in a discussion of poetry, they are made to denounce Byron and Tom Moore in terms hardly appropriate to their own characters (*Phineas Finn* I:151). In a slightly different category is Madame Max, who is introduced as a foreigner—in looks, dress, accent, and above all point of view (*Phineas Finn*, chapter 40)—but who subsequently becomes indistinguishable, in any significant respect, from the English people with whom she mixes.

7 "Both realistic and sensational"

Trollope's subtlest and most exciting explorations of crime and violence are to be found not in the political novels, but in the three major works that appeared during the last ten years of his life: *The Eustace Diamonds*, *The Way We Live Now*, and *Mr. Scarborough's Family*. Each of these centres on a massive criminal fraud which succeeds partly because of its own cleverness and daring, but more because of the general public's willingness to be defrauded, its predisposition to applaud successful dishonesty. The three novels depict a society that often appears to have no gods but money and social success and no pleasures but those to be got from news of crime, scandal, financial wizardry, or social imposture. The gentry are everywhere selling out to adventurers and vulgar financiers. Class barriers and moral standards are crashing in unison, leaving, as casualties, mental and economic cripples at every level of society. Corruption seems almost endemic, and innocence is forced into angry defensive postures that easily become cranky or even crazy. Such is the "way we live now". (And although it is, in particular, the way that London, the commercial and political heart of England, lives, the provinces are no longer as safe from its defilements as Barset had generally proved itself to be. As I have noted, relatively "quiet", rural novels of the same period, novels like *The Vicar of Bullhampton* and *The American Senator*, show deep, divisive passions at work in society; and in *Sir Harry Hotspur of Humblethwaite* the old rural order is in effect destroyed by its contact with the metropolis.)

Though it has become fashionable to do so, however, it is a mistake to regard Carlylean gloom, bitterness, and satirical rage, or a preoccupation with psychological abnormalities, as setting the dominant tone of Trollope's later work. Even in novels as satirical as *The Eustace Diamonds* and *The Way We Live Now*, a substratum of conservative decency persists; and it tends to come out on top in the end. But the tone of the novels is set above all by their comic energy and ingenuity, the excitement Trollope finds in the tor-

tuosities of the human mind, the muted admiration that even the most antisocial deeds of his creatures appear to exact from him. Lizzie Eustace and Auguste Melmotte are great comic creations as well as social portents; and however degenerate the society that spawns and nourishes them, a good deal of its weakness for them, its subversive imaginative sympathy with them, clearly infects both Trollope himself and the reader. So that while, objectively, the world of the novels may often be ugly, vicious, even monstrous, their total effect is neither hysterical nor dispiriting.

Trollope, like James, takes the "great black things of life"[1] for granted, neither wondering nor shuddering at them. He finds nothing unaccountable in monstrous evil any more than in simple goodness. Often it is only a slightly distorted version of the conventional modus vivendi of society in general, and the mental imbalance that produces it is scarcely distinguishable from what seems the normal state of mind. Almost invariably the people in his novels who do the most extraordinary things are in themselves quite ordinary. The sensational impact of their actions, such as it is, is only momentary. They look mysterious and shocking only from without, only because of the superficial contrast they offer to what we take for the normal, the ordinary. Once we look more closely we find their meaning, their moral logic easily comprehensible and quite commonplace. The novels are, in this sense, "at the same time realistic and sensational", as Trollope believed that a "good novel should be" (*Autobiography*, p.194).

The Eustace Diamonds has always been recognized as among the most exciting and carefully plotted of all Trollope's novels. It has many ingredients of a high-life thriller: the strenuous efforts of a titled young lady to keep possession of valuable diamonds that are not legally her own; two attempts by professional thieves to steal the diamonds from her; suspicion that she has arranged the thefts herself, probably in collusion with a lord and a notorious fence; the final loss of the diamonds, reputedly to a Russian princess who has bought them from the thieves or the thieves' agent in Vienna. Out of this "marvellous mass of conspiracy and intrigue" (p.709), Trollope creates a novel that is at once sensational in itself and highly critical of sensationalism—both in fiction and in real life. He also creates a social satire that is not only one of his funniest but perhaps his sharpest and most telling.

Outwardly he makes much of his indifference to the sensational possibilities of his story. In his usual style he ostentatiously "confides" in the reader rather than keep him in suspense. When thieves steal the strongbox from which Lizzie Eustace has previously

removed her diamonds (chapter 44), he assures us in a burst of confidence that—contrary to what we might think—she had neither arranged the theft herself nor had any forewarning of it. After the second, successful attempt to steal the diamonds, he makes a great show of revealing where they are, giving us much unnecessary detail and boasting afterwards that he "states this at once, as he scorns to keep from his reader any secret that is known to himself" (p.473). And whenever he has vital new information to pass on, he is apt to do so with a confidential flourish. It is necessary, for example, that we know the exact whereabouts of the diamonds before the second attempt to steal them, and the disclosure is made with the proud boast: "He who recounts these details has scorned to have a secret between himself and his readers" (p.435). Characteristically, however, all of these confidences leave the most important questions unanswered. If Lizzie was not responsible for the theft of the strong-box, then who was? Suspicion seems to point at her escort, Lord George, and nothing is done to dispel it until the next serial instalment.[2] Similarly, after the successful robbery, we learn that the diamonds are in Mr Benjamin's safe, but not how they got there. As for the whereabouts of the diamonds before the robbery, we already know or can guess it without Trollope's help, and his confidential flourish appears to be simply a means of advertising the importance of the information, hinting loudly that another robbery is imminent: not for him the furtive hints of the expert mystery-writer. He nevertheless took care that in the serial version of the novel the two robberies, the most exciting incidents in his story, should occur at the end of instalments.

Trollope, then, is not altogether sincere in professing to reject sensational methods. But by the very act of openly referring to them he is softening their potential impact. He means us, perhaps, to picture him as at best a rather tremulous and amateurish poacher on other people's fictional preserves, an idea that is borne out by his slighting reference in his *Autobiography* (p.296) to the slapdash way in which he arranged his plot, by contrast to the care Wilkie Collins would have taken over it. It has been argued, indeed, that in *The Eustace Diamonds* he was "consciously satirizing Collins's method as employed in *The Moonstone*".[3] But although there are some striking superficial resemblances between the plots of the two novels—in both of which the owner of valuable diamonds comes under suspicion of having either secreted them or arranged for them to be "stolen" from her—Trollope's most obvious satirical thrusts can hardly be seen as directed at *The Moonstone* in particular. For example, his comic detectives Bunfit and Gager might be taken for caricatures of Collins's Sergeant Cuff, but so, equally, might Bozzle,

the comic detective in *He Knew He Was Right*, which was written before *The Moonstone* appeared. His "doctrine" of "full confidence" between author and reader also antedates not only *The Moonstone* but the sensation novel as a whole. There can be little doubt, however, that *The Eustace Diamonds* is intended partly as a parody of sensation novels in general; and though the parody is not wholly satirical, though it includes elements of emulation as well as of mockery, the mockery is clearly more pronounced.

This is so chiefly because, within the novel, sensationalism as a set of literary conventions is only one aspect of sensationalism as a habit of mind, the habit of mind, seemingly, of a whole society. The story of the diamonds is presented throughout from two conflicting points of view, one of which can be roughly classed as realistic (or, in the novel's words, "materialistic" or "prosaic") and the other as sensational (or "romantic" or "poetic"). From the realistic point of view the whole affair is ugly and pointless, no glamour attaches to either Lizzie Eustace or her diamonds, and the mystery surrounding them is exasperating and morally repugnant. This, in varying degrees, is the view of honest, unimaginative people like Lord Fawn, Lucy Morris, Lady Linlithgow, and Mr Dove. From the sensational point of view Lizzie is a brave and clever woman undergoing cowardly persecution, the diamonds are romantic symbols as well as being worth a lot of money, and the mystery about them is delightful and enlivening. This view is embodied in Lady Glencora Palliser and her set, and up to a point in Frank Greystock and Lord George Carruthers. It is by the value they place on the diamonds, and on Lizzie herself, that we judge most of the characters.

Nominally the diamonds are worth ten thousand pounds, but they have no real money value. If they are family heirlooms they cannot be sold. Even if they are Lizzie's own—if her late husband had intended to make a gift of them to her and had had the right to do so—she cannot sell them; she finds indeed that she cannot even give them away, because her friends consider them too hot to handle. The thieves who steal them lose their freedom to enjoy the proceeds.[4] To the Eustaces they should be valuable as signs of the family's wealth, if not as sentimental emblems; but John Eustace, the de facto head of the family, cares little for either their monetary or their sentimental value. To the family attorney Mr Camperdown they are valuable as symbols of the sanctity of legal arrangements, but it turns out that they symbolize no such thing. To Lizzie they are emblems of her social success, but for this purpose, as the narrator points out, paste diamonds would be more appropriate (p.158). It seems altogether right that in the end, after giving rise to so much anxiety, bitterness, and sensational rumour, the diamonds should prove to be "fictitious" (p.651).

This epithet is applied to them by Mr Dove, whose legal opinion on the ownership of the diamonds—written for Trollope by his friend Charles Merewether[5]—clearly helped determine their moral function in the novel. The law, Mr Dove points out (chapter 25), allows that useful articles such as beds, tables, pots, and pans, and also articles of purely symbolic value such as swords, pennons of honour, and saints' garters and collars may be family heirlooms. But valuable articles like diamonds are recognized by the law only insofar as they can be put to use. They may, for example, be bequeathed to a widow as "paraphernalia"—just as pots and pans may—if they are to be worn by her as part of the dress befitting her station. But although in Mr Dove's eyes the diamonds are a mere "bauble" (p.651), although his classification of them as paraphernalia obviously amuses Trollope, his dry legal mind can also understand—as none of the other characters can—the romantic value that should attach to them:

> "Heirlooms have become so, not that the future owners of them may be assured of so much wealth, whatever the value of the thing so settled may be,—but that the son or grandson or descendant may enjoy the satisfaction which is derived from saying, my father or my grandfather or my ancestor sat in that chair, or looked as he now looks in that picture, or was graced by wearing on his breast that very ornament which you now see lying beneath the glass ... The Law, which, in general, concerns itself with our property or lives and our liberties, has in this matter bowed gracefully to the spirit of chivalry and has lent its aid to romance ... " [p.256]

The explicit contrast that Mr Dove draws here between the spirit of chivalry and romance and the essentially mercenary motives of most of the contenders for the Eustace diamonds reverberates right through the novel. For it is precisely by her appeal to a simulated spirit of chivalry and romance that Lizzie is enabled to hold her ground for so long.

Frank Greystock, her chief stalwart, looks upon himself as her knight whose duty to defend her honour should take precedence over his doubts about the validity of her claim to the diamonds. His knightly duties are his excuse for neglecting his homely little fiancée Lucy Morris. Ironically, however, he normally poses as an enemy to romance. His initial attitude to Lizzie is one of cynical disbelief, and he is rather relieved than otherwise when Lord Fawn, by becoming engaged to her, putatively replaces him as her knight. Later, in a highly revealing scene where he and Lizzie discuss Lancelot and Guinevere (pp.171–72), he upholds Arthur, the "useful, practical man", while she prefers Lancelot, the man with a "heart". To Frank "heart" is simply "a talent for getting into debt, and running away with other men's wives".[6] Subsequently, in a long and characteristic

apology for his hero's shortcomings titled "Too Bad for Sympathy" (chapter 35), Trollope admits that Frank himself is no Arthur. But modern heroes, he insists, inevitably fall short of the old romantic ideals, as even Scott's do. Frank's own chivalric role proves in fact to be very close to that he had ascribed to Lancelot, and it is the expression, essentially, not of idealism but of cynical sensationalism. At the outset he is branded as "not over scrupulous in the outward things of the world", and it is suggested that for this reason his choice of the law as a profession was a wise one (p.32; see also p.117). The evidence is supplied by a scene like that in which, cynically expounding to Lizzie (of all people) his "philosophy" of honesty and dishonesty, he imbues the dishonest man with a panache and a romantic mystery that the honest man lacks (pp.480–81).

There is a further comment on nineteenth-century chivalry in the portrayal of Lord Fawn. In a more distorted form his outlook is quite as sensational and averse to sober truth as Frank's is. He is too chivalrous, too much of a "gentleman", to accuse, or hear anyone else accuse, Lizzie of lying or of sexual impropriety, even when he believes the accusation. And he flinches from any real or imaginary aspersion of his own honour with angry terror (as both Lizzie and Lucy Morris find). For him public dishonour is a worse evil, a more sensational threat, than dishonesty itself.

Lady Glencora Palliser also represents a form of nineteenth-century chivalry in the novel. Like Frank, though more wilfully, she chooses to picture Lizzie as a lady in distress, fighting a lonely and courageous battle for her rights, and she becomes Lizzie's champion in the haut monde. Her motive for doing so is partly to make society obey her whims in defiance of its own judgment, partly to amuse her doting old uncle the Duke of Omnium by adding to the public sensation created by Lizzie's exploits. But at a deeper level it is apparent that she is identifying with Lizzie, sharing the perils of her position, reliving the time in her own past when she too had stood alone against the world in the name of her love for Burgo Fitzgerald. For her, Lizzie's adventures are above all a source of vicarious sensation. They are this also for Lord George Carruthers, who is full of admiration for her until such time as police and public begin to suspect him of participating directly as well as vicariously in her schemes. Indeed, the truth is hardly exciting enough for the police and public, and there is general chagrin when it is found that Lizzie has had no titled accomplice treacherously bent on filching the spoils from her.

At every stage, then, the squalid realities of Lizzie's situation are diluted and sweetened as she becomes a heroine of chivalry or sensational romance. Even John Eustace, whose family she has robbed, pronounces her in the end "a very great woman" (adding, no doubt

with Trollope's concurrence, that she "would make an excellent lawyer" [p.656]). And the narrator, who at the beginning of the novel had been emphatic that she was not to "assume the dignity of heroine" (p.18), becomes so far bedazzled with her as to promote her to it at the end (p.711). The rights and wrongs of her case, seen always in as exciting a light as possible, are debated in the press; shocking and fanciful rumours circulate; and there are even political repercussions, with the Conservatives taking up the cudgels on Lizzie's behalf against the Liberal Lord Fawn when he threatens to jilt her. Manufacturing sensations, in wilful disregard of commonsense and common honesty, has become a nationwide industry.

Lizzie herself is in this respect a typical product and symptom of her society. For it is in her that we see most sharply the barriers that the romantic imagination erects against painful truth. Although she is mostly too frightened to obtain much joy from the sensation she is creating, although it is one of the novel's wittiest ironies that she, who in her imagination revels in romance and sensation, should be altogether dismayed by the dangers that confront her in real life, she nevertheless displays, in the long run, more of the courage of her fantasies, and to this extent more consistency, than most of her audience—enemies and admirers alike.

Lizzie's lying, playacting, and romantic posing are all part of a war on reality. They are her attempt to create a persona that will pass for her true character in her own eyes as well as those of the outside world. Her "guiding motive" is her "desire to make things seem to be other than they [are]" (p.175). To her lies are "more beautiful than truth" (p.719), and her reasons for telling them are often aesthetic rather than utilitarian. So she is not surprised or disappointed when her prospective mother-in-law Lady Fawn fails to be taken in by her performance of the role of dutiful, bible-reading daughter (pp.82–85): acting such a part is its own reward. Nor does she expect that Lord Fawn will believe that her letter rejecting him was really posted before she received his letter rejecting her: "But, with Lizzie Eustace, when she could not do a thing which it was desirable that she should be known to have done, the next consideration was whether she could not so arrange as to seem to have done it" (p.659). Only in her "love" for Frank Greystock is she able to play a part which she finds aesthetically satisfying and which at the same time expresses something like her own true feelings. She clings to him because "there was a feeling of reality in her connection with him, which was sadly wanting to her,—unreal as she was herself,— in her acquaintance with the other people around her" (p.345). Her contempt for dull conventional people like Augusta Fawn and Lucy Morris springs partly from envy. She values her sham friendship for

Augusta because she wishes to be "the possessor of the outward shows of all those things of which the inward facts are valued by the good and steadfast ones of the earth" (p.125). And there are even times when she half-believes that the outward shows might become the inward facts:

> She actually envied the simplicity of Lucy Morris, for whom she delighted to find evil names, calling her demure, a prig, a sly puss, and so on. But she could see,—or half see,—that Lucy with her simplicity was stronger than was she with her craft. She had nearly captivated Frank Greystock with her wiles, but without any wiles Lucy had captivated him altogether. And a man captivated by wiles was only captivated for a time, whereas a man won by simplicity would be won for ever,—if he himself were worth the winning ... Could not she be simple? Could not she act simplicity so well that the thing acted should be as powerful as the thing itself;—perhaps even more powerful? [P.192]

The same anguished cri de coeur is heard later, when she reflects that Lucy is a real diamond—and by way of corroboration Lucy is twice pictured as shedding diamond-like tears (pp.24,174)[7]—whereas Lizzie herself is "paste": "Why could she not force herself to act a little better, so that the paste might be as good as the stone,—might at least seem to be as good?" (pp.584–85).

In moments like these Lizzie recognizes herself as an incurable outsider, a moral outlaw, and in doing so she achieves a certain dignity and pathos, as all Trollope's outsiders do. But in general she plays her game of deception and self-deception with too much zest and skill to elicit pity. Indeed the pose of moral outlaw is one of her favourites; and right to the end, in spite of many disappointments, she keeps alive a residue of her faith in that ideal self which craves only the perfect, though unconventional, freedom of "poetry" ("together with houses, champagne, jewels, and admiration" [p.610]). If the Shelleyan spirit of solitude will not free her from the petty persecutions of society, then perhaps a passionate, savage outlaw, a Corsair, will. Reading Shelley, as she finds in the great comic scene where she memorizes the opening lines of *Queen Mab* (chapter 21), can be an uncomfortable task even in the most picturesque of solitudes. But the poetry itself does not disappoint her. The description of Ianthe's soul "all-beautiful in naked purity" excites her because of the "antithesis conveyed to her mind by naked purity". And in the following lines she prefers to apply the phrase "instinct with inexpressible beauty and grace" not to Ianthe's soul but to the "stains of earthliness" which have "passed away" from it. The "ruin" amid which the soul now stands immortal is to her social ruin, what happens when "people go wrong,—at least women" and "are not asked out any where" (p.195). In part Trollope is satirizing the poetry itself as well as Lizzie, but the nature of her misreadings

brilliantly illustrates his subsequent comment that *The Corsair, Lara,* and *The Giaour* are "a kind of poetry which was in truth more intelligible to her than Queen Mab" (p.234).

For a while she thinks she has found her Corsair in Lord George, who has "no reverence for aught divine or human", who scoffs at marriage vows, and whose eyes "could look love and bloodshed almost at the same time":

> To be hurried about the world by such a man, treated sometimes with crushing severity, and at others with the tenderest love, not to be spoken to for one fortnight, and then to be embraced perpetually for another, to be cast every now and then into some abyss of despair by his rashness, and then raised to a pinnacle of human joy by his courage,—that, thought Lizzie, would be the kind of life which would suit her poetical temperament. [Pp.395–96]

Later she will glimpse some similar Corsair characteristics in Major Mackintosh, the Superintendent of Police who "threatens her with the treadmill" (chapter 71), and in the Jew preacher Mr Emilius, who wins her hand at the end partly because she is not sure that his ardent phrases from the Song of Solomon may not have come from "Juan and Haidée"—than which "nothing could be more opportune" (p.720). Her Corsair fantasy has been seen as a symptom of masochism, of sexual aberration.[8] But if it is this, Lizzie generally has it well under control. She is prudent enough to see that, were she to marry Lord George, he might take to "hurrying about the world without carrying her with him", might do so indeed with another Medora but at Lizzie's expense (p.396). His pose never takes her in completely, any more than her own poses do; and even before he lets her down, by taking peevish, conventional, and altogether un-Corsairlike fright at the threat of becoming implicated in her dishonest schemes, she has come to see that he is "but a pinchbeck lord" (p.457). Both of them—like the public at large—prefer to experience the thrills of moral revolt vicariously.

By the time she agrees to marry Mr Emilius, however, prosaic reality has become almost unbearable to Lizzie. She accepts him almost consciously on aesthetic grounds, in almost wilful defiance of prudence and moral realities. And in the short term at least her doing so is a further "triumph" for her (cf. chapter 72, "Lizzie Triumphs"), a further proof of her ideal self's resilience in the face of rebuffs from fortune and men's eyes. Trollope wisely reserved his account of its subsequent destruction by Mr Emilius for two later novels, *Phineas Redux* and *The Prime Minister.*[9]

Lizzie's loves and wickednesses throw into relief the whole question of society's ability to recognize and cope with passion and violence. In *The Eustace Diamonds* this appears as essentially a question of the value of words. A verbal virtuoso like Mr Emilius can

simulate emotion so well that for Lizzie the thing simulated is better than, perhaps even more real than, the real thing. To her, passion is simply conventional histrionics; and significantly she herself seems real to other people only when she is engaging in histrionics. "When there came to her any fair scope for acting, she was perfect. In the ordinary scenes of ordinary life ... she could not acquit herself well. There was no reality about her, and the want of it was strangely plain to most unobservant eyes. But give her a part to play that required exaggerated strong action, and she hardly ever failed." (p.557) Lizzie's success as an actress shows how, in a society accustomed to verbal evasion, the power of the emotive word becomes absurdly exaggerated.

The same point is illustrated by the extraordinary fear most of the characters have of the word *lie*. Neither Lord Fawn nor Mr Camperdown ever dares accuse Lizzie to her face of lying. Lucy Morris, even in her private thoughts, will not brand Lizzie a liar, but prefers the softer view that "in some matters her friend would condescend—to fib" (p.139). Only when she asks Lucy to give Frank up does Lizzie become an "inveterate liar" (pp.581–82). Major Mackintosh chivalrously reduces Lizzie's lies to "incorrect versions", a locution that Lizzie treasures (pp.617,639). Echoing this, Frank complains feebly after hearing Lizzie's confession, that she has led him to make "so many statements to other people, which now seem to have been—incorrect" (p.642).[10] When Lord George tells her that he may have to break his promise to keep her secret, cynically adding, "What is a broken promise?" she can only reply, "It's a story." (p.573) When Lord Fawn suggests that legal action against Lizzie for the recovery of the diamonds was abandoned only because they were stolen, she angrily asserts that "whoever says so is,—is a storyteller" (pp.553–54). It is only when she is affecting absolute fury that she uses the word lie, as she does to Frank when trying to force him to declare his love for her unequivocally (p.286), and to Lord Fawn himself when trying to intimidate him into renewing his troth to her (p.558). Earlier Lucy Morris had thrown the whole of Fawn Court into commotion by accusing Lord Fawn of "untruth" in stating that Frank Greystock was not a gentleman. To Lucy the "difference between a lie and an untruth" was obvious, but Lord Fawn's outraged response to the accusation had made her perceive that "the less offensive word had come to mean a lie,—the world having been driven so to use it because the world did not dare to talk about lies" (p.259).

Verbal evasion, as Lucy sees, is moral evasion; its rationale is a fear not simply of the grosser evils of human nature, the wilder and more sensational passions that threaten social order, but also of the

most commonplace moral realities. And in a situation where any social peccadillo may be thought too terrible to be called by its proper name, where commotion can be created by the mere use of an emotive word, it follows that real emotions, those which demand passionate expression, can no longer make their full impact by any but the most extravagantly theatrical methods.

This is what Lucinda Roanoke, the heroine of the novel's subplot, finds. When she agrees to marry Sir Griffin Tewett, Lucinda appears to commit herself to passing off a simulated passion as a real one in the same manner as Lizzie. But unlike Lizzie she hates acting and has no taste, even in her imagination, for the cowardly brutality of her Corsair. She has engaged herself to him only because she felt "obliged" to, only because her small fortune is nearly exhausted and marriage is her one means of keeping a place in society. But in choosing a husband she was restricted to the seedy associates of her aunt Mrs Carbuncle, another of Lizzie's jewels, an American adventuress "that nobody knows anything about" (p.422). And even among these people she was "hurried here and hurried there", knowing "nothing of real social intimacies", until she developed "a savageness of antipathy ... to the mode of life which her circumstances had produced for her". She had recognized Sir Griffin as a fool; it takes longer for her to learn "how obstinate, how hard, how cruel to a woman a fool can be" (p.361).

Lucinda has been described as a masochist, inviting comparison in this respect with Lizzie.[11] But if she does gain some perverse satisfaction from the misery into which her engagement plunges her, it is chiefly because no other satisfactions are available to her. There is no reason to doubt her total distaste for Sir Griffin's endearments; nor can it be seen as proof of abnormality, given that Sir Griffin is clearly repulsive not only to her but to nearly everyone else. And while her martyrdom (like Lily Dale's) does give her a moral prestige that she knows how to exploit—a right to hurt others in order to make them acknowledge her own infinitely deeper hurt—there is no lack of evidence that she would avoid the martyrdom if she could. She several times offers to release Sir Griffin from his engagement and does her best to make him wish to be released. She may be deluded in her belief that she could love another man, even a poor one, if she could meet him in a "manner that should be unforced and genuine" (p.361). But it at least points to a sharp distinction between her imaginary desires and Lizzie's. Indeed, in this regard, as in her failure to go through with her masquerade with Sir Griffin and her general revulsion from the society in which she moves (and of which Lizzie herself is a specimen), she is obviously to be contrasted rather than compared with Lizzie.

The more revealing comparison is between Lucinda and Lucy—and the resemblance between their names is of course a pointer to it. Lucy shares not only Lucinda's hatred of and incapacity for shams and evasions but also, though it is less often demanded of her, Lucinda's "heroic" forthrightness and determination. In the episode in which she defies the whole of Fawn Court by refusing to acquit Lord Fawn of untruth she plays a number of Lucinda's characteristic roles: champion of "truth", upholder of the dignity of poverty and inferior social status, martyr to a social code that places propriety above natural love and loyalty, and finally stoical sufferer, too proud to take the easy way out of her suffering. Lucy will not apologize to Lord Fawn until such time as she has completed arrangements to leave Fawn Court and become companion to grim old Lady Linlithgow, thereby ensuring a painful punishment both for herself and for the Fawns—whom, unconsciously, she would rather shame than forgive. Later, in the same spirit, she endures Frank's neglect of her and the tidings of his treacherous attentions to Lizzie with a proud consciousness of her own ability to bear the pain, and of her nobility in refusing to demand explanations from him, that goes some way towards compensating her for her misery. Whatever their other shortcomings, she and Lucinda—and, in a smaller way, Lizzie's companion Miss Macnulty—are the novel's outstanding examples of "natural" honesty and of stoical fortitude in response to society's dishonesty.

Lucy, however, has only Frank and the Fawns and Lady Linlithgow to contend with, all of whom preserve at least a nominal concern for truth. Whereas Lucinda has to make herself understood by Mrs Carbuncle, Sir Griffin, and Lord George, none of whom want to see the truth. Whether perversely or not, Lucinda feels impelled not only to escape Sir Griffin but to make her friends, particularly her aunt, see why she loathes him, why she feels the life she and they are living to be a hell. It is her sense of the moral horror of life with her aunt, not just her aversion to Sir Griffin that she must communicate. Her tragedy is that no matter how plainly she expresses it, her words and gestures make no real impact until they become unmistakably crazed, until she becomes the mad heroine of sensational fiction, or a latter-day Lucy Ashton.[12] Lucinda is presumably the "real heroine" whom we are promised at the beginning of the novel, after it has been explained that neither Lizzie nor Lucy fits the bill (p.19). When she is introduced, much later, the first thing said of her is that her portrait, which had hung in last winter's exhibition, had reminded some people of that of a murderous Brinvilliers (pp.326-27). In the opinion of "a young scamp from Eton", "she's a heroine, and would shoot a fellow as

scon as look at him" (p.328). Even Lord George is confident that if she and Sir Griffin "come to blows", "Lucinda will thrash him" (p.374). But although the potentially violent or homicidal aspect of her heroism is so widely recognized, it is not taken seriously by Lucinda's friends. More than once she threatens, explicitly, that her story will end as Lucy Ashton's had, that if she does not die or go mad she will escape Sir Griffin by "destroying" him (pp.626–27,630). But the intensity of her feelings is not recognized until she repeats the threat on the day set down for her wedding, with a poker held melodramatically in her hand, and then, in the midst of all the consternation she has caused, simply sits mute and frozen, with her Bible before her and a look of "almost idiotic resolution" on her face (p.634). In a world where words have lost their true emotive force, where poses carry more conviction than sincerity, strong emotion can be communicated only by such extravagant theatricality.

Trollope, it is true, usually sees traces of absurdity in the display of strong emotion. They are part of his ironic, unheroic, antisensational view of life. But Lucinda's is an extreme case, and in relation to Lizzie's histrionic "triumphs" a particularly bitter one. After her final breakdown, Lizzie observes airily: "Miss Roanoke has been eccentric, and that has been the long and the short of it" (p.638). Reflecting this lighthearted view of the tragedy, the chapter in which Lucinda's derangement becomes unmistakable is entitled simply "Alas!".

The Way We Live Now, written three years after *The Eustace Diamonds* (in 1873), deals with the same phenomenon: people's cynical admiration for successful dishonesty, their evasion of the tawdry moral realities underlying it for the sake of its surface glamour. But *The Way We Live Now*—Trollope's longest novel—examines the phenomenon both more widely and more deeply. *The Eustace Diamonds*, though it offers glimpses of other worlds, is essentially a satire on the haut monde of London, and for all its pungency it retains a buoyancy, a lightness of touch appropriate to the artificial pleasures of the idle rich. Lizzie Eustace, after all, entertains her world without greatly damaging its moral or material well-being; her career shows up society's existing corruption but hardly deepens or extends it. In *The Way We Live Now*, on the other hand, Melmotte is agent as well as creature of corruption. The infection that he carries is confined to no single social group or habitat but thrives in town and country and among rich and poor alike. It threatens both the prosperity and the moral order of society. *The Way We Live Now* comes closer than any of Trollope's other novels

to admitting the possibility that all existing social institutions may be obsolete and doomed, no longer having any real moral and economic foundations.

Yet although so disillusioned in its vision of modern life, although picturing corruption as nearly all-pervasive, the novel is by no means embittered. Many of its scenes are highly comic, however sombre their implications, and the authorial tone is generally cool and urbane, with few outbursts of anger.

Roger Carbury, the novel's most jaundiced observer of "the way we live now", is carefully portrayed as a man living in the past, in a past so remote as to have acquired, for him, a largely mythical purity. As depicted in earlier Trollope novels, this same past had certainly not glowed with such a moral lustre. In his moated Suffolk manorhouse, so near London yet so rustic, Roger is a lonely figure even among his own order (that of the squirearchy), and it is made clear that he will leave no direct descendants. Economically, too, his is a dying race:

> In the year 1800 the Carbury property was sufficient for the Carbury house. Since that time the Carbury property has considerably increased in value, and the rents have been raised. Even the acreage has been extended by the enclosure of commons. But the income is no longer comfortably adequate to the wants of an English gentleman's household. If a moderate estate in land be left to a man now, there arises the question whether he is not damaged unless an income also be left to him wherewith to keep up the estate. Land is a luxury, and of all luxuries is the most costly. [1:48]

Roger's bitterness, then, is partly that of a doomed social class (to this extent it is shared by his wealthier neighbours, the Longestaffes). And it is compounded when his cousin Hetta accepts the hand of a young City man in preference to his. Both his public and his private circumstances account for his embittered outlook on modern life in general.

Far from endorsing Roger's attitudes, the novel in one scene almost openly disowns them. The scene consists of a brief exchange between Roger and his neighbour the bishop of Elmham, in which the bishop rebuts Roger's pessimism by using the arguments, some of the very words, of an article of Trollope's own attacking "Carlylism":[13]

> "Taking society as a whole, the big and the little, the rich and the poor, I think that it grows better from year to year, and not worse. I think, too, that they who grumble at the times, as Horace did, and declare that each age is worse than its forerunner, look only at the small things beneath their eyes, and ignore the course of the world at large."
> "But Roman freedom and Roman manners were going to the dogs when Horace wrote."

"But Christ was about to be born, and men were already being made fit by wider intelligence for Christ's teaching. And as for freedom, has not freedom grown, almost every year, from that to this?" [II:46]

The bishop's concluding remark, "The world perhaps is managed more justly than you think, Mr Carbury", carries authority in the novel as a whole.

Trollope blamed himself, nevertheless, for having fallen into those errors, characteristic of the satirist, which he had described and parodied twenty years before in *The Warden*. He was, he said, "instigated" to write the novel by what he "conceived to be the commercial profligacy of the age", but he felt afterwards that his "accusations" were "exaggerated" and that the vices he showed were "coloured, so as to make effect rather than to represent truth" (*Autobiography*, pp.303–5). Most contemporary critics agreed with him, the reviewers of the novel in the *Times* and the *Daily Telegraph* being significant exceptions.[14] But while *The Way We Live Now* is perhaps more singlemindedly satirical than any of Trollope's other novels, its satire is seldom likely to seem exaggerated to a modern reader, and there is nothing in its picture of social evils as overcoloured as parts of *The Warden*, *The Bertrams*, and *Doctor Thorne*. Trollope, as usual, finds a few saving graces in nearly all his characters, even in Melmotte, the giant swindler who is the centre and prime exemplar of the commercial profligacy that permeates the whole world of the novel. The few characters who are shown as having no good in them at all—Miles Grendall and Sir Felix Carbury, for instance—are at worst only marginally more vicious than, say, an Undy Scott (in *The Three Clerks*) or a George Vavasor. And following Melmotte's death there is a general purgation of evil. Paul Montague, Hetta's lover, is rescued from the contamination of the City and taken, along with Hetta and their unborn children, under the safe wing of Roger Carbury (who seems in no doubt that his modest means can provide for them all). Sir Felix Carbury, Melmotte's wife and daughter, and the American adventurers Fisker and Mrs Hurtle, all vanish from the English scene. Lady Carbury, the authoress who "touts" her books in the same way as Melmotte touts his imaginary commercial enterprises, and who borrows her laurels on false credit as he borrows cash, is finally rescued from her degradation by the sleek, sensible newspaper editor, Mr Broune. Georgiana Longestaffe is exiled from London and her own worst self by her marriage to a poor curate. And the silly country girl, Ruby Ruggles, at last recognizes the hollowness, the ugliness of Sir Felix in whom, against all the evidence, she had seen glamour, opulence, benevolence, just as society in general had seen them in Melmotte.

The moral norm of the novel's world is not represented by vicious

unprincipled people like Melmotte, Sir Felix, and the Grendalls, any more than it is by inflexible goody-goodies like Roger and his rustic protégé, John Crumb. It is embodied, rather, in people like the serviceable, shrewd, opportunistic Mr Broune and the bishop of Elmham, the goodnatured, lazy, but essentially honest Paul Montague, Dolly Longestaffe, and Lord Nidderdale, and in Hetta Carbury, oldfashioned, decorous, and biddable in everything but her choice of lovers. Mr Broune is prepared to puff both Lady Carbury and (for political reasons) Melmotte, without believing in either; but he is not a knave and certainly not a fool, and he does in the end develop a true, unsentimental affection for Lady Carbury. The bishop of Elmham, though evidently adept at "getting any of the better things which may be going" (II:47), is clearly not to be regarded as a disgrace to his cloth. Paul Montague is as weakly amorous, and at times nearly as gauche, as most of Trollope's jeunes premiers; but he is at least intelligent and straight enough to quickly see through Melmotte and to appreciate the unexciting virtues of Hetta Carbury. Dolly Longestaffe, though almost totally a drone, useless to his family and to society in general, has at any rate one ideal to give him the semblance of a reason for existing: his sense of caste. This has a negative as well as a positive side, leading him, for example, to turn a blind eye to Miles Grendall's cheating at cards rather than expose a member of his own order as unworthy of it, and to calumniate the "vulgar" Jewish banker Mr Brehgert, to whom his sister Georgiana has engaged herself. But it does spur him to unwonted and effective activity when Melmotte fails to pay for one of the family properties that he has bought: Dolly alone is bold enough to hound him, and by doing so brings about his downfall. Lord Nidderdale—son and heir of that Marquis of Auld Reekie who years before had forced his niece, Lady Glencora, into her loveless marriage to Plantagenet Palliser—is willing to forgo both love and pride of rank to win Marie Melmotte's fortune; but he does come gradually to like her and stands by her in the immediate aftermath of her father's disgrace and death. Hetta Carbury may often seem a prig, too good for her world; but her preference for the younger, livelier, less steady Paul Montague over Roger Carbury suggests otherwise. In her superior and censorious moments she is also, at times, shown to be clearly in the wrong, as for example when she opines that Mr Broune has "that air of selfishness which is so very common with people in London;—as though what he said were all said out of surface politeness"; in objecting to this, Lady Carbury for once is on stronger ground than her daughter: "Why should not London people be as kind as other people?" (I:295) The moral of the novel, by no means a utopian or an ungenial one, is perhaps expressed in Lord

Nidderdale's gentle lament for the lost "Paradise" of the Beargarden club, whose members have made it "too hot to hold [them]": "If one wants to keep oneself straight, one has to work hard at it, one way or the other. I suppose it all comes from the fall of Adam." (II:437) Virtue isn't altogether easy even for a Roger Carbury, and Trollope is as modest in his demand for it in *The Way We Live Now* as in most of his novels.

The tolerant restraint that marks his satire also extends to—indeed is inseparable from—his treatment of the more melodramatic parts of his story. None of his other novels containing a comparable amount of potentially sensational material is so unsensational in its total effect; in no others are crime, violence, and rebellious sexual passion more convincingly acclimatized to a generally low emotional temperature. How well the "two streams" of Trollope's fictional art consort in the novel can be seen in his presentation of four of the leading characters: Melmotte, Mrs Hurtle, Sir Felix Carbury, and Georgiana Longestaffe.

All of these, it should be noted at the outset, derive from Victorian sensational archetypes: Melmotte from the criminal who hides his villainy behind a mask of respectability and his terrors behind a mask of prosperity; Mrs Hurtle partly (like Melmotte) from the mysterious stranger, with foreign ways and a murky foreign past, and partly from the ageing and dangerously possessive "other woman"; Sir Felix from the dashing romantic villain who abducts heiresses and seduces country maidens; Georgiana from the young miss driven to rebellious violence by her isolation from the society of eligible men. Trollope, as we should expect, shows them all failing to meet the conventional romantic requirements of their situations, but supplying their world (and the reader) with welcome excitement in the process.

Melmotte is one of the most finely conceived and subtly drawn of all Trollope's characters. For most of the novel he remains a shadowy, half-legendary figure. His reputation for vast wealth invests him with mysterious power. What little we learn about his past and present activities is based on hearsay, and the facts emerge so slowly, so disjointedly that they hardly shake the popular illusion of him as a remote colossus. Some of the early rumours about him prove to be true. It is, for example, confirmed that his daughter is illegitimate, that his wife is a Jewess whom he has married quite recently, and that he has been imprisoned in Hamburg. But most of the stories about his past are neither confirmed nor denied. He is supposed to have fallen foul of the police in Paris and Vienna; and during his election campaign his opponents produce what they believe to be clear evidence of his having been involved in a swindle

connected with an insurance company in Paris. His supporters, however, are able to show that the insurance company in question was actually an Austrian one, and his Austrian exploits, like his American, are never revealed. Many of the rumours that circulate about him must be exaggerated: for example those which credit him with having built a railway across Russia, provisioned the Southern army in the American civil war, and bought up all the iron in England. And apart from the Vera Cruz railway and one or two property deals, we never learn anything precise about even his present business. The very vastness and diversity of his affairs—which he cannot keep track of himself—defies public scrutiny. In the conventional imagination be becomes a figure of almost superhuman immanence and resource; so that one journalist—perhaps with tongue in cheek, but perhaps not—exalts the Vera Cruz ("True Cross") railway, designed to "join one ocean to another", as a work "worthy of the nearest approach to divinity that [has] been granted to men" (I:278).

Until his decline begins, Melmotte is kept hardly less remote from the reader than from the general public. He is not discovered alone for any length of time until well into the second half of the novel, and we are seldom made aware, even for a moment, of what he really thinks when he is engaged in conversation. Even his own family judge him by his "moods" without inquiring into their possible causes. His legendary reputation dwarfs him and screens him from the rest of society; his true identity becomes hidden in the caricature created by his wealth and his secretiveness. Many people feel sure that he is a swindler and some even doubt his money. Everyone recognizes his vulgar brutality. Except in large public gatherings he is socially unacceptable, as Georgiana Longestaffe finds when she consents to be his house-guest. But his magical power of making money, or at least of sustaining an illusion of wealth, can transcend his merely human failings. Whether real or not, his money is seen as something distinct from himself, with a power for good independent of his good intentions. Lady Carbury admires his "beneficent audacity" without any evidence of its beneficence (I:279). Mrs Hurtle enunciates the proposition that "wealth is power" and "power is good" and "the more a man has of wealth the greater and the stronger and the nobler he can be", but takes Melmotte's own "nobility" entirely on trust (I:246). Father Barham looks forward to Melmotte's open adoption of the Catholic faith simply on the strength of a trifling donation made, for vote-winning purposes, to a Catholic charity.

It is not till he has reached his peak of success, when he has begun to "despise mere lords, and to feel that he might almost domineer

over a duke" (I:323), when Lord Alfred no longer feels "aristocratic twinges" at his coarse familiarity (I:330), when he has been chosen to entertain the visiting Emperor of China and to stand as Conservative candidate for Westminster, that Melmotte begins to betray himself. He becomes insufferably arrogant, having come, as we are told, "almost to believe in himself" (II:57). Yet for a long time people continue to tolerate him, and it is only gradually that we are made to see how weakly dependent he is on the illusion of power he has created, how hungry for recognition as a means not only of advancing his commercial success but also of shielding him from his own weakness. In his decline he sometimes looks stupid, irresolute, and vain, so that his clerk Croll can aptly apply to him the fable of the frog and the ox (II:449). But something of the magnitude of his reputation does carry over to the man himself. His consciousness of the greatness of his achievement in graduating from the gutter to the seats of the mighty is not entirely inflated. And he has at least an idea of how he should comport himself under the threat of destruction, at least a glimmering of the duty that his conception of his own "glory" imposes upon him.

The stages in his decline are shown in a sequence of brilliant melodramatic scenes emphasizing the disparity between the man as he really is and the mask that is both his servant and his master. At the beginning of chapter 53, for example, he is discovered alone meditating revenge against Sir Felix for planning to elope with his daughter. Nothing in the glimpse that is allowed of his private thoughts here suggests that he is troubled, and immediately afterwards he is seen behaving with all his usual arrogance, easily convincing Lord Nidderdale that Marie will still be a good match for him, and reassuring Mr Longestaffe that the money for the property he has bought from him will be forthcoming. At the end of the chapter, however, we overhear him conversing for a second or two with his henchman Cohenlupe:

> "I must get that money for Longestaffe," said Melmotte to his friend.
> "What, eighty thousand pounds! You can't do it this week,—nor yet before this day week."
> "It isn't eighty thousand pounds. I've renewed the mortgage, and that makes it only fifty. If I can manage the half of that which goes to the son, I can put the father off."
> "You must raise what you can on the whole property."
> "I've done that already," said Melmotte hoarsely.

This is not the first we have heard of the awkward state of Melmotte's affairs, but the word "hoarsely" brings it home to us. Later we come to recognize Melmotte's larynx as the main chink in his emotional armour: hoarseness is an infallible sign of his momentary loss of self-control (cf. II:255,294,301), and words fail him altogether at his final

appearance in parliament, his most inglorious public display (chapter 83).

In chapter 54, at an India Office reception for the Chinese emperor (who is to be his dinner guest in a few days' time), Melmotte for the first time makes a fool of himself in public, raucously demanding to be introduced to the emperor, and then, when his whim is reluctantly gratified, shuffling past him without a word. (The emperor's "awful quiescence", his ability to live up to his superhuman reputation in spite—as the novel conjectures—of being secretly bored by it, makes him a superb ironic caricature of Melmotte himself: it is even rumoured, facetiously, that he is really a dummy stuffed with hay [II:111], which is what the Melmotte of popular legend in effect is.) But afterwards Melmotte crows to Lord Alfred as if he had brought off a social coup. "Some of you fellows in England don't realise the matter yet; but I can tell you that I think myself quite as great a man as any Prince." Melmotte here is drunk, and this sort of recklessness is not typical of him; but he will eventually see it, correctly, as the chief cause of his downfall. For the reader it is stark evidence that Melmotte's illusion of power is his defence not only against the world, but against reality, including the reality of his own nature.

His growing estrangement from reality is partly to blame for his ignorance of the "horrid rumours" about himself that are gaining currency at this time: rumours of forgery. As a result of this ignorance, he remains unconscious of the danger that his great dinner for the emperor (chapter 59) may fail.[15] In the event, what should have been his most splendid triumph turns into a nightmare as he notes with growing anxiety the absence of many of the people who had clamoured to be invited. He tries, with nagging persistence and in "hoarse whispers", to find out why they have stayed away, asking one friend after another and becoming more and more distraught as he fails to educe an answer. It is a fine dramatic scene, alive with suppressed tension but unnaturally still on the surface. The emperor—"awful, solid, solemn, and silent"—and the empty "Banquo's seats" become terrible in their lifeless immobility, mocking Melmotte's scarcely concealed restiveness. There is hardly any conversation: it is as if Melmotte, the single living creature, were surrounded by ghosts, and the suggested comparison with the banquet scene in *Macbeth* is apposite. (Ironically, Lady Monogram has remarked beforehand that going to a party for the emperor is "no more than going to the play" [I:302].)

The failure of the dinner compels Melmotte to take stock of his position, and immediately after it we for the first time obtain a clear and prolonged view of his private thoughts. What we see is a mix-

ture of stoical courage, far removed from mere bravado, and foolish self-deception; a mixture that continues to govern his conduct right to the end. The resolution to outface his enemies that he now makes is not without heroism, and once or twice later it almost appears that he will have the inner strength to abide by it.

> If he could be there, in one of those unknown distant worlds, with all his present intellect and none of his present burdens, he would, he thought, do better than he had done here on earth. If he could even now put himself down nameless, fameless, and without possessions in some distant corner of the world, he could, he thought, do better. But he was Augustus Melmotte, and he must bear his burdens, whatever they were, to the end. He could reach no place so distant but that he would be known and traced. [II:115–16]

Feelings like these (which inspired one of the best of Luke Fildes's illustrations to the first edition of the novel) will enable Melmotte to meet the electors of Westminster the next day without betraying uneasiness and to continue to face the world with something of his old brashness almost to the end.

Trollope, however, quickly dispels any idea that Melmotte, having hidden so long behind the spectacular facade of wealth and power, having been magnified into a "demi-god" by a sensation-hungry, money-worshipping generation, having presented himself even to the reader as a mysterious and not altogether unimpressive figure, will now be shown in very truth as a man of semiheroic stature. In both of the scenes where he appears in parliament (chapters 69, 83) he will lose control of himself (though his audacity will not completely desert him); and at the nadir of his fortunes his own daughter, whom he has hitherto treated as a mere chattel, will outface him and in effect swindle him out of the money that might have saved him. The scene in which he tries to force her to restore it exposes, almost farcically, his powerlessness when stripped of the air of authority that wealth had given him (II:256–57). It is another fine example of Trollope's mock-sensational treatment of violence. But afterwards Melmotte regains his outward equanimity, losing it only on the last day of his life, when his crimes and his ruin have become common knowledge, and when, rising in a spirit of bravado to make a last speech to the House of Commons, he topples drunkenly over the member sitting in front of him. His final act of defiance is to remain in his place even after this fiasco, not reeling away home for another ten minutes or so. At home he retires to his sitting-room with brandy and water, and is found dead upon the floor the following morning. "Drunk as he had been, ... still he was able to deliver himself from the indignities and penalties to which the law might have subjected him by a dose of prussic acid" (II:319).[16]

Few other major characters in Trollope's novels are dismissed

with such scant ceremony. It is almost as if, having deflated the legend of Melmotte's greatness, Trollope thought his death hardly worth recording. To describe his dying moments in detail would have been to attribute to him an importance that he no longer possesses. But at the same time, by disposing of himself in this manner, before the law can call him to account, Melmotte ensures that the memory of his former glory will not be completely obliterated, as it might have been if he had been subjected to the ignominy of a felon's trial. It is appropriate that he should have withheld his real self from the public gaze—and to some extent from the reader's— right to the last, leaving behind a mass of conjectures and not a little of the sensational aura that clung to his undoubted prowess as a money-maker.[17]

Mrs Hurtle, the second character I have singled out for special attention, is in many ways complementary to Melmotte. Like him she is a foreigner whose past is shrouded in mystery and whom popular rumour credits with hidden, perhaps dangerous power. Gossip garbles and exaggerates her past deeds as it does Melmotte's. In the eyes of a tame, sensation-starved public her capacity for passion and violence becomes magnified in the same way as Melmotte's for conjuring up wealth. Like Melmotte she comes to see herself partly as the popular imagination sees her and to feel that she has a reputation to live up to. But she differs from him, and from nearly everyone in the novel, in that she eventually learns to recognize and accept her true nature, divests herself of the conventionally unconventional mask that she has worn as a defence against the world.

Mrs Hurtle first appears (in chapter 26) as a "widow" whom Paul Montague—Hetta Carbury's undeclared lover and a partner in the Vera Cruz railway—had "once promised to marry". Paul tells her, "hoarsely" (like Melmotte when he betrays anxiety), that he considers their engagement at an end. He had, we are told, "heard that of her past life which, had he heard it before, would have saved him from his present difficulty". Mrs Hurtle, though over thirty, is very beautiful, and aware of her beauty. In no time she has thrown herself at his feet and asked him to kiss her. "Of course he kissed her, not once, but with a long, warm embrace. How could it have been otherwise?" But it is clear that he is no longer in love with her. Initially, all we hear about her, and about her past, is that she is an American, well known on the western seaboard, that in San Francisco she is "regarded as a mystery", that it is not even certain whether there ever was a Mr Hurtle, and that it is known and apparently not disputed that she "had shot a man through the head somewhere in Oregon".

In their first conversation Paul tells her about Melmotte, of whom

she speaks with enthusiasm, comparing him to a Washington, a Napoleon, a "great general" who "rises above humanity" and whose "greatness is incompatible with small scruples" (I:245–46). Paul strongly disagrees. But when the conversation returns, inevitably, to the subject of his former promise to her—which he now wishes to break—she mockingly recalls his righteous disapproval of Melmotte: "And you are the man who cannot bear to hear me praise Augustus Melmotte because you think him dishonest!" (I:249). She then accuses him, twice, of being a liar, tells him that she has passed herself off to her landlady as his fiancée, and makes him promise to visit her again.

Later in the novel he takes her to a play and they discuss the heroine. Mrs Hurtle feels that in real life she would not have wept openly for her lost love as she did on the stage:

> "A woman hides such tears. She may be found crying because she is unable to hide them;—but she does not willingly let the other woman see them. Does she?"
> "I suppose not."
> "Medea did not weep when she was introduced to Creusa."
> "Women are not all Medeas," he replied.
> "There's a dash of the savage princess about most of them." [I:261]

Afterwards we find her telling Paul of her hatred for "what your women call propriety" (I:262), preparing us for the ardour with which she takes her farewell of him after he has seen her to her lodgings. It is already clear that she is passionate, masterful, perhaps violent. But to Paul, and to the reader, her foreignness (of which she makes much) and her alternating poses of "savage princess" and timid, defenceless widow continue to make her disturbing and unpredictable. The "detective's work" of trying to throw more light on her past is "very distasteful" for Paul (I:357), but he must go on with it if he is to free himself. A friend in Liverpool tells him of a report that she is a "queer card", with "a bit of the wild cat in her breeding" (I:355). According to one story she had fought a duel with her husband before separating from him, and he is still alive. (Towards the end it will emerge not only that he is still alive, but also that the legality of her divorce from him—obtained in Kansas—may be in question.) These stories, along with her outbursts of verbal violence ("liar") and her contempt for English propriety, make Paul understandably apprehensive lest he should "incur the fate of the gentleman in Oregon" (I:357).

In the showdown between them, at a hotel in Lowestoft to which she has lured him, Mrs Hurtle seems on the verge of justifying her wildcat reputation (chapter 47). As Paul begins to explain why they must part, her hand clasps a knife that lies on the table beside her.

But for the moment she finds that her tongue can stab as sharply. She admits the truth of the stories about her past, admits that she had shot the man in Oregon and defended herself from her husband with a gun, but insists that on both occasions such measures were necessary. "In this soft civilization of yours you know nothing of such necessity." Paul can see this, and can sympathize. But he can be forgiven for feeling, after hearing of her exploits, that "any ordinary man might well hesitate before he assumed to be her master". He is more than ever convinced that a marriage with her would not suit and gently tells her so. At this she again reaches for the knife, but restrains herself, choosing instead to dismiss him. "My last word to you is, that you are—a liar ... Ten minutes since, had I had a weapon in my hand I should have shot another man." Paul reflects uneasily that it must be "her custom to have a pistol with her" and thankfully makes his escape.

It is one of those near-sensational scenes in which Trollope specializes, scenes in which the descent into violence seems to be blocked by his sense of the absurdity of the situation. In this instance it is Paul's thoughts that register the absurdity: though half-afraid of her, he cannot take her quite seriously, cannot fully believe that passions so exotic and language so excited can have anything to do with him. But in truth, as she shows straight after he has gone, Mrs Hurtle is no fonder of "violence and rough living and unfeminine words" than he is; like most Americans she feels an "almost envious admiration of English excellence"; "to live the life of an English lady would have been heaven to her" (I:449–50). And although she subsequently meditates horsewhipping Paul—or at least threatening to do so—and continues to batter him verbally, gentler feelings prevail in the end. She comes to his rescue when the news of his former relationship with her leads Hetta to spurn him, and in their last farewell, before her return to America, she resists the desire to reproach him and behaves with real dignity.

What makes her so impressive in the novel is not only the mystery, the unresolved contradictions, that surround her for so long, but also the force with which, despite her exoticism, she expresses feelings that nearly all women can share. Her power over Paul—such as it is—illustrates the power of illusion over the conventional mind as surely as does Melmotte's popular fame. But the sensational illusion of herself which she presents, half at the dictate of her unsavoury reputation, does correspond to something real in her own and in every woman's nature. Though not really the savage princess, the wildcat that she seems, she expresses in her atavistic pose a resentment against male domination that must have been shared by many women too proper to acknowledge it. No doubt

there is something preposterous in her threat to horsewhip Paul, but
her defence of herself when he taxes her with the impropriety of the
threat is unanswerable:

> "It is certainly more comfortable for gentlemen,—who amuse
> themselves,—that women should have that opinion. But, upon my word,
> I don't know what to say about that. As long as there are men to fight for
> women, it may be well to leave the fighting to the men. But when a
> woman has no one to help her, is she to bear everything without turning
> upon those who ill-use her? Shall a woman be flayed alive because it is
> unfeminine in her to fight for her own skin? What is the good of being
> feminine—feminine, as you call it? Have you asked yourself that? That
> men may be attracted I should say. But if a woman finds that men only
> take advantage of her assumed weakness, shall she not throw it off? If
> she be treated as prey, shall she not fight as a beast of prey? Oh no;—it is
> so unfeminine!" [II:8]

This tirade could have come equally well from the Signora Neroni,
Lady Laura Kennedy, or (in *The Way We Live Now* itself) Marie
Melmotte; and it is validated, given authority, by the widespread
evidence, in many of Trollope's novels, that modern man has
become too effete to protect his womenfolk as he ought.

Mrs Hurtle makes a sensational impact in the novel partly for the
same reason as Lady Laura does in *Phineas Redux* and Lucinda in
The Eustace Diamonds: because she is a woman of powerful but by
no means ignoble passions in a world afraid of passion.[18] In *The Way
We Live Now* the only characters who express themselves with any
real emotional conviction are Mrs Hurtle, Roger Carbury, John
Crumb, and, in his drunken and violent moments, Melmotte. It is
significant that both Mrs Hurtle and Roger are in love with people
who prefer more tepid lovers. No doubt Hetta and Paul are well
matched, as Mrs Hurtle and Paul or Roger and Hetta would not be.
Hetta's tameness is such that it is an adventure for her to "[trust]
herself all alone to the mysteries of the Marylebone underground
railway" (II:385); her Oregon (or Vera Cruz?) is King's Cross.

Sir Felix Carbury, the most despicable person in the novel, is in
many respects a miniature Melmotte. He is, like Melmotte, a confidence trickster, but his victims are not greedy, gullible men of the
world but romantic young women. The illusions they form about
him enable him to exploit them, partly for mercenary reasons, partly
to gratify his own vanity, just as Melmotte exploits his victims. To
Sir Felix, as to Melmotte and the world at large, there is an excitement in the idea of dishonesty that makes it pleasurable in itself,
regardless of rewards. But like Melmotte, only far more ig-
nominiously, he fails to live up to his own idea of himself. The
Beargarden club, where he plays cards and carries on what he calls
the "game" of living, is to him what Abchurch Lane and the Stock

Exchange are to Melmotte. He lives by gambling, as Melmotte does, and when he wins, as Nidderdale remarks, "he goes on as though he were old Melmotte himself", notwithstanding that he plays "without a rap to back him" (I:359). Like Melmotte, Sir Felix becomes reckless and finally disgraces himself under the influence of drink. The Beargarden circle is ruined by the levanting of Vossner, who had kept it in funds, just as Melmotte is by the levanting of his partner Cohenlupe.

The "great enterprise" of Sir Felix's life is to marry Melmotte's daughter Marie. But he displays none of the zeal one would expect from a gambler playing for such high stakes. The wooing is "weary work" and he gets through it only by studying his words and looks and "repeating them as a lesson" (I:43). But the heiress, a reader of romantic novels who has hitherto been starved of affection, unexpectedly conceives the idea that she is in love with him. In her eyes the romance of the affair is heightened by her father's opposition. But "romance" is not Sir Felix's "game" (I:223), and he regards Melmotte's opposition as a fatal obstacle until Marie tells him of the fortune her father has made over to her as a precaution against bad times. She will share this with Sir Felix if he will elope with her. To his alarm she suddenly reveals a guile and resolution much superior to his own. Her plan to swindle her father fills him with admiration, opening his eyes to the possibilities of dishonesty in somewhat the same way as his detection of Miles Grendall's cardsharping. He finds he can no more resist her plans for him than he had been able, earlier, to resist Melmotte's own.

Marie's mixture of moonstruck innocence, courage, and practical efficiency looks ahead to that of the typical Jamesian innocent: what she "knew" is no less surprising than what James's Maisie or even Maggie Verver "knew"; her corrupt knowledge makes her just as formidable and is just as hard to reconcile with her large residual innocence. She is one of Trollope's best ironical character studies. Like Dolly Longestaffe and Lord Nidderdale, she has the function in the novel of revealing the strength of innocence in a world where it is so little understood as to be credited with no judgment and no capacity for action at all. This is shown not only by her easy mastery of Sir Felix but also by the courage and calculation with which she defies her father, deliberately provoking him to violence on two occasions (chapters 29, 77) as a means of diverting him from his purpose. Later, after Sir Felix has finally failed her, she coolly throws in her lot with the American adventurer Fisker but makes it clear that she will hang on to her own money.

Sir Felix's callow subservience to Marie at the time when she is making arrangements for their elopement shows how little he is cut

out for a hero of romance. But the project would have failed even if
he had been capable of playing his part. As Sir Felix himself laments
(I:460), eloping is no longer so easy as in the days when Gretna
Green offered safety.[19] Amorous fugitives must now escape abroad.
But to do so they must be faster and more secret than the telegraph:
for Melmotte is able, without stirring from his own London hearth,
to have his daughter stopped at Liverpool simply by telegraphing.
"Who," the narrator wonders, "is benefited by telegrams? The newspapers are robbed of all their old interest, and the very soul of intrigue is destroyed." (I:471) Melmotte's is that unheroic, unromantic world of "telegrams and anger" which half-attracts and half-
repels the Schlegel sisters in E.M. Forster's *Howard's End*. But it is
not only the machine but man himself that stands in the way of
romance—as we see when we meet Sir Felix, on the morning he
should have travelled to Liverpool, staggering home blind drunk,
having lost at cards all the money Marie had given him to take her to
America. "The old shap'sh stopped ush," he tells his mother, instinctively giving the traditional romantic explanation (I:478). But
he had never got further on his way to Liverpool than the
Beargarden.

His other romantic adventure comes to a similarly unheroic end.
Ruby Ruggles, the simple farm lass from Suffolk, is like Marie an
avid reader of novels—"thrice-thumbed old novels"—and lives
equally in "ignorance as to the reality of things". As women of her
class (that of Hetty Sorrel) and of a slightly higher class (that of the
Brangwen women in *The Rainbow*) are wont to do, she "builds
castles in the air, and wonders, and longs"; she "is better educated,
has higher aspirations and a brighter imagination" than the men
around her, and "if she be good-looking and relieved from the pressure of want, her thoughts soar into a world which is as unknown to
her as heaven is to us". In her eyes the young squire of the
neighbourhood is "an Apollo" (I:170). For his part Sir Felix pursues
her simply because he thinks it the "proper sort of thing for a young
man to do" (I:173). There is no great reward at stake here, and,
since her romantic dreams of love and ease promise to make her a
ready prey, no great challenge. Picturing himself in the role of conventional romantic villain, he never doubts that she will play her
corresponding role of hapless, helpless victim. But this affair, too,
ends in anticlimax. As he endeavours to drag her off to a bed of sin in
sordid Islington, her rejected lover John Crumb hears her screams,
rushes to the rescue, and beats the would-be villain's face to a pulp.
After this disgrace Sir Felix skulks around London for a while, then
allows himself to be shipped off to Germany (at sensible Mr
Broune's insistence) to join Burgo Fitzgerald in ignominious exile.

If Sir Felix Carbury is Trollope's typically shabby version of the conventional romantic villain, Georgiana Longestaffe is his most notable satirical comment on another stock figure of sensational fiction: the female rebel. As such, she offers obvious parallels to both Mrs Hurtle and Marie Melmotte. Her passions, like those of the French sisters in *He Knew He Was Right*, are in part a burlesque of those of more "serious" characters in the novel. But although essentially a comic character, she is presented a good deal more realistically than the French sisters had been—with much more restrained humour, and more concentration on what is socially typical, and socially portentous, in her character and situation.

The Longestaffes in many respects recall the De Courcys. Like the De Courcys they first came to prominence under the Whigs (though they are now Tories), and their Whiggish values and lifestyle are contrasted unfavourably with the more antique and unpretentious ways of their neighbour Roger Carbury, whose family has held land in Suffolk since (at the latest) the Wars of the Roses. They are to him as the De Courcys were to the Greshams and Thornes, as West Barset was to East. Significantly, however, the Longestaffes, with all their gross faults, are not nearly as harshly satirized as the De Courcys had been.[20] Mr Longestaffe, though mean, silly, haughty, and irascible, at least has glimmerings of selfrespect and of genuine pride. The prejudice against Jews which Georgiana's shortlived engagement to one brings into play is shown to be antiquated and unfair, and in the showdown between them the Jew in question, Brehgert, clearly looks a better man and a better gentleman than Longestaffe himself (II:361–63). But although it hardly squares with his willingness to use Jews to help him out of his social and financial difficulties, Longestaffe's prejudice is at least consistent with his general Conservatism: " ... if he had ever earned for himself the right to be called a Conservative politician by holding a real opinion of his own,—it had been on that matter of admitting the Jews into parliament" (II:93). His social exclusiveness, however misguided, is preferable to the indifference of Lord De Courcy, who seems not to care whom his daughters marry as long as he is relieved of the expense of them.

The Longestaffe girls, like the De Courcy ones, set their matrimonial sights too high and then, when their youthful bloom has faded, find that they must marry beneath them or not at all. "Love", as Lady Carbury explains to her daughter, "is like any other luxury. You have no right to it unless you can afford it. And those who will have it when they can't afford it, will come to the ground like this Mr. Melmotte." (II:326) But equally, as the Longestaffe and De Courcy girls discover, a woman who looks upon

marriage merely as an investment must beware of overreaching herself, living on credit (in the form of rank and stateliness) until her tangible assets, her womanly attractions, are exhausted. Georgiana has nearly reached this stage when her father announces that his powdered footmen and his family's extravagance have left him without the means to keep his London house open for the rest of the season. He breaks the news with a sense of crisis and is gratified when it is received with hysterical dismay, his wife weeping, his elder daughter screaming, and Georgiana threatening outright rebellion (I:123). Later he relents, agreeing that he will bring them back to London if they will stoop to entertain the Melmottes at Caversham, his country seat. But once the Melmottes have left Caversham he renegues on his promise. Georgiana's passion now knows no bounds. She makes the "horrid" threat that she will marry a London tradesman rather than accept permanent exile to the country. She charges her father, to his face, with premeditated treachery. Casting him, appropriately, in the role of a defaulting Melmotte, she insists that she is "not going to be cheated and swindled and have her life thrown away into the bargain" (chapter 21).

Apart from a few of Mrs Hurtle's outbursts, there is nothing in the novel to equal the violence of emotion, or at least of emotional language, aroused by Georgiana's engagement to Brehgert. Even Georgiana can justify herself only by blaming it on the sensational breakdown of the whole social order to which she had been accustomed. For her father to be unable to keep up his London house, everything must be "upset and at sixes and sevens"; it is clear to her that "things have got so that they never will be nice again" (II:140-41). But this tragic view of her plight cuts no ice with Mr Longestaffe. In his eyes Georgiana is "degraded and disgraced" by the engagement. To her mother the proposed marriage is "unnatural" since the Jews are an "accursed race;—think of that, Georgiana;—expelled from Paradise". Her brother Dolly would keep her Lovelace at bay by having her father "lock her up" (II:263,266). There is universal relief, but no real forgiveness, when she breaks off the engagement (upon hearing that Mr Brehgert will not, after all, be able to offer her a house in town).

Georgiana's escape from what all her friends regard as a tragic misalliance parallels the rescue of Ruby Ruggles from Sir Felix and of Paul Montague from Mrs Hurtle. Though not an unambiguously happy ending, it at least represents a consolidation of English genteel values, and of the caste system upon which they are based, in the face of a threat from both within and without. Whether much remains in these values that is really worth preserving, the novel as a

whole leaves in doubt, and it was presumably his feeling that this was so that caused Trollope to accuse himself of satirical exaggeration.[21] But at less exalted levels of society—those of Paul and Hetta, John Crumb and Ruby, even Lady Carbury and Mr Broune—the novel shows that some worthwhile values do persist, however precariously.

In *Cousin Henry* and *Mr. Scarborough's Family* the laws, beliefs, and personal values which the landed gentry see as the foundation of their property and privileges come under attack even more directly than in *The Way We Live Now.* Again, old and sacrosanct institutions are made to yield to new, and law and truth are shown to be easily subvertible by fraud, malice, tacit dishonesty, or mere accident. Yet Trollope's sympathy and understanding enfold the sinners at least as warmly as the saints, and his sadness at the spectacle of human weakness and social decay is lightened by his usual mildly cynical resignation.

Cousin Henry deals with the consequences of a landed proprietor's vacillation between affection and duty. Affection inclines him to leave his estate to his niece, a girl in every respect fit to be lady of the manor. Duty, in the form of his reverence for the "religion" of primogeniture (p.9), tells him that his nephew, a sly, shambling London clerk, should be his heir. Like Sir Harry Hotspur, he thinks to solve his problem by marrying the beloved niece to the nephew. But whereas Emily Hotspur had responded by falling in love with her cousin—all too avidly—Isobel Brodrick detests hers and flatly refuses him. Thereafter the two stories diverge completely. Emily fades away and dies a pathetic death when her lover proves faithless and unprincipled. Isabel, however, doesn't repine even when her cousin Henry is unexpectedly found to be the heir after her uncle's death; nor does Cousin Henry turn out an absolute scoundrel in order to throw her nobility into relief. The novel in fact becomes primarily a study of Henry's failure, because of conscientious scruples, superstitious fears, and social timidity, to prove himself a scoundrel. To do so he must destroy his uncle's lost last will, of which he alone knows the whereabouts. This will had named Isabel as heir after all. Henry's transparent guiltiness eventually leads to its discovery and his dispossession.

The novel's sustained and compelling analysis of Henry's torture of guilt, indecision, and boredom is one of Trollope's finest characterizations. It is remarkable particularly for its compassion and for its restrained and natural exploitation of the sensational possibilities of Henry's situation.[22] Henry is the son of a gambler and a divorcee. He is sly and untruthful and had been sent down from Ox-

ford "for some offence not altogether trivial" (p.8). It is only by a quibble that he can maintain to himself that he has not actually hidden the will, and it is as much his cowardice as his conscience that prevents him from destroying it. Perhaps even more to the point, he has neither the looks, the "feelings", nor the avocations of a gentleman. In the remote, rustic, hierarchical society of Carmarthenshire he is altogether an intruder, snubbed by most and disliked by all of his neighbours. Both what he is and what he stands for are despicable, if not detestable. Yet the novel's scrutiny of him, close and relentless as it is, never appears either cruel or prejudiced. It has the merit of allowing us, consistently and without authorial intrusion, to see him as he sees himself, and it is for this reason, as much as for his lack of evil willpower, that he escapes all the cliché phrases and postures of villainy—or of temptation to villainy—that entrap many of his predecessors in Trollope's novels. The novel ends, indeed, with a readily acceptable plea for compassion towards him, even though he had attempted illegally to retain possession of an estate valued at fifteen hundred pounds a year. It also allows him to retreat unpunished to London where his "wicked deeds" remain unknown and where he will have for consolation the four thousand pounds his uncle did intend him to inherit.

No doubt pity is more easily enlisted for an isolated, ineffectual villain like Henry than for a more socially representative and more practised one like Melmotte or Lopez. But the novel by no means encourages us to underestimate the gravity of the crime which Henry almost commits, that of destroying the will. To the lawyer who finally discovers the will it would be an "atrocity" (p.178), a "deed of darkness" (p.160), to Isabel a "deed of hideous darkness" (p.75). Henry himself is haunted by the conviction that God and nature will never allow his guilt to remain hidden. All he need do to make himself safe is destroy the volume of Jeremy Taylor's sermons in which, with Henry's help, the will had concealed itself. He does not dare to remove the will from the book, for to do so would be to show that he had known all along where it was. But if he were to bury the book, or sink it in a well or in the sea, "it would surely reappear by one of those ever-recurring accidents which are always bringing deeds of darkness to the light" (p.97). His imagination darts uneasily between fears of damnation, fears of worldly disgrace, and what seem like troubled recollections of sensation and Gothic novels (and he is, after all, isolated on a Celtic shore that might well remind him of the setting of some of Melmoth's and Frankenstein's ordeals):

> He dreamt that he was out there in a little boat all alone, with the book hidden under the seats, and that he rowed himself out to sea till he was

so far distant from the shore that no eye could see him. Then he lifted the book, and was about to rid himself for ever of his burden;—when there came by a strong man swimming. The man looked up at him so as to see exactly what he was doing, and the book was not thrown over, and the face of the swimming man was the face of that young Cantor [a neighbouring farmer's son] who had been so determined in his assertion that another will had been made. [P.113]

Later, Henry does almost steel himself to burn the will, but again his nerve fails him. The light of his candle looks to him like hellfire and he would rather face even the terrible Mr Cheekey, the barrister who is to try to wrest his secret from him, than "those eternal flames". At the moment of decision he is Macbeth manqué, frozen by the knowledge that "when done, it could not be undone!" (p.233). There is, then, enough of the sensational in his own view of the situation, as well as in other people's. But the tone of the novel, like that of all Trollope's best novels, remains sober, faintly ironical, at once detached and sympathetic.

Mr. Scarborough's Family is the most memorable expression of the fertile restlessness of Trollope's imagination during the last five years of his life. In other novels, notably *John Caldigate* and *The Landleaguers*, this restlessness shows itself in his return to exotic, adventurous settings such as he had favoured in his earliest, experimental work. In *Marion Fay* he tries his hand at a style of sentimental romance quite new to him, and in *The Fixed Period* he ventures even further afield, into an imaginary country in the distant future. But the marvellous exploits of Mr Scarborough, an English gentleman living very much in the here and now, represent without question the most original, most challenging, and most fully achieved work of his old age.

Mr Scarborough is by any standard an exceptional character. The *Saturday Review* felt him to be "original almost to incredibility" and wondered whether Trollope "did not outrage the canons of his art in seeking to impose on our intelligence such a caricature of humanity", yet admitted that Scarborough "wins us, with most of the people who come about him, in a measure over to his own way of thinking".[23] Contemporary reviewers also remarked upon the daring "ingenuity" of the novel's main plot, which consists, essentially, of the series of acts Mr Scarborough performs with a view to safeguarding his vast property after his death. First he disinherits his wastrel elder son Mountjoy by producing bogus evidence of his illegitimacy (a "marriage" with Mountjoy's mother after Mountjoy's birth). Then he persuades the Jews to accept repayment of the actual sums they had lent Mountjoy, without the vastly larger interest charges which would have swallowed up the whole estate when it

came into Mountjoy's possession. And finally, almost on his deathbed, he restores Mountjoy to the heirship by revealing that he and Mountjoy's mother had in fact been married twice, once before and once after Mountjoy's birth. (Both ceremonies had taken place "abroad" and without publicity.) Not surprisingly, public opinion finds such "Machiavellian astuteness" hard to credit (p.14), just as some of the reviewers did. They might have had less difficulty if they had recognized him as a character with a literary pedigree, a nineteenth-century version of Volpone (as Louis Trevelyan was of Othello).[24] As it is, no one within the novel can think of a better explanation for and description of Scarborough's antics than "romance"—one of the identical twins ("poetry" being the other) to which Trollope's characters habitually attribute all manifestations of excessive emotion or fancy. Thus to Augustus Scarborough the story that Mountjoy, his elder brother, is illegitimate at first seems merely a "romance", a "romantic tale" (pp.9,41); to Harry Annesley, the jeune premier of the novel, it is "what the novel readers would call romantic" (p.43); and Mr Scarborough himself, proud of his rational superiority to the "conventionalities of the world" (p.193), takes ironic delight in pretending to identify himself with the baffled, irrational public for whom his stratagems are a "complication of romances" (p.61).

These overt references to the strangeness of the tale are an orthodox means of both forestalling the reader's incredulity and whetting his appetite for the barely credible. In the opening paragraph of chapter 1 Trollope promises, uncharacteristically, that his introductory chapters will contain "the most interesting ... incidents" of the novel. But he also suggests, characteristically, that the interest will be felt keenly only by "those who look to incidents for their interest in a tale". The implication is that such readers may be disappointed with the subsequent chapters, that the novel does not intend to cater for their tastes. In truth, however, the plot is not only interesting and unusual, but is unfolded in such a way as to keep the reader guessing about the outcome for as long as possible. Indeed, with this object in view, Trollope blatantly cheats, giving us time and again a purported account of Scarborough's thoughts which not only leaves out a major fact that ought to appear in them but also, for a long time, presents a different and false version of the facts. An inveterate ironist will perhaps slip into the habit of pretending that the false is the true even in his private thoughts; and this is perhaps what Scarborough is meant to be doing when he thinks of Mountjoy's illegitimacy as "the truth" (p.7), Mountjoy's blood as that of "a bastard" (p.367), and Augustus as "in truth" his "legitimate heir" (pp.192-93), or when he at one point feels "so

angry with Augustus that he would, if possible, revoke his last decision" (the decision, presumably, to disinherit Mountjoy), "but that, alas! would be impossible" (p.364). Augustus himself doesn't believe it impossible, neither do the Jew moneylenders, and Scarborough several times hints to other characters that it isn't. But although the reader is by these means well prepared for the impossible to happen by the time it does, Trollope must still be convicted of betraying his doctrine of "full confidence" between author and reader and disregarding the demands of imaginative consistency. For he fails to indicate that, in this one instance, the narrator has only a partial and conjectural entrée into the character's mind. This failure could be due to indecision, to his wish to keep his own as well as Scarborough's options open till almost the end. But it seems much likelier that his uncertainty was simply a technical pretence—of the same kind as his pretended ignorance of the guilt of Lady Mason in *Orley Farm* and with the same object: to preserve a semblance of suspense for readers who "look to incidents for their interest in a tale".

The real interest of Mr Scarborough's story, however, clearly resides less in what he does and how he does it than in the morality of his actions as he sees them and as the public sees them. Scarborough is a conscious, highly articulate moral rebel, defying the law on principle and to some extent altruistically, whereas earlier Trollopian hero-villains, such as Lizzie Eustace and Melmotte, had simply defied it instinctively and in the name of selfinterest. His specific targets are the law of entail and the system of primogeniture, which he objects to not merely because they deny him the right to dispose of most of his own goods as he wishes, but also because they take no account of either the moral deserts or the practical competence of possible heirs: they are both immoral and irrational. To free himself of their tyranny and to show up their absurdity, he and his wife had thirty years earlier laid a plan that would enable them to choose which of their sons should be heir. They had, in other words, set up an experiment in lawbreaking as an assertion of their moral freedom. Like his law-abiding attorney Mr Grey, who has a passion for "abstract honesty" (p.141), whose life is governed by "considerations as to radical good or evil" (p.502), Scarborough is by way of being a moral philosopher, the exponent of an ethical theory. The book reminded Hugh Walpole at times of "the author of *Erewhon*";[25] and as we shall see, Scarborough's philosophy is very close to Butlerian hedonism.

First, however, a few words should be said about the novel's subplot, which seems to me to be among the most unfortunate that Trollope ever devised: not only because it is stale and insipid in

itself, but also because it compromises the moral and emotional impact of the main plot. In this respect the part that deals with Mrs
Mountjoy's pointless and needlessly prolonged resistance to her
daughter Florence's love affair with Harry Annesley is less offensive
than that which deals with Mr Prosper's attempts to disinherit
Harry—his nephew, upon whom his property is entailed—by marrying and producing an alternative heir. Florence's problems with her
mother and with her string of vapid and obviously vain suitors at
least have the merit of being quite irrelevant to Mr Scarborough's.
Mr Prosper's, on the other hand, are clearly meant to be compared
and contrasted with Scarborough's. He too sets out to circumvent an
entail, though by legal means and for purely selfish reasons; he too
changes his mind when he comes to recognize that letting the entail
stand will after all conduce to his comfort and dignity better than
circumventing it. Scarborough acts throughout on principle and
with courage and calculation, whereas Prosper is the slave of
wounded pride, weak self-assertiveness, mental and moral debility.
Yet they fail alike in their endeavour to alter the disposition of their
property. This parallel failure ought to be piquant, and would be if
the novel's message were the pettiness of human striving and the
humbling of vanity, or even the widespread social and domestic
evils arising from the system of entails. But in fact Scarborough
would be the last man to impute universal significance to his struggle to preserve his vast estate intact, and his war against the
"conventionalities" of society that interfere with his right to do what
he will with his own is very much a personal one. He is not a social
crusader, is not interested in the socially typical aspect of his
problems, and clearly does not expect his methods of solving them to
set a social precedent. Yet the parallel with Prosper, who is very
much a type character, with typical social problems, and who is an
abject slave to the conventionalities, does seem to invite us to view
Scarborough's story partially within the frame of a "problem novel"
and to assume that a satirical comment on primogeniture, entails,
and conflict between heirs and incumbents must lie close to the
heart of the novel's message. This assumption has, I believe, led
many critics, especially modern ones, to miss the real point of the
Scarborough plot.

   The most characteristic evidence of misunderstanding is the idea
that Scarborough is a bitter man, and one whom Trollope conceived
in a spirit of bitterness. A.O.J. Cockshut, for example, would have it
that Scarborough is a "bitter, sneering old man", a "maniac" obsessed
with property, and that the mood of the book is a "compound of . . .
moderation, bitterness, and self-distrust".[26] L.P. and R.P. Stebbins
assert that in the novel a "titanlike" Trollope "questioned the moral

order and writhed with pain and contempt at his own answer".[27]
Bradford Booth, at the close of the novel, "can imagine a chorus of
leering devils playing an impish obligato to Trollope's sardonic
music".[28] Booth and E.A. Baker both describe the novel as a satire.[29]
But although it is true that Scarborough himself is a satirist and a
serious and articulate critic of society, the novel again and again affirms that, except in one instance, his "sneers and chuckles" (p.170)
are not bitter or malicious, that he is far from indifferent to the affection and good opinion of other people and far from incapable of
winning it, and that his love of money, his concern for his property,
is not motivated by selfishness or avarice and does not take
precedence over his human affections. As I have said, his aversion to
primogeniture and entails is based at least as much on reason and
morality as on selfinterest, and his contempt for the law, particularly
the laws of inheritance, and for the institution of marriage is actuated mainly by his commitment to "natural" justice. Why should
the accident of having been born first enrich one child at the expense of another? Why should a child born out of wedlock be
regarded as having less claim on his parents than a legitimate one?
Natural justice and human affection cry out against such absurdities, and if Scarborough does sometimes cry out against them
satirically, in accents of "cynical raillery",[30] we are never in doubt
that it is his good nature, his native kindness, that provokes the cry.

Scarborough is not only a good-natured man himself; he is also
committed to good nature, along with reason and natural justice, as
the highest ethical values. "All virtue and all vice were comprised by
him in the words good-nature and ill-nature" (p.194). The rules and
forms of religion, like those of law, are mere nonsense in his eyes,
mere "conventionalities". Yet although his lawyer Mr Grey, for
whom the forms of law are the citadels of absolute truth, insists that
Scarborough "hasn't got a God", "believes only in his own
reason,—and is content to do so, lying there on the very brink of
eternity" (p.157), Scarborough himself denies that he is an atheist
(p.202). His son Augustus calls him a pagan—"He will bid you come
and see a pagan depart in peace" (p.67)—but his paganism is a rejection rather of revealed than of natural religion, and he has no
quarrel with Christian ethics. Indeed the climax of the great scene in
which he first expounds his philosophy at length (chapter 21) consists of a defence of his own life as a preparation for "Heaven with
all its bliss":

> "I lived entirely abroad, and made most liberal allowances to all the
> agricultural tenants. I rebuilt all the cottages. Go and look at them. I let
> any man shoot his own game till Mountjoy came up in the world and
> took the shooting into his own hands. When the people at the pottery

began to build I assisted them in every way in the world. I offered to keep a school at my own expense, solely on the understanding that what they call dissenters should be allowed to come there. The parson spread abroad a rumour that I was an atheist, and consequently the school was kept for the dissenters only. The School Board has come and made that all right, though the parson goes on with his rumour. If he understood me as well as I understand him, he would know that he is more of an atheist than I am. I gave my boys the best education, spending on them more than double what is done by men with twice my means. My tastes were all simple and were not specially vicious. I do not know that I have even made anyone unhappy.'' [Pp.201–2]

The last sentence of this, strikingly reminiscent of Trollope's summing up of his own life at the end of his *Autobiography*, might sound smug were it not for the urgent compulsion to justify himself, to make others understand and love him, that underlies all Scarborough's selfdefences. This need for the goodwill of others is the reflex of his own natural benevolence: like the eighteenth-century deist that he essentially is, he has a strong sense of the godlike not only in man and nature generally but also within himself.

The parallel that comes to mind here is with Fielding's Squire Allworthy. He too has two "sons", one a bastard, the other legitimate, one wild and rebellious, the other tame and servile; he too is brought to recognize that the wild one, whom he had angrily cast off, is after all the better man, a natural sinner whereas the tame one is a sinner against nature. Allworthy of course is not consciously a moral rebel as Scarborough is, but the lesson he learns (or ought to have learnt) from his misjudgment of his two "sons" is implicitly the lesson which Scarborough teaches: that there can be no good without good nature. Augustus thinks of himself, at one point in the novel, as a Jacob and of his elder brother Mountjoy as an Esau, and it is true that he is the smooth, artful man while Mountjoy is the artless one, the child of nature, "hairy" both literally and figuratively. Augustus, appropriately, is by training a lawyer, a man of words, and Mountjoy a soldier, a man of action. Augustus, as his name suggests, stands for the pride and presumption of civilized, Apollonian man, Mountjoy for the careless hedonism of natural, Dionysian man. As well as Jacob and Esau, Blifil and Tom Jones, they are Ivan and Mitya Karamazov. So that when Scarborough finally decides to reinstate the natural man Mountjoy as his heir, even though he knows this will probably mean the loss of the property, we are made to feel that he is consciously choosing one type of humanity, one conception of morality, in preference to another.[31]

Scarborough, however, is not an allegorical or mythological figure but a character in a realistic novel, and his decision is neither an easy, morally simple one nor a dispassionate one. To leave his property to good-natured Mountjoy rather than ill-natured

Augustus may accord with what he regards as natural justice, may reward the virtues of loyalty, affection, and unselfishness that commend themselves most highly to his moral reason. But Scarborough is a man of the world, not solely an ethical theorist. And he is sufficiently attached to his worldly goods and family status to summon up almost superhuman energy in trying to protect them after his death. The smooth Augustus, who will obviously guard the property well, has to display innumerable examples of his meanness, malevolence, and ingratitude before Scarborough begins to contemplate deposing him. Almost to the end he considers it unthinkable that the estate should be left to Mountjoy, to be gambled away to the Jews. And his final change of mind is due rather to a heightening of his hatred of Augustus and his affection for Mountjoy than to a lessening of his solicitude about the property. On his deathbed his last words are a prudential plea to Mountjoy to give up gambling.

It is Scarborough's fury against Augustus that has presumably given rise to the idea of him as a bitter man, a "leering devil" whose conduct made Trollope "writhe with pain and contempt". Certainly, the scene in which he meets Augustus for the first time after reinstating Mountjoy as heir is the most melodramatic in the novel, and the melodrama results from the capacity for evil, for devilish cruelty, that is attributed both to him and to Augustus: " ... he managed to turn himself round and look his son full in the face. Such a look as it was! There was the gleam of victory, and the glory of triumph, and the venom of malice." (p.543) When Trollope waxes alliterative and tautological like this, someone is outdoing Herod, and Scarborough clearly is when, a moment later, he professes to be afraid that Augustus will murder Mountjoy: an appropriately lurid climax to a scene that began with the recumbent Scarborough pretending, Volpone-like, that he was too weak to speak above a whisper. The tone of this scene, however, is quite untypical both of Scarborough himself and of the novel. As Augustus remarks on another occasion, "There is a manner of doing evil so easy and indifferent as absolutely to quell the general feeling respecting it" (p.45); and this is Scarborough's normal manner. Even his detestation of Augustus is usually expressed urbanely enough, and his next-to-last words before his death are an evidently sincere plea to Mountjoy to "do something ... for poor Gus" (p.565).

How little there is of the remorseless stage villain in him is shown, time and again, by his ability to charm and disarm his critics and by his acts of supererogatory kindness. One potential critic who is notably silent throughout is the narrator, who lets Scarborough speak for himself—and speak very well—almost without demur and

continues to withhold moral comment even after the devious men-
dacity of his scheme has become fully apparent. Doctor Merton, to
whom Scarborough unburdens himself most often, knows that as a
law-abiding man he ought to be shocked by Scarborough's liber-
tarian beliefs and practices, but he listens spellbound to Scarborough's long exposition and defence of his philosophy in chapter
21, and at other times becomes his moral accomplice—as when he is
"utterly unable to keep from laughing" at Scarborough's assertion
(in a letter to Mr Grey which he is dictating to Merton) that he
"know[s] the strength of an entail" and would "not for worlds ...
venture to meddle with anything so holy" (p.369).

   The only critic of Scarborough who remains implacable to the end
is his lawyer Grey, who denounces the dying man as a liar (p.521)
and parts from him "boiling with anger" (p.525). It has been the
faith of Grey's life, a creed absolutely antithetical to Scarborough's,
that "the law is the law"—independent of personal whim (p.168)—
and that "law and justice may be made to run on all-fours" (p.531).
Though he dislikes Augustus, Grey is determined as a matter of
"duty" (p.180) to ensure his succession to the property. His
daughter Dolly, who regards herself as "the Conscience" and him as
"the Reason" of his legal practice, tries to persuade him to dis-
engage himself from the Scarboroughs altogether rather than risk
being contaminated by them. He tells her, impatiently, that her
morality "goes back to Adam and Eve" (p.156). But her wisdom is
vindicated when it becomes clear that Grey in fact has been seduced
by his curiosity, by the "singularity" of Scarborough's "complicated
farrago of dishonesty" (pp.181,169). He becomes angry with himself
because he cannot regard Scarborough "as an honest man regards a
rascal", cannot feel towards him "that profound dislike which he
was aware such conduct as the squire's ought to have generated"
(p.373). Looking back at the end he feels that Scarborough "had
turned him round his finger" (p.526).

   Part of the reason why Grey and Merton cannot think of Scarborough as a rascal is that a rascal, according to Grey, has something
mean about him (p.516), whereas Scarborough is generous and un-
selfish. He shows this not only in his treatment of his sons but also in
interceding to help the course of Harry Annesley's love affair
(chapters 38–41) and in the warmth with which he thanks Grey for
privately paying one of Mountjoy's gambling debts out of his own
pocket: "you are the sweetest and finest gentleman I ever came
across" (p.478). Breaches of moral and civil law by such a man defy
the censure of all but the most rigid and theoretical moralists—Dolly
Grey for example. He is the goodnatured man to whom the good
nature of others responds almost involuntarily, for whom nature

pleads in despite of morality, as we see in the obituary pronounced over him by Dr Merton:

> "The poor old boy has gone at last, and in spite of all his faults I feel as though I had lost an old friend. To me he has been most kind, and did I not know of all his sins I should say that he had been always loyal and always charitable. Mr. Grey condemns him, and all the world must condemn him. One cannot make an apology for him without being ready to throw all truth and all morality to the dogs. But if you can imagine for yourself a state of things in which neither truth nor morality shall be thought essential, then old Mr. Scarborough would be your hero. He was the bravest man I ever knew. He was ready to look all opposition in the face, and prepared to bear it down. And whatever he did he did with the view of accomplishing what he thought to be right for other people. Between him and his God I cannot judge, but he believed in an Almighty One, and certainly went forth to meet Him without a fear in his heart."[32] [Pp.567–68]

Trollope's last major novel ends, then, not on a note of reactionary and melodramatic bitterness but on one of bemused acquiescence. Scarborough, the most audacious and purposeful of all his outlaws, is also the least outrageous, the most attractive of them. Even Grey, who has been caught, rather like a latterday Mr Harding, in the crossfire between Scarborough and his enemies, consigns himself to the rubbish heap of outworn institutions with only a token protest against the more flexible, more "average" morality of Mr Barry, who takes over his practice. Only Dolly Grey—who wears spectacles as stern German girls do, but as English girls do not (p.148)— remains uncompromising in her prelapsarian purity. But Dolly is potentially even more of an outlaw than Scarborough, as suggested by her threat—spoken with "an air of badinage"—that if she were married to Barry she would "plunge a knife" into him one morning after breakfast (pp.318–19,321). (Later she pretends to fear that the rejected Barry "would cut my throat if he could get hold of me" [p.507], and she tells him, with rather gruesome pride, that she "would burn my hand off for my father" [p.504].) Scarborough, whom she considers "a thoroughly bad man" (p.517), would be horrified by this sort of talk. And no doubt Harry Annesley would be similarly shocked to hear his beloved Florence Mountjoy tell an unwelcome suitor that she would surely kill either him (the suitor) or herself if forced to marry him. Virginally pure idealists like Dolly and Florence run to emotional extremes which pragmatists like Scarborough know how to steer between. However, the love-story of Harry and Florence also ends on a beatific note, in tune with the mellowness of Scarborough's deathbed. Harry, a listless youth who is even less believably a fellow of his college at Cambridge than his namesake in *The Claverings*, rises in the end to Patmorean heights of grace as he pledges himself to his future wife: "May God do so to

me, and more also, if to the end I do not treat her, not only with all affection, but also with all delicacy of observance" (p.488). This is a more poetic vein than Trollope's young men usually manage; but even if it seems too poetic for Harry himself it is appropriate to a novel whose strongest message is the preciousness of natural human affections.[33]

NOTES

1. The phrase was applied to Trollope by Walter Allen: see *New Statesman*, 21 November 1959, p.714.
2. The novel was serialized in the *Fortnightly Review*, in twenty instalments, between 1 July 1871 and 1 February 1873.
3. See H.J.W. Milley, "*The Eustace Diamonds* and *The Moonstone*", *Studies in Philology* 36 (October 1939): 651–63.
4. However, Cockshut's statement that the diamonds are recovered (*Anthony Trollope*, p.181) is incorrect.
5. See *Autobiography*, p.100n. As noted above, Trollope also took legal advice when writing *Lady Anna*.
6. The "volume of poetry" that Frank and Lizzie are discussing is Tennyson's *Elaine*. Stephen Gill and John Sutherland, editors of the Penguin English Library edition of the novel, note (p.774) that Lizzie alludes to "Tennyson when she wants to be thought moral ... ; Byron when she wants to be thought daring; Shelley when she wants to be thought intellectual and spiritual". Examples of her Byronic and Shelleyan phases are discussed below.
7. This point is noted by Stephen Gill and John Sutherland in their introduction to the Penguin English Library edition of the novel.
8. See Cockshut, *Anthony Trollope*, pp.188–92.
9. See *Phineas Redux*, chaps. 55 and 72, *The Prime Minister*, chaps. 54 and 61. Lizzie, it should be noted, had feared all along that a marriage to either Lord George or Mr Emilius might turn out to be bigamous (as her marriage to Mr Emilius actually does). Bigamy would seem to be as common and accepted a threat in her world as in that of the sensation novel.
10. Another memorable euphemism for *lie* is coined by Dean Lovelace in *Is He Popenjoy?* (p.132): "a positive misstatement".
11. Cockshut, *Anthony Trollope*, pp.191–92.
12. Trollope, as Bradford Booth noted ("Trollope on Scott: Some Unpublished Notes", *Nineteenth Century Fiction* 5 [December 1950]: 223–30), had read *The Bride of Lammermoor* at New Year 1871, just after he began *The Eustace Diamonds*. Though Booth does not remark on the resemblance, Lucinda's tragic fate is unmistakably modelled, in crucial respects, on that of Scott's heroine. It also seems reasonable to conjecture that Lady Lovel in *Lady Anna* (written between May and July 1871) was partly modelled on Lucy Ashton's mother. There is an interesting general resemblance between the Deans family in *The Heart of Midlothian* and the Brattle family in *The Vicar of Bullhampton*.
13. "An Essay on Carlylism", *Saint Pauls* 1 (December 1867): 292–305. The essay was provoked particularly by Carlyle's jeremiad on the Second Reform Bill, "Shooting Niagara and Afterwards".
14. See *Times*, 24 August 1875, p.4, and *Daily Telegraph*, 21 August 1875, p.3. According to T.H.S. Escott (*Anthony Trollope*, p.298) and Michael Sadleir (*Commentary*, pp.398–99), a signed leading article in the *Times* by J.T. Delane (editor of the paper) probably gave Trollope the idea for Melmotte. I have not been able to locate the article, but apparently it told the story of an English nobleman who had been lured into speculation and bankruptcy by a swindling Californian colonel. Hiram K. Fisker, the American promoter of the Vera Cruz railway, was presumably meant to remind readers in some respects of James Fisk, the

American swindler who was murdered in January 1872 and who made his fortune largely by illegal dealing in the shares of the Erie railway company. On Fisk, see *Annual Register*, 1872, Part I, pp.286–87.

15. The inclusion of the emperor in the novel was no doubt suggested to Trollope by the visit of the Shah of Persia to England in June–July 1873. The Shah dined at the Guildhall (20 June), but I have not found any record of his having been entertained privately by any representative of British commerce. The first three parts of *The Way We Live Now* were written in May 1873; the remaining seventeen between 1 July and 22 December 1873; the emperor's impending visit is first referred to in part 7 (chap.32). On the Shah's visit, see *Times*, 29 May 1873, p.9, and 19 June–7 July, passim.

16. John Sadleir, MP, had also used prussic acid to put an end to his troubles: see above, chap.4, note 6. Apart from Sadleir, it has been suggested that Melmotte may have been modelled on Dickens's Merdle (in *Little Dorrit*), on George Hudson, the railway king, and on an earlier fictional portrait of Hudson in Robert Bell's *The Ladder of Gold* (1850). See R.B. Martin, *Enter Rumour*, pp.230–41.

17. I have noted elsewhere that Trollope earlier had a different plan: his manuscript papers in the Bodleian show that he originally contemplated having Melmotte stand trial. See "Trollope Changes His Mind; the Death of Melmotte in *The Way We Live Now*", *Nineteenth Century Fiction* 18 (June 1963): 89–91. Melmotte himself "had heard of trials in which the accused criminals had been heroes to the multitude while their cases were in progress" (II:296). But later, as he stood with his razor in his hand, shaving, it had also struck him "how easily might he put an end to it all!" (II:301).

18. One of the best accounts of the emotional reticence that typifies most of Trollope's characters is to be found in "English Character and Manners as Portrayed by Anthony Trollope", *Westminster Review* 67 (January 1885): 53–100.

19. A law passed in 1856 decreed that one of the partners must have resided in the neighbourhood for at least three weeks before a marriage involving a minor could be solemnized.

20. Perhaps, by the time he wrote *The Way We Live Now*, Trollope had softened a little towards the De Courcys themselves: the only member of the family who appears in any of his later novels, Lady Rosina, is sympathetically presented and is honoured by the friendship of no less fastidious a person than Plantagenet Palliser (especially in *The Prime Minister*).

21. In *The Prime Minister*, which he began only a few months after finishing *The Way We Live Now*, Trollope can perhaps be seen trying to atone in some measure for this "exaggeration". Plantagenet Palliser, from whom the novel takes its title, is his idea of a "perfect gentleman", and part of the proof of Palliser's gentlemanliness is the rigid sense of caste that makes him spurn adventurers and social climbers and shudder at the "vulgarity", the indiscriminate condescension, of his wife. Contrasted to Palliser is Ferdinand Lopez, the central character of the novel's other main plot, who is merely an adventurer, but who does succeed, where Brehgert failed, in carrying off the daughter of a proud old English family. Society as a whole, however, never opens its arms to Lopez as it does to Melmotte. He is instinctively detested and distrusted by conservative people like old Mr Wharton, his wife's father. And whereas Roger Carbury's Suffolk, where the old-fashioned virtues still obtain, is a rural backwater cut off from the mainstream of social life, the Hereford of the Whartons and their friends the Fletchers is a potent and salutary influence even in London. Except for the heroine, Emily Wharton, only the foolish and vulgar are taken in by Lopez. Once he shows himself in his true colours, ruin quickly overtakes him: he throws himself under a train and is, as the narrator exultantly puts it, "knocked into bloody atoms". Throughout, the novel implicitly endorses the fanatical pride and exclusiveness, the bitter and sensational mistrust of outsiders (especially Jews) which characterize the Wharton-Fletcher mentality. As a result it in fact becomes altogether more "exaggerated" and unfair, less balanced and realistic, than its predecessor. Its melodramatic bitterness is a throwback to Trollope's earliest and worst days of "tilting at windmills".

22. The novel was highly praised on both scores in a perceptive review in the *Saturday Review* 48 (25 October 1879): 515–16. Julian Hawthorne, son of the great

romancer whom Trollope so deeply admired, reviewed the novel in the *Spectator* 52 (18 October 1879): 1320. His review includes one of the best general descriptions of Trollope's art of realistic sensationalism. He is not identified as the author of the review in *Trollope: the Critical Heritage*, ed. Donald Smalley (London: Routledge and Kegan Paul, 1969), but it was incorporated in his *Confessions and Criticisms* (Boston: Ticknor, 1887).

23. *Saturday Review* 55 (19 May 1883): 642–43.
24. On Trollope's fondness for the Jacobean drama and on the resemblance between Scarborough and some of the villainous supermen of Massinger, Middleton, Jonson, and Beaumont and Fletcher, see Bradford A. Booth, *Anthony Trollope*, pp. 130–31.
25. Hugh Walpole, *Anthony Trollope* (London: Macmillan, 1929), p.172.
26. Cockshut, *Anthony Trollope*, pp. 139,234,151.
27. L.P. and R.P. Stebbins, *The Trollopes: the Chronicle of a Writing Family* (London: Secker and Warburg, 1947), p.327.
28. Booth, *Anthony Trollope*, p.131. Whether Booth intended the reminiscence of *The Egoist* is not clear.
29. Booth, *Anthony Trollope*, p.130; E.A. Baker, *The History of the English Novel* (London: Witherby, 1937) VIII: 154. The "malevolence" of the novel reminded Hugh Walpole of Peacock as well as Butler (*Anthony Trollope*, p.172).
30. Cf. Sadleir, *Commentary*, p.397.
31. A similar moral choice may be implicit in Violet Effingham's preference for the hairy Lord Chiltern over the "smooth" Phineas Finn—which one feels is also Trollope's own preference.
32. It may be significant that the last sentence of this tribute is missing from the serial version of the novel in *All the Year Round*. As a morally conservative family paper, *All the Year Round* may well have baulked at such explicit defence of Scarborough as a religious man. See my note on this matter in *Notes and Queries*, Feburary 1977.
33. The lovers in *The Claverings* were also Florence and Harry. If so much spurious biographical evidence had not already been squeezed out of Trollope's novels, one would be tempted to speculate that, consciously or unconsciously, Trollope hoped for a marriage between his wife's orphan niece Florence Bland, who had come to live with him and his wife in the 1860s and who acted as his amanuensis towards the end of his life, and his elder son Harry, who was still unmarried at the time of Trollope's death and who on at least one occasion had got into an embarrassing amorous entanglement—befitting a Trollopian jeune premier (see G. Haight, *The George Eliot Letters* [London: Oxford University Press, 1956] V: 351,357).

8 "Things done in the wilds"

No doubt there was a feeling with many that anything done in the wilds of Australia ought not "to count" here at home in England. [*John Caldigate*, p.399]

Trollope's writing career began with two novels set in Ireland and ended with a third. In between, he set two further novels mainly in Ireland, four others on the Continent,[1] two wholly or in part in Australia, one partly in America, and one in an imaginary country of the future, Britannula. A very high proportion of his short stories also have foreign settings.

None of these essays in exoticism has ever, to my knowledge, been ranked among his major or most distinctive achievements, and none was an outstanding popular success. His perseverance with them is not easily explained, except in terms of his desire to show off his knowledge of out-of-the-way people and places. But in general, although their local colour seems authentic enough, their insight into the psychology and customs of foreign races is disappointingly shallow and cool. Trollope boasted that in *Nina Balatka* and *Linda Tressel* "Prague is Prague, and Nuremburg is Nuremburg" (*Autobiography*, p.177), but even in these, the most exotic of his novels, the mores of Trollopian England are seldom far beneath the exotic surface. In the Irish and Australian novels, too, the English class system and genteel English courtship rituals tend to prevail, incongruously, in societies quite alien in speech, custom, and physical environment. In *The Kellys and the O'Kellys*, for example, a group of Anglo-Irish aristocrats sort out their minor dynastic and amorous perplexities in a world which seems, inexplicably, to have no moral connexion with that in which their neighbour, Barry Lynch, perpetrates rabid Irish villainies. A similar, even more blatant imaginative disjunction is apparent in *Castle Richmond*, where most of the Anglo-Irish remain absorbed in their private emotional problems, not callously indifferent but, it seems, simply blind to the famine which is carrying off the peasantry all around them. In *The Landleaguers*, which Trollope left uncompleted at his death,

violence and stunted sympathies are almost endemic—among Irish, Anglo-Irish, Jews, and Americans alike—but amid all the horror and brutality a pair of lovers daintily practise all the standard shufflings of a slow-motion Trollopian courtship. And *Harry Heathcote of Gangoil*, as I have pointed out elsewhere,[2] ends with a most unconvincing consolidation of English middle-class values in the teeth of the levelling, divisive influence of life in the Australian bush.

Speaking of *Nina Balatka* and *Linda Tressel*, Trollope remarked that they contained "more of romance proper than had been usual with me" (*Autobiography*, p.177) He presumably had in mind the near-suicide of Nina and the tragic death, from heartbreak, of Linda. But objectively it is hard to see that Nina, at the nadir of her fortunes, is unhappier than Emily Wharton or Emily Hotspur at the nadir of theirs; and at least nobody resorts to the "romantic" expedient of trying to kill her or her lover, as the enemies of Alice Vavasor and Anna Lovel do in prosaic England. Indeed, the hostility between Jews and Gentiles which is the chief source of her troubles is not noticeably fiercer than that which comes to the surface in upper-class England when Emily Wharton and Georgiana Longestaffe become engaged to Jews. Similarly the religious persecution which both Nina and Linda encounter from scandalized friends and relatives is scarcely more savage than that which Hester Bolton suffers in *John Caldigate*; and Linda's death, which Trollope acknowledged to be "lachrymose" (*Autobiography*, p.176), is not more so than Emily Hotspur's. In *The Golden Lion of Granpère*, the other Continental novel, the European system of patriarchal authority and arranged marriages topples before the urgency of young love just as surely as traditional hindrances do before English lovers. The Europe that we see in the "Continental" novels is very much less romantic than the remote hideaway for bigamous marriages, illicit liaisons, and all manner of unnamable vices that figures in many of the novels set mainly in England.

What Trollope would call romance does bulk larger in his Irish, Australian, and American settings and clearly constitutes one of the chief attractions these settings have for him. Two of the Irish novels deal with a state of virtual civil war in which violence and murder are commonplace. A third, *Castle Richmond*, includes one of Trollope's juiciest and most farfetched tales of bigamy and blackmail. And the fourth, *The Kellys and the O'Kellys*, boasts the most thoroughgoing and outlandish of all his villains. This villain, it is true, is an old Etonian, and both the blackmailers and the suspected bigamists in *Castle Richmond* are English. But in both novels there is clearly an implicit assumption that sensational scandals and outré behaviour are less shocking, more to be expected in Ireland than in

England: even if the Irish social situation does not directly produce them, it accommodates and assimilates them with much less fuss than England could. The bigamy case in *John Caldigate*, which I shall be looking at in detail, rests on the same assumption, though less comfortably. Without quite being given to understand that Australia is beyond the reach of English social laws, the reader is finally expected to accept as more or less normal and venial there misbehaviour which Trollope would never ask him to condone in England. A similar expectation underlies the bigamy plot of *Dr. Wortle's School*: in America, where a spouse is always likely to disappear without trace, and where, as sober Mr Peacocke finds on a train journey through the Wild West, even a gentleman needs to be able to defend himself against attack by gun and knife, the possibility of accidental, innocent bigamy is obviously many times higher than in a stable society like England.

   Trollope's most common difficulty with his foreign settings is that of deciding just how foreign, how exotic and romantic, to make them. In novels where he is explicitly or implicitly contrasting foreign ways with English, he is apt to exaggerate the contrast and to concentrate on its superficial aspects. The villainies of Barry Lynch in *The Kellys and the O'Kellys* and the wild-west scenes in *Dr. Wortle's School* are only the crudest and most extreme examples. Both appeal blatantly to simple romantic stereotypes, relying on these, rather than on any exploration of individual responses to unusual social situations, to account for conduct and attitudes so outrageously at variance with English standards. The Continental novels at least avoid this weakness, and they do so because their implicit aim, despite Trollope's intention to render the romance and distinctively foreign quality of the life they depict, is in fact to translate this life into familiar English terms. Thus Trollope's unusually sympathetic picture of Jewish ghetto life in *Nina Balatka*, antedating that in *Daniel Deronda* by nearly a decade, depends in part on a playing down of its distinctive Jewishness—whether by choice or because of authorial ignorance. His unusually sympathetic attitude to the Catholic religion in *Linda Tressel*—unusual not so much for him personally as for a Victorian protestant—is very much a corollary of the hatred of protestant puritanism which 'had been bred in him in England (and which also conditions his unexpected Catholic bias in the Irish novels). Again, in *The Golden Lion of Granpère* the capacity for change and compromise which he attributes to the Continental system of arranged marriages and strict paternal authority—and which other Victorian novelists, from Thackeray and Meredith down, altogether deny it—reads like a fairly direct superimposition of the conventions of the English love-story on a

foreign one. In general, as I have suggested, the Continental novels exhibit the opposite fault to that of the others with foreign scenes and settings: the fault of exaggerating the essential resemblances, rather than the differences, between English life and foreign. It is only in the very small group of novels in which he is genuinely concerned with the moral interaction of different ways of life, and in particular with the doubts that may be cast on the authority of English standards by experience of foreign ones, that he for the most part avoids these two forms of exaggeration. The remainder of my discussion will be devoted to the novels that I place in this group: *An Eye for an Eye*, *John Caldigate*, and *The Fixed Period*.

Among the Irish novels, the singling out of *An Eye for an Eye* rather than *The Macdermots of Ballycloran* perhaps calls for explanation. The ambiguous position of Thady Macdermot and his sister Feemy, decayed gentry caught in a no man's land between the warring Irish peasantry (represented by illegal potheen makers) and the Anglo-Irish establishment (represented, albeit tawdrily, by customs officers) certainly highlights a conflict of different national temperaments and ways of life. It infuses, as one critic has noted,[3] an almost Hardyesque sense of "historical determinism" into the conventional romantic tale of a brother (Thady) killing his sister's seducer (the revenue officer Captain Ussher). Even the local colour that is laid on so thickly and obtrusively—with setpiece descriptions of a village wedding (I, chapter 12), a race meeting (II, chapter 7), and Carrick-on-Shannon on assizes day (III, chapter 6)—can be seen as a necessary part of the groundwork of the tale. So too, for once, can the frequent authorial excursuses, on matters such as the plight of the Irish poor, landlord-tenant relationships, Maria Edgeworth's Irish novels, and the Maynooth grant.[4] All the social and historical scene-setting deepens our awareness of the nets in which Thady and Feemy are entangled. At the climax of the novel, however, this awareness, and our whole sense of the inevitability of their tragedy, is rudely jolted for the sake of a melodramatic effect. Feemy dies in "premature parturition" before she can deliver the testimony that might have saved Thady from the gallows. The reader thus learns, for the first time, that she had not, after all, resisted Captain Ussher's advances as an English girl of her social pretensions almost certainly would have done; the elopement to which Thady had put a stop—by killing Ussher under the impression that he was abducting Feemy—had not been Ussher's last desperate expedient to obtain his way with her; indeed, retrospectively, the reader is bound to protest that he could not have had any motive for agreeing to it at all. The eleventh-hour disclosure of Feemy's pregnancy, then, not only gives

a gratuitously sensational twist to the climax of the novel but also affronts our whole conception of the social divisions—deriving from international ones—that underlie and give point to the Macdermots' tragedy. It is, in fact, a particularly sad example of one of the flaws that I have noted as typical of Trollope's exotic novels: for essentially the trouble with Feemy's pregnancy is that at the last minute it seems to imply that both she and Ussher have all along been much more "Irish", much remoter from "English" ways of thinking and behaving, than the reader had ever been led to suppose.

In this respect *An Eye for an Eye*, another tale of an Irish girl's seduction—this time by an Englishman—and of the killing of her seducer, plays much fairer with the reader. As an artistic expression of the poison affecting personal relationships between members of an oppressed race and their oppressors, it defines the moral differences and resemblances between the two races more consistently and more believably than *The Macdermots*. Fred Neville loves Kate O'Hara and would like to marry her, but he is heir to an English earldom and she, though a lady by birth and education, is impoverished and Irish. There is also a religious difference, she being Catholic and he of evangelical protestant stock. At the back of his mind, too, there is a fear of seeming to reenact the disgraceful conduct of a previous heir to the earldom, who had married "a wretched painted prostitute from France" (I:15–16). This fear is exacerbated when he learns that the girl's father is an ex-convict. Such a connexion, he manages to convince himself, puts it out of the question that she should ever become his countess, but he toys with the idea of a "morganatic" marriage. When the old Irish priest to whom he proposes the scheme rejects it angrily as "a counterfeit marriage", there is no course left for Fred but to admit his perfidy. The girl's mother avenges her daughter's shame by pushing him from the top of a cliff near her cottage, on the wild western coast of Ireland.

An Eye for an Eye is the most purely romantic of all Trollope's novels (its only rival being *Marion Fay*), and though even its English scenes are heavily atmospheric, the main sources of romance are obviously the wild Irish setting and the context of English misprision and devaluation of things Irish. It is difficult, for example, to imagine Trollope opening any of his English novels with an introduction in which a mad lady stalks about a private asylum incessantly muttering, "An eye for an eye" [5] And it is almost unthinkable that he would have allowed an English gentleman to seduce an English lady, as opposed to an Irish one, without showing himself to be a heartless scoundrel—rather than "simply a self-indulgent spoiled young man" as Fred Neville is (I:204).

Yet for all its romance *An Eye for an Eye* is resolutely realistic in

its judgment of moral issues. The nemesis that overtakes Fred
Neville is an Englishman's punishment for his stunted sympathies
towards and complacent ignorance about people of another race.
Ireland is an outlet for Fred's romantic escapism, a funkhole from
his social responsibilities. There, he assumes, even the clergy will ab-
solve him from rigour of conscience. Because the old priest, Father
Marty, lives "in a village in the extreme west of Ireland, listening
night and day to the roll of the Atlantic and drinking whisky
punch", Fred expects to find him "romantic, semi-barbarous, and
perhaps more than semi-lawless in his views of life" (II:33). Fred, as
Trollope has noted before (I:172), is a reader of romantic novels, and
the romantic Ireland of the novelist appears to have seduced him
just as surely as he has seduced Kate O'Hara: "Irish priests have
been made by chroniclers of Irish story to do marvellous things; and
Fred Neville thought that this priest, if only the matter could be
properly introduced, might be persuaded to do for him something
romantic, something marvellous, perhaps something almost lawless.
In truth it might have been difficult to find a man more practical or
more honest than Mr. Marty." (II:34–35) *An Eye for an Eye*, then, is
both a romance and, up to a point, a didactic warning against
romance, an implicit plea to English readers to acknowledge the
Irish as real people, people like themselves. This plea emerges
sharply and naturally from a simple, compact, and balanced study of
two contrasted, but not totally unlike, ways of life.

John Caldigate, like *An Eye for an Eye*, measures a young man's
romantic delusions about a foreign way of life against the more
prosaic reality. But again, for all its moral realism, the novel skilfully
exploits the romantic possibilities inherent in the collision of a raw,
primitive society—in this case Australia—with a settled,
sophisticated one. Indeed, just as *An Eye for an Eye* has claims to
being Trollope's most successful romance, *John Caldigate* is
probably his most wholehearted and accomplished attempt at a sensation novel.

   John Caldigate comes down from Cambridge bored, heavily in
debt, and virtually estranged from his father. The family estate in
Cambridgeshire, Folking, strikes his jaundiced eye as a "washy
fen" He considers it absurd that, "with so wild and beautiful a
world around him", he should be doomed to waste half his life at
Folking waiting for his father to die (p.20). The "wild and beautiful
world" that especially beckons to him is New South Wales. "There
was gold being found at this moment among the mountains of New
South Wales, in quantities which captivated his imagination. And
this was being done in a most lovely spot, among circumstances

which were in all respects romantic" (p.9). Romanticism, it is clear, is Caldigate's ailment, and in more senses than one; for he is also an incurable sentimental philanderer. What he must learn is to distinguish between genuine and illusory romance.

His education begins on the goldfields. On the ship that takes him to Australia he embarks on another of the vague sentimental flirtations that are one of the marks of his false romanticism. Later, however, it becomes more than a flirtation, when the woman, who calls herself Mrs Smith, joins him on the goldfields and becomes his mistress and business partner. She is a major part of the moral trial, the confrontation with reality, which Australia will eventually be seen to have represented for him. But the nature of their relationship is not revealed to the reader until four (or five)[6] years later, some time after his return to England. In the meantime we are left free to suppose that what Caldigate considers the true romance of his life has been realized with his return "laden with gold" to England, his reconciliation with his father, and his marriage to Hester Bolton. This, he had assured himself before leaving England, "should be his romance" and as far as we know he has more or less kept his vow to "cling to it" in Australia (p.18). It is only when Mrs Smith comes to England, claiming that he had married her on the goldfields and accusing him of bigamy, that the reality, as distinct from the romance, of his Australian experiences becomes fully apparent.

From his first arrival in Australia, though, it is clear that not all of Caldigate's romantic expectations have been fulfilled. Nobble, one of the "lovely spots" where gold had been found "among the mountains of New South Wales", turns out to be the "foulest place" he "had ever seen" (p.79).[7] Its streets are deep in "mud and slush" when he arrives, ironically recalling the muddy fields around Folking which had seemed so dreary to him. Ahalala, where he and his friend commence their mining operations, proves even more primitive. But the young men soon strike gold, and Caldigate eventually returns to England a rich man. Unlike his companion, who has taken to drink and vanished into the Queensland bush, he seems to have emerged morally unscathed, perhaps even strengthened, by his exposure to the temptations of life almost beyond the confines of civilization. If there is any moral danger confronting him, it seems to be that of complacency. It may be only as a stratagem that he tells the mother of an English girl who supposes herself to have some claim on him that he is "wedded" to his Australian gold-mine, and that it is an "imperious mistress" (pp.144,146). But we sense something very confused in his romantic values when he likens his courtship of Hester Bolton to his quest for gold: "Having found

where the gold lay at this second Ahalala,—that the gold was real gold,—he did not doubt that he would be able to make good his mining operations" (p.134). Seemingly, gold has become the emblem of his success in love as well as in worldly matters; but to the reader it soon becomes apparent that it is more fittingly an emblem for the moral damage he has suffered on the goldfields. With a superb ironical appropriateness, the woman who had shared his life on the goldfields does return to England as an "imperious mistress" claiming to be "wedded" to him, and does succeed for a time in separating him from Hester, from the wife of his "true" romance. When her emissaries first come to Folking, the surrounding fields are again "flat, plashy, and heavy-looking with the mud of February" (p.260); earlier Caldigate had remarked complacently that he "had been able to topdress the English acres with a little Australian gold" (p.217), but it is clear the topdressing also includes some Australian mud.

Caldigate is put on trial for bigamy, found guilty, and sent to gaol, and it is not until he has been there some months that fresh evidence establishes his innocence. Hester and his father stand by him throughout, but her family and most of his friends are convinced of his guilt. Public opinion, for the most part, is more lenient, considering that "anything done in the wilds of Australia ought not 'to count' here at home in England" (p.399). Such a view, assuming as it does that moral standards were less stringent in the Australian bush than in England, naturally commends itself to Caldigate, who had gone to Australian in search of more "conventional freedom" than England allowed. Before his imprisonment he had angrily denied that there had been anything "disgraceful" in his conduct (p.226), was astonished that people could believe him guilty "against the whole tenor of my life and character" (p.241), and had complained that "any man might be made the victim of a conspiracy" in the same way as he had been (p.357). That promising to marry a woman and allowing her to call herself his wife are acts for which he may fairly expect retribution, even though they were committed in the "wilds of Australia", he seems unable to see. Trollope's publisher, John Blackwood, protested that Caldigate was so "cold self satisfied and self reliant" at this stage that it was "impossible to sympathise with him",[8] and some of the English reviewers felt that he failed to show sufficient remorse, and was not severely enough punished, either for his treachery to Mrs Smith or for his "inconstancy" to Hester.[9] (One reviewer observed tartly that "unswerving constancy is assumed to be an exclusively female virtue".[10]) Even after his spell in gaol, while he can now understand why so many people had believed him guilty and can acknowledge

that his own "early follies" have brought about all his troubles (pp.605–6), he shows no real contrition.

In this sense the expectations built up in the first half of the novel are hardly realized. It is clear that Trollope's sympathy for his hero and his aversion to the puritanical Boltons—Caldigate's most implacable enemies—soften and at times distort his judgment. Even the fact that Caldigate had lied about his relationship with Mrs Smith both to his wife's brother and to his wife—"He had seen her [Mrs Smith] again in Sydney, where he had found her exercising her profession as an actress. That had been all." (p.187)—is not held against him and causes him no loss of sleep. Presumably the suspicions that his wife's family had entertained about his colonial career are still to be regarded as a sign rather of their puritanical nasty-mindedness than of proper parental prudence. At one point, too, the novel appears to endorse Caldigate's own view that the most serious of his offences was fornication (p.380), although if this were true the moral outrage displayed by the Boltons and others would seem merely ridiculous.

In some ways, however, the novel gains more than it loses from its equivocalness about the hero's culpability. Whether or not this was what Trollope intended, Caldigate's alienation from "English" moral standards is impressively rendered, and the point is made that these standards have only a tenuous hold even on English society. The belated disclosure of Caldigate's affair with Mrs Smith may seem hard to reconcile with the conception that we have previously formed of his character, and perhaps even of the extent to which such deviations from English sexual rules are countenanced on the goldfields. Trollope must be accused of cheating here, as he did in *The Macdermots of Ballycloran*. But once the initial shock of the disclosure is overcome, the new and heightened sense we receive, progressively, of the differences between life in a frontier environment and life at home compels belief and admiration. By the end we are almost persuaded that the worst of Caldigate's follies was neither breach of promise nor fornication—which in the circumstances were easily excusable—but his complacency in failing to see that they might catch up with him in England and that if they did they must appear more culpable to other eyes, ignorant of the realities (as the novel sees them) of bush life, than to his own. That this complacency. though shaken, is not completely uprooted even by his trial and imprisonment can be taken as showing how deeply the "wilds of Australia" have left their mark on his moral nature.

John Caldigate is probably the most sensational of Trollope's novels both in matter and in manner. And although, as we have seen, part of the sensational effect is achieved by cheating, many of

the most dramatic scenes are subtle and realistic. Among these must be included Caldigate's first sight of Crinkett, the leader of the conspiracy against him, sleeping on a park bench in Cambridge (p.245), the appearance of two of the conspirators at the christening of Caldigate's baby (chapter 27), and the long "imprisonment" of Hester by her mother at Puritan Grange, the home of the Boltons (chapters 31, 33–36). In such scenes, though emotion is muted, though voices are hardly ever raised, though the circumstances are rich in Hitchcockian incongruities (the disturber of Caldigate's peace lying blissfully asleep), the novel's central moral antitheses are dramatized with great power. The uncouthness of the Australians and the ugly gloom of Puritan Grange are beautifully set off against the amenities of upper-class English country life (with which they nevertheless establish their spiritual connexion); and Caldigate's complacent conviction of the irrelevance, the inconsequence, the dormancy of his Australian past is beautifully mocked in the image of the sleeping Crinkett and in the uneasy festivities of the christening (which cannot wash away the stain of the goldfields where his rebirth as an English squire began). No doubt the Tichborne Case, which Mrs Smith refers to when she compares herself to "the claimant" (p.532), provided part of the inspiration for the novel's mixture of farce and drama, its juxtapositions of antipodean wild-life and English high-life. But the evocation of the goldfields and the dramatization of their intrusion into prosaic rural England rank among Trollope's most original and effective pieces of writing.

The subject of a man's past sins crossing the ocean to catch up with him recurs in *Dr. Wortle's School.* One of Dr Wortle's teachers, Mr Peacocke, an ordained clergyman, had married an American woman—in America—only to find that her first husband, whom she had believed to be dead, was still living. Scandal breaks out, and the school is faced with "ruin" as most of the pupils are withdrawn by their parents. Dr Wortle's confrontation with the pharisees, when he refuses to sack Peacocke, has some resemblances to John Caldigate's with the Boltons. In particular its moral significance is blurred in the same way by Trollope's obvious partisanship, which leads him to overlook inconsistencies in Wortle's attitudes while losing no opportunity to emphasize those in his enemies'. On impulse, and speaking man to man, Wortle can assure Peacocke that to him Mrs Peacocke is "as pure as the most unsullied matron in the country" (p.106). In private, however, he admits to himself that it would be against his principles, against commonsense, to sacrifice his school for the Peacockes' sake, and that unless they can now regularize their position by marrying legally they will sooner or later have to go: indeed

they may have to even if they do become man and wife (cf. p.100)
His position in fact is very like that of Clara Amedroz in *The Belton
Estate*, who would never have allowed herself to become intimate
with Mrs Askerton if she had known of her sinful past, but who "on
impulse" resolves to stand by her once she is assailed by scandal. It
is a position that we can applaud for its humaneness and fidelity
without feeling that we are compromising or calling into question
any basic sexual rules. In *John Caldigate*, by contrast, the rules are
questioned both implicitly and explicitly: Caldigate can see nothing
"disgraceful" about his entanglement with Euphemia Smith, and
public opinion, in agreeing with him that English social laws have
no absolute value and authority, acknowledges that the wilds are not
only across the sea but latent within all of us.

The Fixed Period (1882), written only two years before Trollope's
death, is the most ambitious and, in conception at least, the most imaginative of his essays in exoticism. Its subject is the attempt, in the
year 1981, in the South Pacific republic of Britannula, to introduce a
system of legal euthanasia of all men and women upon their
reaching their sixty-eighth birthday.[11] The attempt fails when the
British, the former rulers of Britannula, are induced by some of the
more elderly members of the population to send in a gunboat and a
governor to re-establish imperial authority and to quash republican
laws which are inimical to those of the mother country.

In the early chapters Britannula does appear genuinely exotic, a
genuine Utopia, and the florid polemical style of the first-person
narrative—by Fidus Neverbend, president of the republic—has a
convincingly Swiftean flavour. (Readers of *Blackwood's* in which the
novel was serialized, anonymously, would have been slower to
recognize Trollope as the author than readers of those two earlier
Blackwood's stories, *Nina Balatka* and *Linda Tressel*.) Once the
dialogue begins, however, and once the familiar triangle of callow
young lovers appears on the scene, the three oceans and four genera-
tions that separate Britannula from Trollope's England shrink rapid-
ly. Britannula may be ruled by a president who could have
graduated from the Grand Academy of Lagado, the inhabitants may
call their schools "didascalions" and their shillings "decimals', may
get about on steam tricycles, employ a steam catapult in lieu of a
bowler when playing cricket, and rashly entrust their rights to a
single-chamber legislature. But their gentlemen are still gentlemen,
private property and its privileges remain safe, mid-Victorian
courting customs still prevail, and there are no skyscrapers, no
aeroplanes, no internal combustion engines, no radio. The height of
twentieth-century technology is the telephone, the gramophone,

and a 250-ton steam swivel-gun. Military might is shared equally by two power blocs, England and France on the one hand and Russia and America on the other. England itself, though it now has an elected house of lords, still loves a lord; its prime minister is Gladstone's great-grandson, and his colonial secretary, the Duke of Hatfield, is apparently the grandson of Lord Salisbury, albeit "a strong anti-Church Liberal" (I:14). The touring party from the Marylebone Cricket Club (beaten by the colonials as the MCC had been beaten in Australia in 1877) still includes too many gentlemen and too few players. No doubt most literary visions of Utopia and of the future contain similar incongruities and anachronisms, especially when it is part of their intention to satirize existing customs. But Trollope detains us so long in Britannula—at least twice as long as he needs to—and eventually makes us so at home in it that our initial surprise at its mingled strangeness and familiarity is altogether dissipated: Trollope's copious matter-of-factness domesticates even Utopia.

As a result the more fantastic elements of the story, notably the marathon cricket-match, tend to lose their satirical point and to appear facetious and overdone—in much the same way as does the satirical fantasy of *Brown, Jones and Robinson*.[12] Worse still, what promised to be the main interest of the novel, namely the type of mind that could conceive and the type of community that could accept the idea of fixing the period of every human life, ceases to be either a serious or an amusing matter long before the end of the novel. Fidus Neverbend begins as a Swiftean projector justifying his crazy scheme primarily on "politico-economical" grounds, secondarily on humanitarian ones. But by the time he has been revealed as an ordinary family man—whose wife nags him about the scheme, whose son publicly opposes it, whose future daughter-in-law almost charms him out of it, and who is quite able to see, if not to feel, the arguments against his modest proposal—his craziness on the question of euthanasia comes to appear simply a mild, unaccountable idiosyncrasy. That he justifies himself by appealing to "utility" and the greatest happiness principle, that he is a republican who sees himself following in the footsteps of the great radicals and scientists of the past, that his republic has evidently cut itself adrift from the mother country prematurely, that the legislature which approved the fixed period is subject to no house of review: these are all circumstances which at one time or another seem to throw some light on his aberration and on the moral of the tale. By the end, however, neither the moral, the psychological, nor the politico-economic significance of his behaviour is at all clear, and Britannula itself fails to explain it. Both Neverbend and Britannula turn out too ordinary

to be the source of such an extraordinary idea as the fixed period.

It is fitting that a discussion of Trollope's art and scope should finish with his one attempt at a utopian novel, for *The Fixed Period* is perhaps the climactic example of his lifelong refusal to accept the limitations of his style and imagination.

NOTES

1. Including *La Vendée*, a historical romance. *La Vendée*, like Trollope's costume drama, *The Noble Jilt*, bears sad witness to his admiration for Sir Henry Taylor's verse-drama, *Philip van Artevelde* (1834). It is a total failure, both as an evocation of the past and as a picture of.foreign life.
2. Trollope's *Australia*, ed. P.D. Edwards and R.B. Joyce (Brisbane: University of Queensland Press, 1967), appendix 3.
3. Polhemus, *The Changing World of Anthony Trollope*, pp. 13–14.
4. The British government had approved state assistance for the Roman Catholic seminary at Maynooth in 1844. Trollope in the novel supports this move on the grounds that the Catholic church, unlike the Anglican, was continuing to win new adherents and that better educated priests would be less fanatical (III:84–85). There is some biting satire at the expense of the established church— and implicit sympathy for the Catholic—in *The Kellys and the O'Kellys*, chap. 38. In both *The Kellys and the O'Kellys* and *The Landleaguers* the follies of the Church of England in Ireland are epitomized in the fatuous bigotry of a parson called Armstrong.
5. In true romantic fashion, the introduction is in fact an epilogue—the only example of this device in Trollope's fiction.
6. The novel is inconsistent on this point: see pp.132,152.
7. On the real-life originals of the goldmining scenes in the novel, and the relationship between Trollope's factual and fictional accounts of such scenes, see Edwards and Joyce (eds.), Trollope's *Australia*, pp.765–67.
8. Bodleian MS., Don. c.10, p.54.
9. See, for example, *Saturday Review* 48 (16 August 1879): 216–17, and *Spectator* 52 (19 July 1879): 916–17.
10. *Saturday Review* 48 (16 August 1879): 216.
11. It has long been recognized that Trollope probably got the idea for this system from Massinger's play *The Old Law*. See Booth, *Anthony Trollope*, pp.129–30.
12. Bradford Booth (*Anthony Trollope*, p.130) also suggested a comparison between the grotesqueries of *Brown, Jones and Robinson* and those of *The Fixed Period*. I refer briefly to *Brown, Jones and Robinson* in chap.4 above.

Appendix 1

The Barset Novels and History

In *Barchester Towers* the short-lived Conservative ministry which just fails to survive long enough to appoint Archdeacon Grantly as bishop of Barchester recalls the Derby ministry which was in power from February to December 1852. And though its fall takes place in a different month, the identification is confirmed by a subsequent reference to the rebellion of the protectionist rump which brought the ministry down; here the historical rather than the fictional date is given—November 1852 (p.194). Further confirmation is provided by references to the "first threatenings of a huge war"—obviously the Crimean—which "hung heavily over the nation" as the new Whig-Peelite government came to office (p.12), and to Dr Proudie's membership of the "University Improvement Committee" (p.32) which makes proposals for reform at Oxford (pp.92, 328–29, 392). All of these suggest 1852–53 as the period covered by the novel. *Doctor Thorne*, the next novel in the series, covers the period 1854–57, beginning with Frank Gresham's twenty-first birthday (1 July 1854) and ending with his wedding in April, nearly three years later. *Framley Parsonage*, which followed *Doctor Thorne*, begins at a time when Frank's marriage is "hardly as yet more than six months old" (p.81) and when Dr Proudie, who had been appointed to the bishopric coveted by Archdeacon Grantly, has been "four or five" years in Barchester (p.16). These two facts, along with indications of the lapse of time within the novel, suggest 1857–58 as the period; and this is confirmed by references to contemporary historical events, notably the Indian Mutiny and the enforced retirement, "some months afterwards", of the Whig prime minister Lord Brock (Palmerston) who was credited with having handled it so successfully (pp.84–87). We are also told that Mr Sowerby has represented West Barset ever since the Reform Bill, a period of twenty-five years (pp.398–400). In *The Small House at Allington*, there is very little reference to contemporary history, but we do learn that Lord Brock has returned as prime minister (as Palmerston did in 1859). From the dating of some letters—"186-"—and from such details as Lady Dumbello's being "as yet ... little more than two years married"

(pp.154–55) and Mr Harding's being now well over seventy (p.147), we can, by looking back to earlier novels, establish 1860–61 as the period.[1] In *The Last Chronicle of Barset* this sort of evidence is not as reliable: contradictory statements are made as to the time that has elapsed since the jilting of Lily Dale in *The Small House at Allington* (I: 154, 242; II: 21), and both Grace Crawley and little Johnny Bold (I: 7, 439) appear to have put on more years than have actually passed since they were introduced in earlier novels. But other evidence based on comparison with earlier novels—for example, Mr Crawley's present age as compared with his age when he appeared in *Framley Parsonage* (I:6), the ten years' duration of his curacy at Hogglestock, to which he was appointed by Arabin eighteen months after Arabin became dean of Barchester (I:5), and the present age of Mr Harding (II:175)—does seem to point to 1865 as both the earliest possible commencing date and the most likely one. This evidence, in turn, is supported by the novel's references to contemporary history: Johnny Eames and Major Grantly, on a train journey, read the *Pall Mall Gazette*, which was founded in 1865 (I:281);[2] the American Civil War is either still in progress or very recently concluded (II:36); there is a change of ministry, as there was in 1865 when Palmerston stepped down (II:110); and Venice is still under Austrian rule, which ended in 1866 (II:313).

NOTES

1. This makes the amusing allusion to Lady Dumbello as the "Woman in White" (I:233) highly topical: Collins's novel was published in August 1860.
2. No doubt their reading would have included one of Trollope's own hunting or travelling or clerical sketches, all of which came out in the *Pall Mall* in 1865 and early 1866.

Appendix 2

The Palliser Novels and History

In *Can You Forgive Her?*, written in 1863–64, there are a number of thinly veiled allusions to events and personalities of the Palmerston-Gladstone ministry of 1859–65. The chancellor of the exchequer, Finespun, whose longstanding disagreements with the prime minister, Lord Brock, lead to rumours that he will soon resign and be replaced by Plantagenet Palliser, clearly has much in common with Gladstone, just as the Conservative leader in the House, Sidonia, is obviously Disraeli. Finespun differs with the prime minister over "the expediency of repealing what were left of the direct taxes of the country" (II:11) and later over "French wines" and the sending of "some political agent" to France (II:440); similarly, Gladstone's dislike of income tax, his wholehearted support of the Cobden trade treaty with France (1860) and general desire for friendlier relations with that country conflicted with Palmerston's policy of hostility towards France and increased military expenditure. Later, when Plantagenet Palliser is prime minister, he too has to fight jingoistic demands—from Sir Orlando Drought—for the building of four great battleships; and, like Gladstone, resents having to work with men like Sir Orlando when his private preference is for men "who discussed the evils of direct taxation" (*The Prime Minister* I:299). It is true that Finespun disappears after *Can You Forgive Her?* and that Gladstone's part is subsequently played, more or less, by Gresham; but so too does Sidonia disappear, to be replaced by Daubeny. Such discrepancies are explained, I suggest, by a change of purpose and emphasis between *Can You Forgive Her?* and the later novels of the series, a change which, among other things, results in our being given a much closer view of Gresham and Daubeny than we had had of Finespun and Sidonia. Gresham and Daubeny are characters where Finespun and Sidonia were only names, and to have retained the name Sidonia would have been too blatantly to identify a real-life politician as the model for a fictional character.

Phineas Finn, like *Can You Forgive Her?*, presents a version of

parliamentary happenings at the time when it was being written and immediately before. It is an elaborately garbled version, though still a recognizable one, of the parliamentary history of the years 1865–67. (The novel was written between November 1866 and May 1867.) The minority Conservative ministry of Lord de Terrier and Daubeny is clearly modelled on the Derby-Disraeli ministry, which had been in office since June 1866, with the difference, however, that it gives way to a Whig-Liberal ministry quite early in the novel and after only fifteen months in office, whereas the Derby-Disraeli ministry followed a shortlived Whig-Liberal one and still held power when the writing of the novel was completed. The crisis over the formation of the new Whig-Liberal ministry of Mildmay and Gresham (1:101–5) roughly parallels that which attended the formation of the Russell-Gladstone ministry in October 1865. Mildmay's abortive Reform Bill, though not identical in its provisions, and though defeated by a different combination of forces, inevitably recalls Russell's bill of 1866, and Mildmay's deep emotional commitment to it is very similar indeed to Russell's commitment to his. The public agitation for reform in the novel, culminating in the disturbance outside parliament when the radical Turnbull's carriage "stops the way" (chapter 25), is obviously based on the agitation that led up to the Hyde Park Riot of July 1866.[1]

In *The Eustace Diamonds*, written between *Phineas Finn* and *Phineas Redux*, a Liberal ministry is still in power, though uneasily. It has fallen by the beginning of *Phineas Redux*.

By the time *Phineas Redux* was written (1870–71), Disraeli's Reform Bill had been passed (1867) and Gladstone's first ministry, which took office in 1868, had disestablished the Irish Church (1869). But although both these real-life changes are referred to as faits accomplis several times in the novel, they are clearly the models for the chief measure before parliament during the actual period of the novel: Mr Daubeny's effort to "dish the Whigs" by introducing a bill to disestablish the English church.[2] True, his effort fails, whereas Disraeli's had succeeded spectacularly. But this is only one of several instances in which Trollope withholds from his Conservatives spoils that their real-life counterparts had won. Daubeny's apparent reluctance to resign after his failure recalls the widespread suspicion aroused by Disraeli's continuance in office for over six months after his defeat in the house early in 1868—a defeat which he suffered, like Daubeny, on a disestablishment measure, though unlike Daubeny's this was not his own but an opposition measure. Daubeny, again like Disraeli, has all along headed a minority government, having come into office only because of a split among the Liberals on a question of electoral reform: in the novel the ques-

tion is the ballot, in real life it was the best method of broadening
the franchise.

The Prime Minister has fewer correspondences to real-life
parliamentary history than its three predecessors. In order to give his
favourite political character Plantagenet Palliser, now Duke of Omnium, the opportunity of leading the nation for three years, Trollope
was obliged to invent a situation without any recent parallel: no
coalition such as the duke heads had ruled since 1852. At the time
when the novel was written, between April and September 1874,
Disraeli had just won his greatest electoral victory, but there is no
sign of a Conservative revival in the novel. Though his government
is a coalition, the prime minister is a Liberal, and when he is
defeated a Liberal government under Gresham follows. In spirit the
duke's ministry belongs to the early 1870s, the period which in real
life saw the gradual decline of Gladstone's first ministry. The duke
himself, as I have already pointed out, shares some of Gladstone's
most distinctive attitudes, and he is at his most Gladstonian in *The
Prime Minister*, where the exercise of power accentuates his
touchiness, impatience, and self-righteousness.[3] Like Gladstone's his
government offends the powerful brewers and its "strength" is "im-
paired" as a result (I:136–37). The demagogic campaign of his
lieutenant, Sir Orlando Drought, for "the Salvation of the Empire"
by the building of "four bigger ships of war than had ever been built
before" (I:360–61) recalls another of the causes of discontent in the
ranks of Gladstone's ministry. The idea that Trollope has in effect
deposed Gladstone's first ministry half-way through its term of office to make way for the duke's coalition is also supported by such
"historical" evidence as the circumstance that voting at elections is
now by ballot (introduced, in real life, in 1872) and the existence in
parliament of a Home Rule party (the Home Rule movement having
been launched in 1870).

The Duke's Children, the last novel in the series, is a step further
removed from real-life history than *The Prime Minister* in that it not
only invents a further sequence of ministries without historical
parallel but refrains from allusions that would roughly date its action. It was written in 1876 when Disraeli was securely in power. But
in the novel, though the Conservatives are in office, they are led no
longer by Daubeny but by Lord Drummond, and their fortunes are
already declining when the novel opens. The "great Conservative
reaction in the country" (I:196) that swept them into office had
revealed itself, apparently, no more than two years ago. But there
has already, for reasons unexplained, been a subsequent election at
which a Liberal recovery began. At the end of the novel the Conservatives are again supplanted after less than three years of ascen-

dancy. Writing in 1876, Trollope can hardly have expected Disraeli's government to be similarly shortlived; but in any case, if he wished to remind the reader of recent history, he would not have given the Conservatives a new and colourless leader, or had them submit themselves to a seemingly pointless election with no historical parallel. Nor would he, for the first time in the series, have avoided any allusion—even veiled allusion—to recent legislation or to topical political questions.[4]

NOTES

1. These comments were written before I had had the chance to read John Sutherland's excellent introduction and notes to the Penguin English Library edition of *Phineas Finn*. Sutherland draws attention to a number of other allusions to the politics mainly of the years 1865–67. He also suggests another possible real-life model for Phineas, the Irish MP Samuel Chichester Fortescue (see note 98, pp.745–46).
2. In real life a similar measure actually was brought before parliament in 1871, not long after the writing of the novel was completed, but it was quickly thrown out.
3. However, he also remains, as Blair G. Kenney has shown ("Trollope's Ideal Statesmen: Plantagenet Palliser and Lord John Russell", *Nineteenth Century Fiction* 20 [December 1965]: 281–85), a disciple of his first "mentor" Mr. Mildmay, who is modelled on Lord John Russell.
4. There was no doubt a certain topicality about the remark (1:201) that most people's idea of "patriotism" is a "feeling that they would like to lick the Russians, or to get the better of the Americans in a matter of fisheries or frontiers". 1876, when the novel was written, was the year of the crisis over the "Eastern Question" and anti-Russian feeling was strong. (Later in the year Trollope appeared on the same public platform as Gladstone to speak up in favour of the Russians: see *Times*, 9 December 1876, pp.7–8). The fisheries dispute with the US was also in the news in 1876: see *Annual Register* 1876, part 1, p.104. However, both this dispute and Russophobia were of long standing; they do not help us to date the novel precisely.

Index